Core 2

for Edexcel

D1635761

CAMBRIDGE
UNIVERSITY PRESS

The School Mathematics Project

SMP AS/A2 Mathematics writing team David Cassell, Spencer Instone, John Ling, Paul Scruton, Susan Shilton, Heather West

SMP design and administration Melanie Bull, Carol Cole, Pam Keetch, Nicky Lake, Jane Seaton, Cathy Syred, Ann White

The authors thank Sue Glover for the technical advice she gave when this AS/A2 project began and for her detailed editorial contribution to this book. The authors are also very grateful to those teachers who commented in detail on draft chapters.

PUBLISHED BY THE PRESS SYNDICATE OF THE UNIVERSITY OF CAMBRIDGE
The Pitt Building, Trumpington Street, Cambridge, United Kingdom

CAMBRIDGE UNIVERSITY PRESS
The Edinburgh Building, Cambridge CB2 2RU, UK
40 West 20th Street, New York NY 10011–4211, USA
477 Williamstown Road, Port Melbourne, VIC 3207, Australia
Ruiz de Alarcón 13, 28014 Madrid, Spain
Dock House, The Waterfront, Cape Town 8001, South Africa

http://www.cambridge.org/

© The School Mathematics Project 2004
First published 2004

Printed in the United Kingdom at the University Press, Cambridge

Typeface Minion   *System* QuarkXPress®

A catalogue record for this book is available from the British Library

ISBN 0 521 60534 2 paperback

Typesetting and technical illustrations by The School Mathematics Project

The authors and publisher are grateful to London Qualifications Limited for permission to reproduce questions from past Edexcel examination papers. Individual questions are marked Edexcel. London Qualifications Limited accepts no responsibility whatsoever for the accuracy or method of working in the answers given.

Using this book

Each chapter begins with a **summary** of what the student is expected to learn.

The chapter then has sections lettered A, B, C, … (see the contents overleaf). In most cases a section consists of development material, worked examples and an exercise.

The **development material** interweaves explanation with questions that involve the student in making sense of ideas and techniques. Development questions are labelled according to their section letter (A1, A2, …, B1, B2, …) and answers to them are provided.

D Some development questions are particularly suitable for discussion – either by the whole class or by smaller groups – because they have the potential to bring out a key issue or clarify a technique. Such **discussion questions** are marked with a bar, as here.

K **Key points** established in the development material are marked with a bar as here, so the student may readily refer to them during later work or revision. Each chapter's key points are also gathered together in a panel after the last lettered section.

The **worked examples** have been chosen to clarify ideas and techniques, and as models for students to follow in setting out their own work. Guidance for the student is in italic.

The **exercise** at the end of each lettered section is designed to consolidate the skills and understanding acquired earlier in the section. Unlike those in the development material, questions in the exercise are denoted by a number only.

Starred questions are more demanding.

After the lettered sections and the key points panel there may be a set of **mixed questions**, combining ideas from several sections in the chapter; these may also involve topics from earlier chapters.

Every chapter ends with a selection of **questions for self-assessment** ('Test yourself').

Included in the mixed questions and 'Test yourself' are **past Edexcel exam questions**, to give the student an idea of the style and standard that may be expected, and to build confidence. Occasionally, exam questions are included in the exercises in the lettered sections.

Contents

1 Dividing polynomials

In this chapter you will learn how to
- divide a polynomial expression by a linear one
- use the remainder and factor theorems to factorise polynomial expressions

A Polynomials: revision

A polynomial is an expression that can be written in the form
$a + bx + cx^2 + dx^3 + ex^4 + fx^5 + \dots$ where $a, b, c, d, e \dots$ are constants.

You have seen in Core 1 that the sum, difference or product of two polynomials is also a polynomial.

Example 1

Polynomials are given by $f(x) = x^5 - 3x$ and $g(x) = x^4 + 2x^3 - 1$.
Expand and simplify $f(x)g(x)$.

Solution

$f(x)g(x) = (x^5 - 3x)(x^4 + 2x^3 - 1)$

$= x^9 + 2x^8 - x^5 - 3x^5 - 6x^4 + 3x$

$= x^9 + 2x^8 - 4x^5 - 6x^4 + 3x$

$\times$	x^4	$2x^3$	-1
x^5	x^9	$2x^8$	$-x^5$
$-3x$	$-3x^5$	$-6x^4$	$3x$

Exercise A (answers p 126)

1 A polynomial is given by $f(x) = x^4 - 2x^3 + 5x - 1$.
Evaluate each of these.

(a) $f(1)$ (b) $f(0)$ (c) $f(2)$ (d) $f(-1)$ (e) $f(\tfrac{1}{2})$

2 Expand and simplify each of these.

(a) $(3x + 5)(x^2 - 3x + 1)$ (b) $(2x^2 + 3)^2$

(c) $(x - 2)(x^2 + 2x + 4)$ (d) $(1 - x)(2x^3 + 2x^2 + 2x + 3)$

3 Polynomials are given by $p(x) = 2x^2 - 3$ and $q(x) = x^3 + x^2 - 4$.
Expand and simplify each of these.

(a) $p(x)q(x)$ (b) $(p(x))^2$ (c) $(q(x))^2$

4 A polynomial is given by $f(x) = 2x^3 - 3x^2 - 11x + 6$.

(a) Evaluate each of these.

    (i) $f(0)$ (ii) $f(2)$ (iii) $f(3)$ (iv) $f(-2)$ (v) $f(\tfrac{1}{2})$

(b) Sketch the graph of $y = f(x)$.

B Division (answers p 126)

The sum, difference or product of any two integers is always another integer.
We know that this isn't true for dividing two integers – sometimes there is a remainder.

A statement such as $57 = 4 \times 14 + 1$ tells us that dividing 57 by 4 leaves a remainder of 1.

We know that the sum, difference or product of any two polynomials is also a polynomial.
Now we will consider whether or not dividing polynomials will work in the same way as
dividing two integers. Will there sometimes be a remainder here too?

B1 (a) Work out the missing polynomial in the statement
$$x^2 + 7x + 12 = (x + 3)(\qquad).$$

(b) Hence, write down the expression equivalent to
$$(x^2 + 7x + 12) \div (x + 3).$$

B2 Find the missing polynomial in each statement below.

(a) $3x^2 + 10x + 3 = (x + 3)(\qquad)$

(b) $2x^2 + x - 3 = (x - 1)(\qquad)$

D

B3 Can you find the missing polynomials in the statements below?

(a) $x^3 + 3x^2 + 7x + 5 = (x + 1)(\qquad)$

(b) $x^3 - 2x^2 - 17x - 6 = (x + 3)(\qquad)$

(c) $x^3 - 3x^2 - 7x - 15 = (x - 5)(\qquad)$

B4 Find the missing polynomial in each statement below.

(a) $x^2 + 2x + 1 = x(\qquad) + 1$

(b) $x^2 + 4x + 7 = (x + 1)(\qquad) + 4$

(c) $x^2 - 8x + 13 = (x - 3)(\qquad) - 2$

D

B5 (a) Can you complete the statement below so that R is an integer?
$$x^2 + 6x + 7 = (x + 5)(\qquad) + R$$

(b) What is the remainder after dividing $(x^2 + 6x + 7)$ by $(x + 5)$?

B6 (a) Can you complete the statement below so that R is an integer?
$$x^2 - 10x + 31 = (x - 3)(\qquad) + R$$

(b) What is the remainder after dividing $(x^2 - 10x + 31)$ by $(x - 3)$?

B7 (a) Can you complete the statement below so that R is an integer?
$$x^2 - 10x + 11 = (x - 3)(\qquad) + R$$

(b) What is the remainder after dividing $(x^2 - 10x + 11)$ by $(x - 3)$?

B8 (a) Can you complete the statement below so that R is an integer?
$$8x^2 + 6x + 3 = (2x + 1)(\qquad) + R$$

(b) What is the remainder after dividing $(8x^2 - 6x + 3)$ by $(2x + 1)$?

To divide $(x^3 - x^2 + x + 15)$ by $(x + 2)$, we need to find the missing polynomial and the value for R in the statement

$$x^3 - x^2 + x + 15 = (x + 2)(\qquad) + R$$

We can use a 'reverse table' method to find the missing expressions.

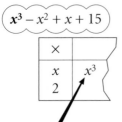

×	
x	x^3
2	

This must be x^3 as it's the term with the highest power of x …

… so this is x^2 …

×	x^2
x	x^3
2	

×	x^2
x	x^3
2	$2x^2$

… and this is $2x^2$.

×	x^2
x	x^3
2	$2x^2$

The sum of the circled expressions must be $-x^2$ …

… so this is $-3x^2$ …

×	x^2	
x	x^3	$-3x^2$
2	$2x^2$	

… this is $-3x$ …

×	x^2	$-3x$
x	x^3	$-3x^2$
2	$2x^2$	

×	x^2	$-3x$
x	x^3	$-3x^2$
2	$2x^2$	$-6x$

… and this is $-6x$.

×	x^2	$-3x$
x	x^3	$-3x^2$
2	$2x^2$	$-6x$

The sum of the circled expressions must be x …

… so this is $7x$ …

×	x^2	$-3x$	
x	x^3	$-3x^2$	$7x$
2	$2x^2$	$-6x$	

… this is 7 …

×	x^2	$-3x$	7
x	x^3	$-3x^2$	$7x$
2	$2x^2$	$-6x$	14

… and finally this is 14.

So $x^3 - x^2 + x + 14 = (x + 2)(x^2 - 3x + 7)$

We need to add 1 to each side to obtain the correct polynomial so

$$x^3 - x^2 + x + 15 = (x + 2)(x^2 - 3x + 7) + 1$$

Hence $(x^3 - x^2 + x + 15) \div (x + 2) = (x^2 - 3x + 7)$ with a remainder of 1.

Alternatively, we can use a 'long division' method and work as in numerical long division.

$$\begin{array}{r}
x^2 - 3x + 7 \\
x + 2 \overline{\smash{\big)}\ x^3 - x^2 + x + 15} \\
\underline{x^3 + 2x^2\phantom{{}+x+15}} \\
-3x^2 + x\phantom{{}+15} \\
\underline{-3x^2 - 6x\phantom{{}+15}} \\
7x + 15 \\
\underline{7x + 14} \\
1
\end{array}$$

This also shows that $(x^3 - x^2 + x + 15) \div (x + 2) = (x^2 - 3x + 7)$ with a remainder of 1.

Exercise B (answers p 126)

1 Find the result of each of these.
Some have remainders and some divide exactly.

(a) $x^3 + 4x^2 + 7x + 9$ divided by $x + 1$

(b) $x^3 + 2x^2 - 9x + 2$ divided by $x - 2$

(c) $x^3 - 6x^2 + 11x - 31$ divided by $x - 5$

(d) $2x^3 + 5x^2 + 5x + 9$ divided by $x + 2$

(e) $3x^3 - x^2 - 7x + 5$ divided by $x - 1$

(f) $5x^3 + 13x^2 - 7x - 5$ divided by $x + 3$

(g) $x^3 + 2x^2 - x - 2$ divided by $x + 2$

2 Find the result when $x^3 - 2x - 1$ is divided by $x + 1$.
(It might help to think of the cubic expression as $x^3 + 0x^2 - 2x - 1$.)

3 Find the result of each of these.

(a) $x^3 - 13x + 12$ divided by $x - 1$

(b) $x^3 + x + 12$ divided by $x + 2$

(c) $2x^3 + 7x^2 - 9$ divided by $x + 3$

(d) $3x^3 - 5x + 1$ divided by $x - 2$

(e) $4x^3 - x^2 + 3$ divided by $x + 1$

4 Find the result when $x^3 - 1$ is divided by $x - 1$.

5 A polynomial is defined by $f(x) = x^3 + 7x^2 + 7x - 15$.

(a) Show that f(x) divides by $x + 5$ exactly.

(b) Hence write f(x) as a product of two expressions, one linear and one quadratic.

(c) Factorise the quadratic expression.
Hence write the polynomial f(x) as the product of three linear expressions.

6 A polynomial is defined by $p(x) = x^3 - 6x^2 + 5x + 12$.

   (a) Find the remainder when $p(x)$ is divided by

      (i) $x - 2$ (ii) $x - 1$ (iii) x (iv) $x + 1$ (v) $x + 2$

   (b) Which of the expressions in (a) is a factor of $p(x)$?

   (c) Hence write $p(x)$ as a product of two expressions, one linear and one quadratic.

   (d) Factorise the quadratic expression.
      Hence write the polynomial $p(x)$ as the product of three linear expressions.

   (e) Solve $p(x) = 0$.

7 Find the result of each of these.

   (a) $6x^3 - 20x^2 - 21x + 10$ divided by $3x - 1$

   (b) $4x^3 + x^2 - 12x - 3$ divided by $4x + 1$

   (c) $2x^3 + 13$ divided by $2x + 1$

C Remainders and factors (answers p 126)

A division results in a **quotient** and a remainder.

For example, $39 \div 7 = 5$ remainder 4
                     In this case, the quotient is 5 and the remainder is 4.

Another example is $48 \div 6 = 8$ remainder 0
                     Here the quotient is 8.
                     As the remainder is 0 we know that 6 is a factor of 48.

C1 A polynomial is defined by $p(x) = x^3 + 2x^2 - 9x + 10$.

   (a) (i) Divide $p(x)$ by $x - 2$ and write down the remainder.

      (ii) Calculate $p(2)$.

      (iii) What do you notice?

   (b) (i) Divide $p(x)$ by $x + 1$ and write down the remainder.

      (ii) Calculate $p(-1)$.

      (iii) What do you notice?

   (c) For various values of a

      (i) Divide $p(x)$ by $x - a$ and write down the remainder.

      (ii) Calculate $p(a)$.

      (iii) What do you notice?

      (iv) Can you explain this?

When $p(x) = x^3 + 2x^2 - 9x + 10$ is divided by $x - 2$,
there is a quotient of $x^2 + 4x - 1$ and a remainder of 8.

Hence we can write $p(x) = (x - 2)(x^2 + 4x - 1) + 8$.

If $x = 2$ is substituted, then $(x - 2) = 0$.
So the quotient is multiplied by 0, leaving $p(2) = 8$ which is the remainder.

In general, suppose that $p(x)$ is a polynomial in x and that
dividing $p(x)$ by $(x - a)$ gives a quotient of $q(x)$ and a remainder R.

Then we can write $\quad p(x) = (x - a)q(x) + R$

This gives us $\quad\quad\quad p(a) = 0 \times q(a) + R = R$

That is, $\quad\quad\quad\quad\quad p(a) = R$

This result is called the **remainder theorem** and can be summarised:

When $p(x)$ is divided by $(x - a)$, the remainder is $p(a)$.

C2 A polynomial is defined by $p(x) = x^3 + 5x^2 - 2x - 2$.

    (a) Use the remainder theorem to work out the remainder when $p(x)$ is divided by $x - 1$.

    (b) Confirm your result by dividing $p(x)$ by $x - 1$.

C3 A polynomial is defined by $f(x) = x^3 - x^2 - 7x + 3$.
    Find the value of $f(3)$. What does this tell you?

C4 A polynomial is defined by $p(x) = x^3 + 3x^2 - 10x - 24$.

    (a) Use the remainder theorem to work out the remainder when $p(x)$ is divided by

        (i) $x - 1$ **(ii)** x **(iii)** $x + 1$ **(iv)** $x + 2$ **(v)** $x + 3$

    (b) Use your results to write down a factor of $p(x)$.

    (c) Write $p(x)$ as the product of a linear and a quadratic expression.

    (d) Factorise the quadratic and write $p(x)$ as the product of three linear factors.

    (e) Hence solve the equation $x^3 + 3x^2 - 10x - 24 = 0$.

    (f) Sketch the graph of $y = x^3 + 3x^2 - 10x - 24$.

For a given polynomial $p(x)$, if $p(a) = 0$ then $(x - a)$ is a factor of $p(x)$.
The converse is also true: if $(x - a)$ is a factor of $p(x)$, then $p(a) = 0$.

This result is called the **factor theorem**.

C5 A polynomial is defined by $p(x) = 2x^3 - 5x^2 + x - 12$.
    Use the factor theorem to find one linear factor of $p(x)$.

Example 2

A polynomial is given by $p(x) = x^3 + 4x^2 + x - 6$.
Show that $(x + 3)$ is a factor of $p(x)$ and express $p(x)$ as a product of three linear factors.

Solution

To show that $(x + 3)$ is a factor, evaluate $p(-3)$.

$$p(-3) = (-3)^3 + 4 \times (-3)^2 + (-3) - 6$$

$$= -27 + 36 - 3 - 6$$

$$= 0$$

So $(x + 3)$ is a factor of $p(x)$.

Now write $p(x)$ as the product of $(x + 3)$ and a quadratic factor.

$p(x) = (x + 3)(x^2 + x - 2)$ *With practice, you will be able to write down the quadratic factor straight away by realising that the coefficient of x^2 must be 1, the constant term must be -2 and hence the coefficient of x must be 1 (to achieve $4x^2 + x$ in the expansion).*

$= (x + 3)(x + 2)(x - 1)$ *The quadratic factorises. This will not always be the case.*

Example 3

Factorise $p(x) = x^3 - 5x^2 + 5x + 3$ completely.
Hence solve $p(x) = 0$, giving all solutions as exact values.

Solution

In any linear factor of the form $(x - c)$, the value of c must be a factor of 3 (the constant term in $p(x)$).
So first evaluate $p(1), p(3), p(-1)$ and $p(-3)$ to look for linear factors.

$p(1) = 1 - 5 + 5 + 3 = 4$ so $(x - 1)$ is not a factor.
$p(3) = 27 - 45 + 15 + 3 = 0$ so $(x - 3)$ is a factor.

Now write $p(x)$ as the product of $(x - 3)$ and a quadratic factor.

$p(x) = (x - 3)(x^2 - 2x - 1)$ *The quadratic expression does not factorise so you have now factorised $p(x)$ completely. It has only one linear factor.*

So $p(x) = 0 \implies (x - 3)(x^2 - 2x - 1) = 0$

$\implies (x - 3) = 0$ which gives $x = 3$ or

$(x^2 - 2x - 1) = 0$ which gives $x = \dfrac{2 \pm \sqrt{8}}{2} = \dfrac{2 \pm 2\sqrt{2}}{2} = 1 \pm \sqrt{2}$

So the equation $p(x) = 0$ has solutions $x = 3, 1 + \sqrt{2}, 1 - \sqrt{2}$.

 When factorising a cubic polynomial, once you have found a linear factor, then the quadratic factor can be found by comparing coefficients.

Exercise C (answers p 127)

1 Use the remainder theorem to find the remainder when $x^3 - 3x^2 + x - 10$ is divided by $x - 4$.

2 A polynomial is given by $p(x) = x^3 + 5x^2 - 17x - 21$.
(a) By finding the value of $p(3)$, show that $(x - 3)$ is a factor of $p(x)$.
(b) Express $p(x)$ as a product of three linear factors.

3 A polynomial is given by $f(x) = x^3 - 4x^2 - 7x + 10$.
(a) By finding the value of $f(-2)$, show that $(x + 2)$ is a factor of $f(x)$.
(b) Factorise $f(x)$ into the product of three linear factors.

4 A polynomial is given by $q(x) = x^3 + 6x^2 - 13x - 42$.
(a) Show that $(x + 7)$ is a factor of $q(x)$.
(b) Express $q(x)$ as a product of three linear factors.
(c) Hence solve the equation $q(x) = 0$.

5 A function is defined as $f(x) = x^3 + 4x^2 - 11x + 6$.
(a) Factorise $f(x)$ completely.
(b) Hence solve the equation $x^3 + 4x^2 - 11x + 6 = 0$.
(c) Sketch the graph of $y = x^3 + 4x^2 - 11x + 6$.

6 A polynomial is given by $p(x) = x^3 + x^2 + 3x - 5$.
(a) Show that $(x - 1)$ is a factor of $p(x)$.
(b) Express $p(x)$ as a product of one linear and one quadratic expression.
(c) (i) Find the value of the discriminant of the quadratic expression.
(ii) Hence show that the equation $p(x) = 0$ has only one real solution.

7 A polynomial is given by $p(x) = x^3 + x^2 - 7x - 7$.
(a) Show that $(x + 1)$ is a factor of $p(x)$.
(b) Express $p(x)$ as a product of one linear and one quadratic expression.
(c) Hence, solve the equation $p(x) = 0$.
(Give any non-integer solutions as exact values.)

8 Factorise these cubics completely. (Some have only one linear factor.)
(a) $x^3 + 4x^2 - 7x - 10$ (b) $2x^3 + 5x^2 - x - 6$ (c) $x^3 - x^2 - 3x + 2$
(d) $x^3 + 7x^2 + 14x + 8$ (e) $2x^3 + 2x^2 - 5x - 5$ (f) $x^3 + 8x^2 + 21x + 18$

9 Factorise these cubics completely.
(a) $x^3 - 64x$ (b) $x^3 + 64$

D Dividing by $(bx - c)$ (answers p 127)

D1 A polynomial is defined by $f(x) = 4x^3 - 6x^2 + 2x - 7$.

(a) Use the remainder theorem to find the remainder when $f(x)$ is divided by $(x - 2)$.

(b) (i) What do you think the remainder will be when $f(x)$ is divided by $(2x - 4)$?

(ii) Now divide $f(x)$ by $(2x - 4)$ and work out the remainder. Were you right?

(c) What do you notice about the remainders when $f(x)$ is divided by $(x - 2)$ and $(2x - 4)$? Can you explain this?

D2 A polynomial is defined by $g(x) = 8x^3 + 4x^2 + 6x - 11$.

(a) Find the remainder when $g(x)$ is divided by $\left(x - \frac{1}{2}\right)$.

(b) (i) What do you think the remainder will be when $g(x)$ is divided by $(2x - 1)$?

(ii) Now divide $g(x)$ by $(2x - 1)$ and work out the remainder. Were you right?

(c) What do you notice about the remainders when $g(x)$ is divided by $\left(x - \frac{1}{2}\right)$ and $(2x - 1)$? Can you explain this?

D3 A polynomial is defined by $p(x) = 9x^3 + 12x^2 - 3x - 1$.

(a) Find the remainder when $p(x)$ is divided by $\left(x + \frac{1}{3}\right)$.

(b) (i) What do you think the remainder will be when $p(x)$ is divided by $(3x + 1)$?

(ii) Now divide $p(x)$ by $(3x + 1)$ and work out this remainder. Were you right?

(c) What do you notice about the remainders when $p(x)$ is divided by $\left(x + \frac{1}{3}\right)$ and $(3x + 1)$? Can you explain this?

D4 What do you think will be the remainder when

(a) $4x^3 + 3x^2 + x - 1$ is divided by $2x - 1$

(b) $2x^3 + x^2 - 6x + 3$ is divided by $2x + 1$

(c) $3x^3 + 5x^2 + x - 4$ is divided by $3x - 1$

In general, suppose that $p(x)$ is a polynomial in x and that dividing $p(x)$ by $(bx - c)$ gives a quotient of $q(x)$ and a remainder R.

Then we can write $\qquad p(x) = (bx - c)q(x) + R$

When $x = \frac{c}{b}$ then $bx - c = 0$, so $p\left(\frac{c}{b}\right) = 0 \times q(x) + R$

That is, $p\left(\frac{c}{b}\right) = R$

When $p(x)$ is divided by $(bx - c)$, the remainder is $p\left(\frac{c}{b}\right)$.

(Note that $x = \frac{c}{b}$ is the solution of the equation $bx - c = 0$.)

D5 Work out the remainder when

(a) $6x^3 + 3x^2 + x - 4$ is divided by $2x - 1$

(b) $4x^3 + x^2 - x$ is divided by $4x + 1$

(c) $2x^3 + 5x^2 + x - 2$ is divided by $2x - 1$

(d) $27x^3 + 1$ is divided by $3x + 1$

Example 4

What is the remainder when $f(x) = 2x^3 + 5x^2 - 7x - 3$ is divided by $(2x - 1)$?

Solution

$2x - 1 = 0 \implies x = \frac{1}{2}$ so the remainder is the value of $f\left(\frac{1}{2}\right)$.

$$f\left(\tfrac{1}{2}\right) = 2 \times \left(\tfrac{1}{2}\right)^3 + 5 \times \left(\tfrac{1}{2}\right)^2 - 7 \times \left(\tfrac{1}{2}\right) - 3$$
$$= 2 \times \tfrac{1}{8} + 5 \times \tfrac{1}{4} - 7 \times \tfrac{1}{2} - 3$$
$$= \tfrac{1}{4} + \tfrac{5}{4} - \tfrac{7}{2} - 3$$
$$= -5$$

So the remainder is –5.

Example 5

A polynomial is given by $p(x) = 3x^3 + 10x^2 - 3x - 2$.
Find the remainder when $p(x)$ is divided by $(3x + 1)$.
Hence, express $p(x)$ as a product of a linear and a quadratic factor.

Solution

$3x + 1 = 0 \implies x = -\frac{1}{3}$ so the remainder is the value of $p\left(-\frac{1}{3}\right)$.

$$p\left(-\tfrac{1}{3}\right) = 3 \times \left(-\tfrac{1}{3}\right)^3 + 10 \times \left(-\tfrac{1}{3}\right)^2 - 3 \times \left(-\tfrac{1}{3}\right) - 2$$
$$= 3 \times \left(-\tfrac{1}{27}\right) + 10 \times \left(\tfrac{1}{9}\right) + 1 - 2$$
$$= -\tfrac{1}{9} + 1\tfrac{1}{9} + 1 - 2$$
$$= 0$$

Since the remainder is 0 we can write $p(x)$ as the product of $(3x + 1)$ and a quadratic factor.

$\quad p(x) = (3x + 1)(x^2 + 3x - 2)$ *The coefficient of x^2 must be 1, the constant term must be –2 and hence the coefficient of x must be 3 (to achieve $10x^2 - 3x$ in the expansion).*

Exercise D (answers p 128)

1 Find the remainder when

  (a) $2x^3 + x^2 - 7x + 7$ is divided by $2x - 1$

  (b) $4x^3 - 4x^2 - 2x + 1$ is divided by $2x + 1$

  (c) $3x^3 + 11x^2 - 3x - 1$ is divided by $3x - 1$

2 A polynomial is given by $p(x) = 2x^3 + 7x^2 - 10x + 3$.

  (a) Find the remainder when $p(x)$ is divided by $(2x - 1)$.

  (b) Express $p(x)$ as a product of one linear and one quadratic factor.

3 A polynomial is given by $f(x) = 6x^3 + 31x^2 + 3x - 10$.

  (a) Find the remainder when $p(x)$ is divided by $(3x + 2)$.

  (b) Express $p(x)$ as a product of three linear factors.

*4 Factorise each polynomial completely.

(a) $12x^3 + 4x^2 - 3x - 1$ (b) $9x^3 - 4x + 1$ (c) $8x^3 - 1$

E Further problems

Example 6

A polynomial is given by $f(x) = 2x^3 + ax^2 + 6x + 3$, where a is a constant.
When $f(x)$ is divided by $(x - 2)$, there is a remainder of 7.
Find the value of a.

Solution

Dividing $f(x)$ by $(x - 2)$ gives a remainder of 7 so $f(2) = 7$

$$\Rightarrow \quad 2 \times 2^3 + a \times 2^2 + 6 \times 2 + 3 = 7$$

$$\Rightarrow \quad 16 + 4a + 12 + 3 = 7$$

$$\Rightarrow \quad 31 + 4a = 7$$

$$\Rightarrow \quad a = -6$$

Example 7

The polynomial $f(x) = x^3 + ax^2 - 4x + b$ has a factor $(x + 2)$.
When $f(x)$ is divided by $(x - 3)$, there is a remainder of 30.
Find the values of a and b.

Solution

$(x + 2)$ is a factor so $f(-2) = 0$

$$\Rightarrow \quad (-2)^3 + a \times (-2)^2 - 4 \times (-2) + b = 0$$

$$\Rightarrow \quad -8 + 4a + 8 + b = 0$$

$$\Rightarrow \quad 4a + b = 0$$

Dividing by $(x - 3)$ gives a remainder of 30 so $f(3) = 30$

$$\Rightarrow \quad 3^3 + a \times 3^2 - 4 \times 3 + b = 30$$

$$\Rightarrow \quad 27 + 9a - 12 + b = 30$$

$$\Rightarrow \quad 9a + b = 15$$

We now have two equations in a and b that you can solve simultaneously.

$$9a + b = 15$$
$$4a + b = 0$$

Subtracting gives

$$5a = 15$$

$$\Rightarrow \quad a = 3$$

Substituting in the second equation gives

$$12 + b = 0$$

$$\Rightarrow \quad b = -12$$

Exercise E (answers p 128)

1 The polynomial f(x) is given by f(x) = $x^3 + 2x^2 + kx - 1$, where k is a constant.
When f(x) is divided by ($x - 2$), there is a remainder of 17.
Find the value of k.

2 Given that ($x + 1$) is a factor of p(x) = $x^3 + ax^2 - 6x + 5$, find the value of
the constant a.

3 When the polynomial $x^3 + bx^2 + bx + 5$ is divided by $x + 2$, there is a remainder of 5.
Find the value of b.

4 Given that $x - 3$ is a factor of $ax^3 + 2ax^2 + 3ax - 54$, find the value of the constant a.

5 The polynomial p(x) is given by p(x) = $2x^3 + kx^2 - 7x + 3$.
When p(x) is divided by ($2x - 1$), there is a remainder of 1.
Find the value of the constant k.

6 The polynomial $x^3 + px^2 + qx - 40$ has factors ($x - 5$) and ($x + 1$).
Find the values of p and q.

7 The polynomial q(x) = $x^3 + ax^2 + bx - 6$ has factors ($x - 3$) and ($x + 2$).
Find the values of a and b.

8 The polynomial f(x) = $x^3 + px^2 - 4x + q$ has a factor of ($x + 3$).
When f(x) is divided by ($x - 1$), there is a remainder of 4.
Find the values of p and q.

9 The polynomial $hx^3 - 10x^2 + kx + 26$ has a factor of ($x - 2$).
When the polynomial is divided by ($x + 1$), there is a remainder of 15.
Find the values of h and k.

10 The polynomial f(x) is given by f(x) = $4x^3 + ax^2 + bx + 2$.
($4x + 1$) is a factor of f(x).
When f(x) is divided by ($x - 1$), there is a remainder of 20.
Find the values of a and b.

11 The polynomial p(x) is given by p(x) = $9x^3 + 12x^2 + hx + k$.
When p(x) is divided by ($3x - 1$), there is a remainder of 2.
When p(x) is divided by ($x + 2$), there is a remainder of -5.
Find the values of h and k.

*12 The diagram shows a cubic curve.
It cuts the axes at the points shown.

Write the equation of the curve in
the form $y = ax^3 + bx^2 + cx + d$.

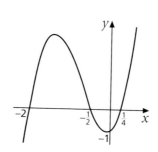

Key points

- The **remainder theorem** says that when a polynomial p(x) is divided by ($x - a$) the remainder is p(a). (p 11)

- When a polynomial p(x) is divided by ($bx - c$) the remainder is $p\left(\dfrac{c}{b}\right)$. (p 14)

- The **factor theorem** says that
  if p(a) = 0 then the polynomial p(x) has a factor ($x - a$) and
  if the polynomial p(x) has a factor ($x - a$) then p(a) = 0. (p 11)

- When factorising a cubic polynomial, once you have found a linear factor, then the quadratic factor can be found by comparing coefficients. (p 12)

Mixed questions (answers p 128)

1 Divide $x^3 + 4x^2 + x + 32$ by $x + 5$.

2 (a) Using the factor theorem, show that ($x + 3$) is a factor of $x^3 - 3x^2 - 10x + 24$.

Edexcel

   (b) Factorise $x^3 - 3x^2 - 10x + 24$ completely.

3 A polynomial is given by p(x) = $x^3 - 12x + 16$.

   (a) Use the factor theorem to show that ($x - 2$) is a factor of p(x).

   (b) Sketch the graph of y = p(x), showing clearly where the graph meets each axis.

4 Find the remainder when $4x^3 + 8x^2 - 3x + 1$ is divided by ($2x - 1$).

5 f(x) = $ax^3 + bx^2 - 7x + 14$, where a and b are constants.

   Given that when f(x) is divided by ($x - 1$) the remainder is 9,

   (a) write down an equation connecting a and b.

   Given also that ($x + 2$) is a factor of f(x),

   (b) Find the values of a and b.

Edexcel

6 (a) Find a linear factor of the polynomial p(x) = $x^3 - 2x^2 - 3x + 6$.

   (b) Solve p(x) = 0, giving your answers correct to 2 d.p.

7 The polynomial $x^3 + px^2 + qx - 50$ has factors ($x + 5$) and ($x - 5$). Find the values of p and q.

8 The polynomial f(n) is given by f(n) = $n^3 + n^2 - 7n + k$, where k is a constant. ($n - 3$) is a factor of f(n).

   (a) Find the value of k.

   (b) Factorise f(n) as the product of a linear factor and a quadratic factor.

   (c) Show that there is only one real value of n for which f(n) = 0.

Test yourself (answers p 128)

1 (a) Using the factor theorem, show that $(x + 2)$ is a factor of $x^3 - 2x^2 - 5x + 6$.

(b) Factorise $x^3 - 2x^2 - 5x + 6$ completely.

2 (a) Factorise $p(x) = x^3 - 7x^2 + 14x - 8$ completely into linear factors.

(b) Sketch the graph of $y = p(x)$.

3 $f(x) = 4x^3 + 3x^2 - 2x - 6$.

Find the remainder when $f(x)$ is divided by $(2x + 1)$.

Edexcel

4 $f(x) = 2x^3 + 5x^2 - 8x - 15$.

(a) Show that $(x + 3)$ is a factor of $f(x)$.

(b) Hence factorise $f(x)$ as the product of a linear factor and a quadratic factor.

(c) Find, to two decimal places, the two other values of x for which $f(x) = 0$.

Edexcel

5 $f(x) = x^3 + ax^2 + bx - 10$, where a and b are constants.

When $f(x)$ is divided by $(x - 3)$, the remainder is 14.

When $f(x)$ is divided by $(x + 1)$, the remainder is -18.

(a) Find the value of a and the value of b.

(b) Show that $(x - 2)$ is a factor of $f(x)$.

Edexcel

6 $f(x) = x^3 - x^2 - 7x + c$, where c is a constant.

Given that $f(4) = 0$,

(a) find the value of c,

(b) factorise $f(x)$ as the product of a linear and a quadratic factor.

(c) Hence show that, apart from $x = 4$, there are no real values of x for which $f(x) = 0$.

Edexcel

7 $f(x) = px^3 + 6x^2 + 12x + q$.

Given that the remainder when $f(x)$ is divided by $(x - 1)$ is equal to the remainder when $f(x)$ is divided by $(2x + 1)$,

(a) find the value of p.

Given also that $q = 3$, and p has the value found in part (a),

(b) find the value of the remainder.

Edexcel

8 $f(n) = n^3 + pn^2 + 11n + 9$, where p is a constant.

(a) Given that $f(n)$ has a remainder of 3 when it is divided by $(n + 2)$, prove that $p = 6$.

(b) Show that $f(n)$ can be written in the form $(n + 2)(n + q)(n + r) + 3$, where q and r are integers to be found.

(c) Hence show that $f(n)$ is divisible by 3 for all positive integer values of n.

Edexcel

2 Equation of a circle

In this chapter you will learn how to
- form and interpret the equation of a circle
- find the tangent and normal to a circle
- decide whether a straight line intersects a circle and find points of intersection

A A circle as a graph (answers p 129)

A1 Use Pythagoras's theorem to find the distance of each of these points from the origin $(0, 0)$.

(a) $(15, 8)$ (b) $(-6, -8)$ (c) $(12, -3.5)$ (d) $(-10, 10.5)$

A2 The diagram shows a circle with centre $(0, 0)$ and radius 13 units.

(a) Use Pythagoras to decide whether each of the following points lies inside the circle, on the circle or outside the circle.

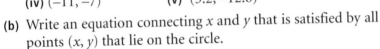

(i) $(6.6, 11.2)$ (ii) $(-12, 5)$ (iii) $(9, 9)$

(iv) $(-11, -7)$ (v) $(3.2, -12.6)$

(b) Write an equation connecting x and y that is satisfied by all points (x, y) that lie on the circle.

A3 Use a graph plotter to draw the graph of your equation from A2 (b). (With some graph plotters you may need to rearrange the equation to give y in terms of x. This form of the equation will contain a square root, so the graph will need to be drawn in two sections, one using the positive square root and the other using the negative square root.)

A4 A circle has the equation $x^2 + y^2 = 49$. Give its centre and radius.

A circle with radius r and centre $(0, 0)$ has the equation $x^2 + y^2 = r^2$.

Notice that this formula still works if x or y is negative.

A5 Use Pythagoras to find the distance of the point $(5, 5)$ from the point $(2, 1)$.

A6 A circle is drawn with centre $(2, 1)$ and radius 5.

(a) Use Pythagoras to decide whether each of the following points lies inside the circle, on the circle or outside the circle.

(i) $(-2, 4)$ (ii) $(5, -3)$ (iii) $(2, -4)$ (iv) $(6.8, 2.4)$

(v) $(-2, -3)$ (vi) $(7, 1)$ (vii) $(-2, -1)$

(b) Give three other points that lie on this circle.

If (x, y) is a general point on the circle in question A6, the right-angled triangle shown has width $(x - 2)$ and height $(y - 1)$.

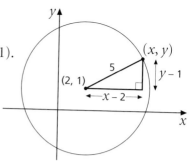

From Pythagoras, $(x - 2)^2 + (y - 1)^2 = 5^2$.
This is the equation of this circle.

A7 Show that $(x - 2)^2 + (y - 1)^2 = 5^2$ still works as the equation for the circle, even if the point (x, y) is to the left of the circle's centre or below it.

A8 If your graph plotter will accept an equation in the form $(x - 2)^2 + (y - 1)^2 = 5^2$, use it to draw the graph of the equation.

Here, (x, y) is a point on a general circle with centre (a, b) and radius r.
The right-angled triangle has width $(x - a)$ and height $(y - b)$.
From Pythagoras's theorem, $(x - a)^2 + (y - b)^2 = r^2$.
The following is true in general:

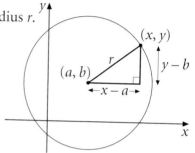

A circle with radius r and centre (a, b) has the equation
$(x - a)^2 + (y - b)^2 = r^2$.

This is sometimes called the 'cartesian equation' of a circle, after the French mathematician and philosopher René Descartes (1596–1650) who pioneered coordinate geometry of the kind you are doing in this chapter.

A9 Give the cartesian equation for a circle with radius 4 and centre $(5, -2)$.

A10 Give the centre and radius of a circle with the equation $(x + 4)^2 + (y - 7)^2 = 6^2$.

Notice that circle C' with centre (a, b) is the image of circle C with centre $(0, 0)$ after a translation by $\begin{bmatrix} a \\ b \end{bmatrix}$.

Notice too that the equation for C' results from replacing x by $(x - a)$ and y by $(y - b)$ in the equation for C.

This corresponds with work you did in Core 1 on translating graphs.

An equation of a circle can have its brackets expanded and its numerical terms gathered together. So, for example, the equation of A10 becomes
$$x^2 + 8x + 16 + y^2 - 14y + 49 = 36$$
which becomes $\quad x^2 + 8x + y^2 - 14y + 29 = 0$.

A11 In the same way, expand your answer to A9 and then gather its numerical terms together.

The expanded equation for a circle generally takes the form $x^2 + y^2 + cx + dy + e = 0$, when c, d and e are numerical values. The order of terms can of course vary.
Note the following:

- The x^2 and y^2 terms must have the same coefficient and the same sign (so in practice you usually see x^2 and $+ y^2$).

- There are no terms such as xy.

- The x and y terms and the constant term (e above) may be absent.

You can experiment on a graph plotter to see what curves you get if you break the first two conditions.

If you are given the equation of a circle in expanded form you can use 'completing the square', which you met in Core 1, to 'put the brackets back' and so find the centre and radius of the circle. This is shown in the following example.

Example 1

Write the circle equation $x^2 - 2x + y^2 + 4y + 1 = 0$ in the form $(x - a)^2 + (y - b)^2 = r^2$ and hence give the coordinates of its centre and its radius.

Solution

Complete the square for the x^2 and x terms. $x^2 - 2x = (x - 1)^2 - 1$

Complete the square for the y^2 and y terms. $y^2 + 4y = (y + 2)^2 - 4$

So the original circle equation is $(x - 1)^2 - 1 + (y + 2)^2 - 4 + 1 = 0$

Tidy the numerical values. $(x - 1)^2 + (y + 2)^2 - 4 = 0$

Rearrange so the radius term is visible. $(x - 1)^2 + (y + 2)^2 = 2^2$

So the centre is at $(1, -2)$ and the radius is 2 units.

Exercise A (answers p 129)

1 Write an equation for each of these circles in the form $(x - a)^2 + (y - b)^2 = r^2$.

   (a) Centre $(6, 3)$, radius 4   (b) Centre $(-2, 0)$, radius 5

   (c) Centre $(1, -6)$, radius 3   (d) Centre $(-2, -2)$, radius 7

2 For each of these circle equations

   (i) give the coordinates of the centre and the radius

   (ii) expand and simplify the equation

   (a) $(x - 2)^2 + (y - 6)^2 = 16$ (b) $(x + 3)^2 + (y - 4)^2 = 25$

   (c) $(x - 4)^2 + y^2 = 7$ (d) $(x + 1.5)^2 + (y - 0.5)^2 = 4$

3 Find the equation of a circle that has its centre at $(-2, -3)$ and passes through the point $(1, 1)$. (Hint: first find the radius.)

4 A circle has the line segment from $(-10, 0)$ to $(16, -10)$ as a diameter. Find the equation of the circle.

5 Find the equation of a circle that has the line segment from $(-7, -1)$ to $(-1, -3)$ as a diameter.

6 State, with reasons, whether the point $(-1, 2)$ lies inside, on or outside the circle $(x - 1)^2 + (y - 4)^2 = 9$.

7 Find the radius and the coordinates of the centre of the circle given by each of these equations.

(a) $x^2 - 4x + y^2 - 2y + 1 = 0$ (b) $x^2 - 2x + y^2 + 6y + 1 = 0$

(c) $x^2 + 10x + y^2 - 4y + 18 = 0$ (d) $x^2 + y^2 - 10y - 24 = 0$

(e) $x^2 + y^2 + 8x - 6y - 11 = 0$ (f) $x^2 - x + y^2 - 7y + 8\frac{1}{2} = 0$

8 Which of these could not be the equation of a circle?

A $x^2 + y^2 - 6y = 0$ **B** $x^2 + 8x + 2y^2 + 4y - 16 = 0$

C $y^2 - 12y = 4x - x^2$ **D** $x^2 - 16x + y^2 - 2y + 15 = 0$

9 Find the equation of the circle that has a radius of 4 units and the same centre as the circle $x^2 - 12x + y^2 + 29 = 0$.

10 (a) Show that the circle $x^2 + 6x + y^2 - 4y = 0$ goes through the origin $(0, 0)$.

(b) A diameter has one end at the origin. Where is its other end?

*11 $P\,(9, 2)$ and $Q\,(-5, 4)$ are points on the circle $x^2 - 4x + y^2 - 6y - 37 = 0$.

(a) Show that P and Q are the ends of a diameter of the circle.

(b) Point $R\,(a, 8)$, where a is positive, is a third point on the circle. Find a.

(c) Calculate the gradients of PR and RQ. What do these values show?

(d) What general property of a circle accounts for your result in (c)?

*12 Show that the equation $x^2 + 2x + y^2 - 6y + 14 = 0$ does not represent a circle.

B Tangent and normal to a circle

A **tangent** to a circle is a straight line that just touches it.

A radius from the centre to where the tangent touches the circle is perpendicular to the tangent.

The **normal** to a circle (or any other curve) is a line drawn at right angles to the tangent where it touches.

A normal to a circle always goes through the centre of the circle so a diameter (and hence two radii) are part of it.

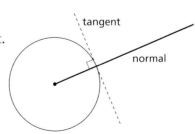

Example 2

A circle has its centre at C (3, 3) and has a radius of 2 units.
From the point P (10, −3) a tangent is drawn that touches the circle at Q.
Find the length of PQ.

Solution

Draw and label a sketch.

Using Pythagoras, $CP = \sqrt{7^2 + 6^2} = \sqrt{85}$.

*Notice that triangle CPQ is right-angled and
has two of its sides given and one to be found.*

Using Pythagoras, $PQ = \sqrt{CP^2 - CQ^2} = \sqrt{85 - 4} = 9$ units.

*Note that another tangent, the same length, could be drawn on the
other side of the circle.*

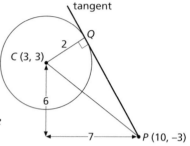

Example 3

C (−2, 1) is the centre of a circle and S (−4, 5) is a point on the circumference.
Find the equations of the normal and tangent to the circle at S.

Solution

The gradient of SC is $\dfrac{1-5}{-2-(-4)} = \dfrac{-4}{2} = -2$

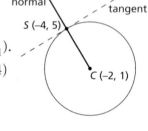

The line through (x_1, y_1) with gradient m has equation $\quad y - y_1 = m(x - x_1)$.
The equation of SC (and therefore of the normal) is $\quad y - 5 = -2(x + 4)$

$$\Rightarrow \qquad y - 5 = -2x - 8$$
$$\Rightarrow \qquad y = -2x - 3$$

If the gradient of the normal is m, the gradient of the tangent is $-\dfrac{1}{m}$.
The gradient of the tangent is $-\dfrac{1}{-2} = \frac{1}{2}$.
Use $y - y_1 = m(x - x_1)$ again.
The equation of the tangent is $\quad y - 5 = \frac{1}{2}(x + 4)$

$$\Rightarrow \qquad y - 5 = \frac{1}{2}x + 2$$
$$\Rightarrow \qquad y = \frac{1}{2}x + 7$$

Exercise B (answers p 130)

  1 P (6, 7) is a point on a circle with its centre at (−3, 1).

    (a) Find the equation of the normal to the circle at P.

    (b) Find the equation of the tangent to the circle at P.

2 (a) Find the radius and centre of a circle with equation $x^2 - 4x + y^2 - 4y = 0$.

   (b) A tangent to the circle has gradient -1. Find **two** points at which it could touch the circle and hence two possible equations for the tangent.

3 The circle C, with centre (a, b) and radius 5, touches the x-axis at $(4, 0)$ as shown in the diagram.

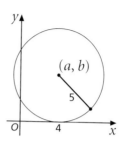

   (a) Write down the value of a and the value of b.

   (b) Find a cartesian equation of C.

   A tangent to the circle, drawn from the point $P\,(8, 17)$, touches the circle at T.

   (c) Find, to three significant figures, the length of PT.

                                                               Edexcel

4 A circle with its centre at $(2, 1)$ has the line $x + 2y = 9$ as a tangent.

   (a) Find the equation of a line through the centre, perpendicular to this tangent.

   (b) Solve the equations of the two straight lines simultaneously to find the point where the circle touches the tangent.

   (c) Find the equation of the circle.

5 The line with equation $y = \frac{1}{3}x + 5$ is a tangent to a circle with centre $(-2, 1)$. Find the equation of the circle.

*6 A circle has the equation $x^2 - 8x + y^2 - 4y + 3 = 0$.

   (a) Find the coordinates of its centre.

   (b) The point $P\,(a, b)$ lies on the circle. Express, in terms of a and b,

      (i) the gradient of the normal at P

      (ii) the gradient of the tangent at P

*7 Circle A has its centre at $(2, 1)$ and passes through the point $T\,(6, 4)$. Circle B has twice the radius of circle A and touches it externally at T.

   (a) Draw a sketch. What can you say about the two line segments from T to the centres of the circles?

   (b) Give the coordinates of the centre of circle B.

   (c) Write the equation of each circle.

C Intersection of a straight line and a circle (answers p 131)

C1 A circle has the equation $x^2 - 16x + y^2 - 2y + 15 = 0$.
A straight line has the equation $y = x + 1$.

   Solve these as a pair of simultaneous equations to find where the circle and the line cross. First substitute $x + 1$ for y in the equation of the circle.

C2 Using the same approach, try to find where these lines cross the circle given in C1.

   (a) $y = x + 3$ **(b)** $y = x + 5$

C1 gives a quadratic equation in x and hence two solutions, $x = 1$ and $x = 7$.
The corresponding solutions for y are $y = 2$ and $y = 8$.
Drawing on paper or with a graph plotter shows that these solutions represent
the points $(1, 2)$ and $(7, 8)$ where the line intersects the circle.

C2 (a) gives a quadratic that has one solution, $x = 3$, from which $y = 6$.
Drawing shows that the point $(3, 6)$ is where the line just touches the circle.
The line is a tangent to the circle.

Notice the factorised quadratic has two brackets the same, so the result $x = 3$
can come from either of them. We sometimes say the equation has a
'repeated' solution (or 'root').

In C2 (b) the quadratic does not factorise; and it cannot be solved by the
formula because its **discriminant** is negative. We say it has 'no real roots'.
(Reminder: the discriminant of the quadratic equation $ax^2 + bx + c = 0$ is
the expression $b^2 - 4ac$.)
Drawing shows that the line fails to intersect or touch the circle.

The discriminant is also useful for distinguishing between the intersecting
and touching cases, as the following summary indicates.

- Two different (distinct) real roots (solutions) $\Leftrightarrow$ line intersects circle
  In this case the discriminant of the equation is positive.

- One real root (or a 'repeated root') $\Leftrightarrow$ line is a tangent to circle
  Here the discriminant is zero.

- No real roots $\Leftrightarrow$ line fails to meet circle
  The discriminant is negative.

(The symbol $\Leftrightarrow$ means 'implies and is implied by'; so in each of these
three cases the geometrical fact follows from the algebraic fact and the
algebraic fact follows from the geometrical fact.)

Example 4

A line has the equation $x - y + 1 = 0$.
A circle has the equation $x^2 - 6x + y^2 = 0$.
Determine whether the line intersects the circle, is a tangent to it or fails to meet it.

Solution

Rearrange the equation for the line. $\qquad y = x + 1$

Substitute for y in the circle equation. $\qquad x^2 - 6x + (x + 1)^2 = 0$

$\Rightarrow \qquad x^2 - 6x + x^2 + 2x + 1 = 0$

$\Rightarrow \qquad\qquad\qquad 2x^2 - 4x + 1 = 0$

The discriminant is $(-4)^2 - 4 \times 2 \times 1 = 8$
As this is greater than zero the line intersects the circle.

When a line intersects a circle, the line segment between the points of intersection is called a **chord**.

The perpendicular from the centre of the circle to a chord bisects the chord.

Conversely, the perpendicular bisector of a chord goes through the centre of the circle. This fact can be useful if you are given points on the circle and are required to find its centre, as the following example shows.

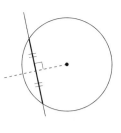

Example 5

A circle has its centre on the y-axis and passes through the points P $(-3, 3)$ and Q $(-1, -1)$. Find its equation.

Solution

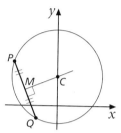

Draw a sketch.
Mark in the perpendicular bisector of the chord PQ.
It will pass through the centre of the circle.

Label some points so you can refer to them.   Let M be the mid-point of PQ.
Let C be the centre of the circle (on the y-axis).

Find what you need to get the equation of MC. M is $\left(\dfrac{-3 + -1}{2}, \dfrac{3 + -1}{2}\right)$, which is $(-2, 1)$.

$$\text{gradient of } PQ = \frac{-4}{2} = -2$$

$$\Rightarrow \text{gradient of } MC = \tfrac{1}{2}$$

The equation of MC is given by

Use $y - y_1 = m(x - x_1)$ with the point M. $y - 1 = \tfrac{1}{2}(x + 2)$

$$\Rightarrow y - 1 = \tfrac{1}{2}x + 1$$

$$\Rightarrow y = \tfrac{1}{2}x + 2$$

The y-intercept of a line with this equation is 2.
So the centre of the circle is at $(0, 2)$.

Find the radius using Pythagoras. $r = PC = \sqrt{3^2 + 1^2} = \sqrt{10}$

So the equation of the circle is $x^2 + (y - 2)^2 = 10$.

Exercise C (answers p 131)

1 In each of the following the equation of a line and of a circle is given. Without solving for points of intersection or contact, determine whether the line intersects the circle, is a tangent to it or fails to meet it.

   (a) $x + y = 3$
       $x^2 + y^2 - 6 = 0$

   (b) $y = 5 - 2x$
       $x^2 + y^2 - 8x - 4y + 15 = 0$

   (c) $y = x + 1$
       $x^2 + y^2 - 6x - 4y + 4 = 0$

   (d) $x + y = 4$
       $x^2 + y^2 + 4x + 2y - 12 = 0$

2 In each of the following the equations of a line and a circle are given.
Find the coordinates of any points of intersection or tangential contact,
or if the line fails to meet the curve state this fact.

(a) $y = 2x + 1$
$x^2 - 8x + y^2 - 8y + 22 = 0$

(b) $2x + y = 4$
$x^2 + 4x + y^2 - 8 = 0$

(c) $y = 20 - 3x$
$x^2 - 6x + y^2 - 2y = 0$

(d) $x + y = 4$
$x^2 - 2x + y^2 - 4y + 4 = 0$

3 A circle has the equation $x^2 - 10x + y^2 + 2y - 24 = 0$.

(a) Find the position of its centre.

(b) Find where the circle cuts the axes.

(c) Sketch the circle.

4 (a) Solve the following pair of simultaneous equations.

$y = x - 1$
$x^2 + 8x + y^2 + 2y + 9 = 0$

(b) Hence describe with reasons how the straight line with equation $y = x - 1$ and
the circle with equation $x^2 + 8x + y^2 + 2y + 9 = 0$ are related geometrically.

5 A circle C has centre $(3, 4)$ and radius $3\sqrt{2}$.
A straight line l has equation $y = x + 3$.

(a) Write down an equation of the circle C.

(b) Calculate the exact coordinates of the two points where
the line l intersects C, giving your answers in surds.

(c) Find the distance between these two points.

Edexcel

6 A circle cuts the x-axis at $(4, 0)$ and $(14, 0)$, and cuts the y-axis at $(0, 6)$ and $(0, 8)$.
Find its equation.

7 A circle has centre $(0, 1)$ and radius $\sqrt{85}$.
$P(9, a)$ and $Q(b, 8)$, where a and b are positive, are points on the circle.

(a) Find the values of a and b.

(b) Find the equation of the line through the centre of the circle, perpendicular
to the chord PQ, and verify that this line passes through the mid-point of PQ.

*8 A circle has the equation $x^2 + 8x + y^2 + a = 0$.
A straight line has the equation $y = \sqrt{3}x$
Find the value of a for which the line is a tangent to the circle.

*9 Find the centre, radius and equation of the circle passing through
the points $(5, 1)$, $(-3, 9)$ and $(-7, -3)$.

*10 Two circles, C and D, have the same centre but different radii.
$P(3, 3)$ and $Q(1, -3)$ are points on C.
$R(-3, 7)$ and $S(1, 3)$ are points on D.
Find the centre of the two circles.

Key points

- A circle with centre $(0, 0)$ and radius r has the equation $x^2 + y^2 = r^2$.
  A circle with centre (a, b) and radius r has the equation $(x - a)^2 + (y - b)^2 = r^2$.
  The second equation is obtained from the first by replacing x by $(x - a)$
  and y by $(y - b)$; the second circle is the image of the first after translation by $\begin{bmatrix} a \\ b \end{bmatrix}$.　(p 21)

- A line from the centre of a circle to where a tangent touches the circle is
  perpendicular to the tangent. A perpendicular to a tangent is called a normal.　(p 23)

- Solving simultaneously the equations for a line and a circle results in
  a quadratic equation. The number of roots of this equation is related to
  the geometrical situation as follows:

  two distinct real roots (discriminant > 0) $\Leftrightarrow$ line intersects circle

  a repeated root (discriminant $= 0$) $\Leftrightarrow$ line is a tangent to circle

  no real roots (discriminant < 0) $\Leftrightarrow$ line fails to meet circle　(p 26)

Test yourself (answers p 131)

1 Write an equation for each of these circles in the form $x^2 + y^2 + cx + dy + e = 0$.

(a) Centre $(4, 1)$, radius 2　　　　(b) Centre $(-2, -3)$, diameter 6

(c) Centre $(2.5, 4)$, diameter 4　　　(d) Centre $(1, -7)$, radius $\sqrt{7}$

2 Find the radius and coordinates of the centre of the circle given by each of these.

(a) $x^2 - 4x + y^2 - 2y - 31 = 0$　　(b) $x^2 + y^2 + 6y - 16 = 0$

(c) $x^2 + 4x + y^2 + 8y + 17 = 0$　　(d) $x^2 + y^2 - 3x - 5y - \frac{1}{2} = 0$

3 A circle has centre $(-1, -2)$ and radius $\sqrt{13}$.

(a) Verify that the point $P(1, 1)$ lies on the circle.

(b) Find the equation of the normal to the circle at P.

4 A circle C has equation $x^2 + y^2 - 10x + 6y - 15 = 0$.

(a) Find the coordinates of the centre of C.

(b) Find the radius of C.

Edexcel

5 (a) The line l goes through the point $P(5, 9)$ and has gradient 2.
Find its equation.

(b) The circle C has equation $x^2 - 8x + y^2 - 4y + 15 = 0$.
Solve the equations for l and C simultaneously and
explain how your solution shows that l is a tangent to C.

(c) Find, as a surd, the length from P to where l touches the circle.

3 Sequences and series

In this chapter you will learn
- what is meant by a geometric sequence
- how to find the sum of a finite geometric series
- how to find the sum of an infinite geometric series

A Geometric sequences (answers p 132)

A1 On Katy's first birthday, her uncle gives her 5p.
He promises to double the amount he gives her each birthday until she is 18.

(a) How much money has he promised to give her on her 18th birthday?

(b) Can you find an expression for the amount of money he gives on her nth birthday?

The amounts of money that Katy gets can be written as a sequence:

5, 10, 20, 40, 80, ...

The sequence has a simple structure – each term is found by multiplying the previous one by a fixed number. The multiplier is sometimes called the **common ratio**.

A sequence with a structure like this is called a **geometric sequence**.

A2 Which of the sequences below are geometric sequences?
Find the value of the common ratio for each geometric sequence.

A   5, 15, 45, 135, ...

B   2, 8, 32, 176, ...

C   6, 2.4, 0.96, 0.384, ...

D   3, 4, $5\frac{1}{3}$, $7\frac{1}{9}$, ...

E   3, −6, 12, −24, ...

F   4, −6, 8, −10, ...

A3 Find the next two terms of the geometric sequence 8, 12, 18, 27, ...

A4 What is the 8th term of the geometric sequence 15, 9, 5.4, 3.24, ... ?

A5 Find the 6th term of the geometric sequence 3, $1\frac{1}{2}$, $\frac{3}{4}$, $\frac{3}{8}$, ...

A6 What is the 20th term of the geometric sequence 3, 6, 12, 24, ... ?

A7 Find the 2nd term of the geometric sequence 4, ___ , ___ , 108, 324.

A8 Each of these is a geometric sequence of positive numbers.
Find the missing terms in each one.

(a) 16, ___ , 1, $\frac{1}{4}$, $\frac{1}{16}$

(b) 2, ___ , 50, ___ , ___

(c) ___ , 18, ___ , 72, ___

(d) 2, ___ , ___ , 128, ___

A9 The first term of a geometric sequence is 2.
The 4th term of the same sequence is −128.
What is the 2nd term in this sequence?

The geometric sequence 2, 6, 18, 54, 162, ... can be defined by $u_1 = 2$, $u_{n+1} = 3u_n$.
The terms follow this pattern:

$$u_1 = 2 \qquad\qquad = 2 \times 3^0 \qquad\qquad \text{(since } 2 \times 3^0 = 2 \times 1 = 2)$$
$$u_2 = 2 \times 3 \qquad\qquad = 2 \times 3^1$$
$$u_3 = 2 \times 3 \times 3 \qquad\qquad = 2 \times 3^2$$
$$u_4 = 2 \times 3 \times 3 \times 3 \qquad = 2 \times 3^3 \text{ ... and so on}$$

This gives us the nth term $u_n = 2 \times 3^{n-1}$.

In general, the geometric sequence with first term a and common ratio r can be written

$$a, \ ar, \ ar^2, \ ar^3, \ ...$$

and the nth term is ar^{n-1}.

Example 1

The sequence 7, 21, 63, 189, ... is geometric.
What is the 10th term?

Solution

Using a for the first term and r for the common ratio we have $a = 7$ and $r = \frac{21}{7} = 3$.
The 10th term is

$$ar^9 = 7 \times 3^9$$
$$= 7 \times 19\,683$$
$$= 137\,781$$

Example 2

The 3rd term of a geometric sequence is 10 and the 8th term is 320.
Find the common ratio and the first term.

Solution

Using a for the first term and r for the common ratio

The 3rd term is ar^2. $\qquad\qquad ar^2 = 10$

The 8th term is ar^7. $\qquad\qquad ar^7 = 320$

Dividing gives $\qquad \dfrac{ar^7}{ar^2} = \dfrac{320}{10}$

$\Rightarrow \qquad r^5 = 32$

$\Rightarrow \qquad r = \sqrt[5]{32} = 2 \qquad \sqrt[5]{32} = 32^{\frac{1}{5}}$ *and can be evaluated on a calculator.*

Now substitute $r = 2$ in $ar^2 = 10$ to give $\qquad a \times 2^2 = 10$

$\Rightarrow \qquad 4a = 10$

$\Rightarrow \qquad a = 2.5$

So the first term is 2.5 and the common ratio is 2.

Example 3

What is the nth term of the geometric sequence $25, \ 10, \ 4, \ 1.6, \ \ldots$?

Solution

Using a for the first term and r for the common ratio we have $a = 25$ and $r = \frac{10}{25} = 0.4$.

So the nth term is $25 \times (0.4)^{n-1}$.

Exercise A (answers p 132)

1 The 2nd term of a geometric sequence is 7.
  The 7th term is 224.

  (a) Find the 15th term.

  (b) Find an expression for the nth term of the sequence.

2 The nth term of a geometric sequence is $2 \times 5^{n-1}$.

  (a) Write down the first four terms of the sequence.

  (b) What is the common ratio?

3 A geometric sequence has first term 40 and common ratio 0.6.
  Find the value of the 20th term, giving your answer to three significant figures.

4 The 3rd term of a geometric sequence is 5 and the 6th term is $\frac{5}{8}$.
  Find the common ratio for this sequence.

5 The 2nd term of a geometric sequence is -12 and the 5th term is 324.

  (a) Show that the common ratio of the sequence is -3.

  (b) State the first term of the sequence.

6 The first term of a geometric sequence is 54 and the 4th term is 16.
  Find the common ratio.

7 The first term of a geometric sequence is 1.5 and the 5th term is 24.
  Find the two possible values for the common ratio.

8 In the year 2000, the hedgehog population on an island is 500.
  The population is estimated to increase in a geometric sequence with common ratio 1.02.

  (a) Find the predicted hedgehog population in 2020.

  (b) By what percentage is the hedgehog population increasing each year?

9 On Ken's first birthday, his mother deposits £1000 in a savings account for him.
  The annual rate of interest is 3%.
  No more money is deposited in or withdrawn from this account.

  (a) Show that on Ken's 5th birthday, he has £1125.51 in his account.

  (b) How much does he have on his 10th birthday?

  (c) Find an expression for the amount of money in this account on his nth birthday.

10 A geometric sequence has a common ratio of 5.
The sum of the first three terms is 37.2.
Find the first term.

11 The first term of a geometric sequence is 3.
The sum of the first three terms is 129.
Find the possible values of the common ratio.

12 A geometric sequence has first term 81 and 4th term 3.
Show that the nth term of the sequence is 3^{5-n}.

B Geometric series (answers p 132)

D **B1** Imagine a board with 16 squares on it.
There is 1p on the first square, 2p on the second square,
4p on the third square, 8p on the fourth square, and so on.

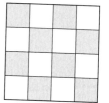

(a) Without doing any calculation, estimate
the total amount of money on the board.

(b) Work out how much money is on the last square.

(c) Can you work out how much money is on the whole board?

The money problem in B1 (b) above can be solved by finding the sum
$$S = 1 + 2 + 4 + 8 + \dots + 16\,384 + 32\,768$$
Writing the numbers as powers of 2 we have
$$S = 1 + 2 + 2^2 + 2^3 + \dots + 2^{14} + 2^{15}$$
Doubling this sum gives
$$2S = 2 + 2^2 + 2^3 + 2^4 + \dots + 2^{15} + 2^{16}$$
Now, subtracting gives
$$2S - S = (2 + 2^2 + 2^3 + 2^4 + \dots + 2^{15} + 2^{16}) - (1 + 2 + 2^2 + 2^3 + \dots\dots + 2^{15})$$
Most of the terms cancel, leaving
$$S = 2^{16} - 1$$
So $S = 65\,536 - 1 = 65\,535$, giving a total of £655.35 on the board.

D **B2** (a) Use a method similar to the one above to show that
$$1 + 3 + 3^2 + 3^3 + \dots + 3^{10} = \frac{3^{11} - 1}{2}.$$

(b) Hence evaluate $1 + 3 + 3^2 + 3^3 + \dots + 3^{10}$.

B3 Evaluate the sum $1 + 3 + 3^2 + 3^3 + \dots + 3^{12}$.

B4 How many terms are in the sum $1 + 5 + 5^2 + 5^3 + \dots + 5^8$?

B5 How many terms are in the sum $1 + 8 + 8^2 + 8^3 + \dots + 8^{n-1}$?

A **geometric series** is the sum of the terms of a geometric sequence.

The sum $1 + r + r^2 + r^3 + \ldots + r^{n-2} + r^{n-1}$ is a geometric series with n terms.

The first term is 1 and the common ratio is r.

Let $\qquad S = 1 + r + r^2 + r^3 + \ldots + r^{n-2} + r^{n-1}$

Multiplying by r gives

$$rS = r + r^2 + r^3 + r^4 + \ldots + r^{n-1} + r^n$$

Now, subtracting gives

$$rS - S = (r + r^2 + r^3 + r^4 + \ldots + r^{n-1} + r^n) - (1 + r + r^2 + r^3 + \ldots + r^{n-1})$$

$\Rightarrow \qquad S(r-1) = r^n - 1$

$\Rightarrow \qquad S = \dfrac{r^n - 1}{r - 1}$

The sum of the first n terms of a geometric series with first term a and common ratio r is

$$S = a + ar + ar^2 + ar^3 + \ldots + ar^{n-2} + ar^{n-1}$$

$\Rightarrow S = a(1 + r + r^2 + r^3 + \ldots + r^{n-2} + r^{n-1})$

$\Rightarrow S = \dfrac{a(r^n - 1)}{r - 1}$

Using sigma notation we can write this as $\displaystyle\sum_{i=1}^{n} ar^{n-1} = \dfrac{a(r^n - 1)}{r - 1}$.

Example 4

Find the sum of the first 10 terms of the geometric series $2 + 6 + 18 + \ldots$

Solution

The first term is $a = 2$ and the common ratio is $r = 3$.

The sum of the first 10 terms is $\dfrac{2 \times (3^{10} - 1)}{3 - 1} = 59\,048$.

Example 5

Evaluate $\displaystyle\sum_{i=1}^{15} 1.5 \times 2^{i-1}$.

Solution

$\displaystyle\sum_{i=1}^{15} 1.5 \times 2^{i-1} = 1.5 + 3 + 6 + \ldots + 1.5 \times 2^{14}$ is a geometric series with 15 terms.

The first term is $a = 1.5$ and the common ratio is $r = 2$.

The sum is $\dfrac{1.5 \times (2^{15} - 1)}{2 - 1} = 49\,150.5$

Exercise B (answers p 132)

1 Find the sum of the first 15 terms of the geometric series $1 + 4 + 16 + \dots$

2 Add the first 12 terms of the geometric series $5 + 10 + 20 + \dots$

3 Evaluate $\displaystyle\sum_{i=1}^{10} 6^{i-1}$.

4 Show that the first 10 terms of the geometric series $8 + 4 + 2 + 1 + \frac{1}{2} + \dots$ add to give 15.98 (to two decimal places).

5 Show that the sum of the first 12 terms of the geometric series $1 - 3 + 9 - 27 + \dots$ is $-132\,860$.

6 Calculate the sum of the first 15 terms of each of these geometric series. Where appropriate, give your answer correct to four decimal places.

(a) $24 + 12 + 6 + 3 + \dots$

(b) $3 - 6 + 12 - 24 + \dots$

(c) $6 + 4 + \frac{8}{3} + \frac{16}{9} + \dots$

(d) $36 - 9 + \frac{9}{4} - \frac{9}{16} + \dots$

7 Evaluate $\displaystyle\sum_{i=1}^{15} 1.6 \times (0.3)^{i-1}$ correct to four significant figures.

8 Evaluate the sum $1 + 3 + 3^2 + 3^3 + \dots + 3^{14}$.

9 Legend tells that the Shah of Persia offered a reward to the citizen who introduced him to chess. The citizen asked merely for a number of grains of rice according to the rule:

1 grain for the first square on the chessboard,
2 grains for the second square,
4 grains for the third square,
8 grains for the fourth square and so on.

(a) How many grains of rice did he request?

(b) If a grain of rice weighs 0.02 g, what weight of rice did he request?

10 Evaluate the sum of the geometric series $3 + 6 + 12 + \dots + 3072$.

11 A sequence is defined by $u_1 = 7$, $u_{n+1} = \dfrac{u_n}{4}$.

Evaluate $\displaystyle\sum_{i=1}^{20} u_i$ correct to three decimal places.

12 An account pays 4% interest per annum.

(a) A sum of £1 is invested in this account at the beginning of a year. No more money is invested and none is withdrawn. What is the total amount of money at the end of 20 years?

(b) The sum of £200 is invested in the same way in the same account. What is the total amount of money at the end of 20 years?

13 The sum of the first x terms of the geometric series $2\frac{1}{4} + 4\frac{1}{2} + 9 + 18 + \dots$ is $1149\frac{3}{4}$. Find the value of x.

C Sum to infinity (answers p 133)

You could use a spreadsheet for questions C1 to C4.

C1 Let S_n be the sum of the first n terms of the geometric series $1 + 2 + 4 + 8 \dots$
- **(a)** Evaluate S_{10}, S_{11} and S_{12}.
- **(b)** Describe what happens to S_n as n gets larger and larger.

C2 Repeat question C1 for the geometric series $1 - 3 + 9 - 27 + \dots$

C3 Let S_n be the sum of the first n terms of the geometric series $6 + 3 + 1\frac{1}{2} + \frac{3}{4} \dots$
- **(a)** Evaluate $S_{10}, S_{11}, S_{12}, S_{13}$ and S_{14}.
- **(b)** What do you think happens to S_n as n gets larger and larger?

C4 Repeat question C3 for the geometric series $1 - \frac{2}{3} + \frac{4}{9} - \frac{6}{27} + \dots$

Let S_n be the sum of the first n terms of the geometric series $5 + \frac{5}{3} + \frac{5}{9} + \frac{5}{27} + \dots$
Can we predict what will happen to S_n as n gets larger and larger?
The series is geometric with first term 5 and common ratio $\frac{1}{3}$.

So $S_n = \dfrac{5 \times \left(\left(\frac{1}{3}\right)^n - 1\right)}{\frac{1}{3} - 1} = \dfrac{5 \times \left(\left(\frac{1}{3}\right)^n - 1\right)}{-\frac{2}{3}} = -\frac{15}{2} \times \left(\left(\frac{1}{3}\right)^n - 1\right)$.

Now, as n gets larger and larger $\left(\frac{1}{3}\right)^n$ gets closer and closer to 0.

So S_n gets closer and closer to $-\frac{15}{2} \times (0 - 1) = \frac{15}{2}$.

We say   'As n tends to infinity then S_n converges to a limit of $\frac{15}{2}$'

or   'The sum to infinity of the series is $\frac{15}{2}$.'

As we have seen, not all geometric series have a 'sum to infinity'.
For example, the sum $1 + 2 + 4 + 8 + \dots$ does not converge to a limit.
A geometric series has a sum to infinity if r^n converges to 0 and this happens only if $-1 < r < 1$.
We can write this as $|r| < 1$, which means the size of r (ignoring negative signs) is less than 1.

> **K** A geometric series has a sum to infinity only if $-1 < r < 1$ (that is, $|r| < 1$).

In general, the sum of the first n terms of a geometric series is $\dfrac{a(r^n - 1)}{r - 1}$.

Now if $-1 < r < 1$ then, as n tends to infinity, r^n converges to 0

and so $\dfrac{a(r^n - 1)}{r - 1}$ converges to $\dfrac{a(0 - 1)}{r - 1} = \dfrac{-a}{r - 1} = \dfrac{a}{1 - r}$.

> **K** If $-1 < r < 1$ then the sum to infinity of the geometric series $a + ar + ar^2 + \dots$ is $\dfrac{a}{1 - r}$.

Sum to infinity is sometimes written S_∞.

Example 6

Find the sum to infinity of the geometric series $1 + \frac{2}{3} + \frac{4}{9} + \frac{8}{27} + \ldots$

Solution

The first term is $a = 1$ and the common ratio is $r = \frac{2}{3}$.

So the sum to infinity is $\dfrac{1}{1 - \frac{2}{3}} = \dfrac{1}{\frac{1}{3}} = 3$.

Example 7

The 2nd term of a geometric series is -4 and the sum to infinity is 9.
Find the first term of this series.

Solution

The first term is a and the common ratio is r.

The 2nd term is -4. $\qquad\qquad ar = -4$

The sum to infinity is 9. $\qquad\qquad \dfrac{a}{1-r} = 9$

Multiply both sides by $1 - r$. $\qquad\qquad a = 9(1 - r)$

Multiply by r to obtain ar on the left. $\qquad\qquad ar = 9r(1 - r)$

Substitute $ar = -4$. $\qquad\qquad -4 = 9r - 9r^2$

$$\Rightarrow \qquad 9r^2 - 9r - 4 = 0$$

$$\Rightarrow (3r + 1)(3r - 4) = 0$$

$$\Rightarrow \qquad r = -\tfrac{1}{3} \ \text{ or } \ r = \tfrac{4}{3}$$

Since there is a sum to infinity, $\frac{4}{3}$ is not a possible ratio as it is greater than 1.

So the common ratio is $-\frac{1}{3}$ and hence the first term is $-4 \div -\frac{1}{3} = 12$.

Exercise C (answers p 133)

1 For each geometric series below find the common ratio and,
where possible, calculate the sum to infinity.

(a) $14 + 7 + \frac{7}{2} + \frac{7}{4} + \ldots$

(b) $9 + \frac{9}{10} + \frac{9}{100} + \frac{9}{1000} + \ldots$

(c) $1 - 2 + 4 - 8 + \ldots$

(d) $4 - 3 + \frac{9}{4} - \frac{27}{16} + \ldots$

2 The first term of geometric series is 5 and the 2nd term is 1.
Find the sum to infinity.

3 The first term of a geometric series is 100 and the sum to infinity is 120.
Find the common ratio.

4 Two consecutive terms in a geometric series are 12 and 8.
The sum to infinity is 81. Find the first term.

5 The 2nd term of a geometric series is -6 and the sum to infinity is 8.
What is the first term of the series?

*6 The terms of a geometric series are all positive.
The sum of the first two terms is 15 and the sum to infinity is 27.
What are the first two terms of the series?

Key points

- A geometric sequence is one where each term can be found by multiplying the previous term by a fixed number (the common ratio). (pp 30–31)

- The nth term of a geometric sequence $a, ar, ar^2, ar^3, \dots$ is ar^{n-1} where a is the first term and r is the common ratio. (p 31)

- When the terms of a geometric sequence are added together they form a geometric series $a + ar + ar^2 + ar^3 + \dots + ar^{n-1}$.

  The sum of the first n terms of a geometric series is $\dfrac{a(r^n - 1)}{r - 1}$. (p 34)

- If $-1 < r < 1$ the sum to infinity of a geometric series is $\dfrac{a}{1 - r}$. (p 36)

Mixed questions (answers p 133)

1 The 4th term of a geometric series is 104 and the 7th term is 13.

  (a) What is the common ratio?

  (b) Find the first term of the series.

  (c) Find the sum to infinity of the series.

2 The 3rd term of a geometric sequence is 15 and the 4th term is 75.

  (a) Find the first term.

  (b) Write down an expression for the nth term.

  (c) Find the value of the 8th term.

  (d) What is the sum of the first 8 terms of the sequence?

3 Evaluate each of these.

  (a) $\displaystyle\sum_{n=1}^{15} 10 \times \left(\tfrac{3}{2}\right)^{n-1}$

  (b) $\displaystyle\sum_{p=1}^{10} 2 \times (-3)^{p-1}$

4 The 3rd term of a geometric series is 54 and the 6th term is 16.

  (a) Show that the common ratio is $\tfrac{2}{3}$.

  (b) Find the sum to infinity of the series.

5 A geometric series has first term 25 and 4th term $\frac{8}{5}$.

Find the common ratio and the sum to infinity of the series.

6 A company made a profit of £64 000 in the year 2001.
The company predicts that the yearly profits will increase in a geometric sequence with common ratio 1.03.

(a) What does the company predict that the profits will be, to the nearest £100,

(i) in 2002   (ii) in 2008

(b) Find the total predicted profit for the years 2001 to 2011.

7 A hospital offers Catherine a 30-day course of ultraviolet light therapy for her eczema. On day n of the course, she is to have t_n seconds of treatment, where

$$t_n = 69 \times 1.100\,21^{n-1}$$

(a) How long, to the nearest second, will Catherine's treatment be on

(i) day 10   (ii) day 30

(b) How much time will she spend in total having this treatment for her eczema?

8 Evaluate the sum $\displaystyle\sum_{i=0}^{20} \frac{1}{4} \times 2^i$.

9 The 2nd term of a geometric series is 80 and the 5th term of the series is 5.12.

(a) Find the common ratio and the first term of the series.

(b) Find the sum to infinity of the series, giving your answer as an exact fraction.

(c) Find the difference between the sum to infinity of the series and the sum of the first 14 terms of the series, giving your answer in the form $a \times 10^n$, where $1 \leq a < 10$ and n is an integer.

Edexcel

10 The 2nd and 4th terms of a geometric series are 20 and 3.2 respectively. Given that all the terms are positive, find the sum to infinity of the series.

11 A geometric series has a common ratio of $-\frac{1}{3}$. Its sum to infinity is 600.

(a) Find, to 2 d.p., the difference between the 10th and 11th terms.

(b) Write down and simplify an expression for the sum of the first n terms of the series.

(c) Show that, when n is even, the sum of the first n terms is less than 600.

*12 The first term of a geometric series is 48.
The sum of the first, 3rd and 5th terms is 63.
The 2nd term is negative. Find its value.

*13 A fractal is a pattern that can be divided into parts that are each a smaller copy of the whole pattern.

The 'box fractal' is shown below in its first few stages of development.

B_0 is a black square.
B_1 is derived by dividing B_0 into nine squares and removing four of them as shown.
B_2 is derived from B_1 by treating each black square in the same way.

Imagine this process continuing indefinitely.

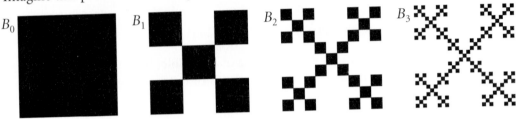

The area of B_0 is 1 square unit.

(a) Find the total area of the black squares in each of B_1, B_2, B_3, ...
Show that, as n tends to infinity, the area of the black squares in B_n converges to 0.

(b) (i) Show that the length of one side of B_0 is 1 unit.

(ii) If the perimeter of each of B_1, B_2, B_3, ... is the total perimeter of the black squares, show that, as n tends to infinity, the length of this perimeter tends towards infinity.

*14 Koch's fractal 'snowflake' curve is shown below in its first few stages of development. It was first described by Helge von Koch in 1904.

F_0 is an equilateral triangle.
F_1 is derived by trisecting each edge of F_0 and replacing the centre third of each edge by two sides of an equilateral triangle.
F_2 is derived from F_1 in the same way.

Imagine this process continuing indefinitely.

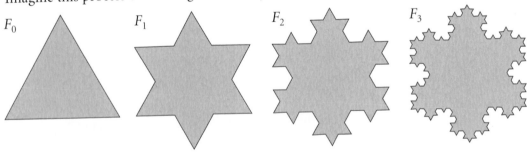

(a) When the area of F_0 is 1 square unit, find the areas of F_1, F_2, F_3, ...
Show that, as n tends to infinity, the area of F_n converges to a limit.
State the limiting value.

(b) Let the length of each side of F_0 be x units.
Does the perimeter of F_n converge to a limit too?

Test yourself (answers p 134)

1 The 3rd and 4th terms of a geometric series are 6.4 and 5.12 respectively.
Find

   (a) the common ratio of the series,

   (b) the first term of the series,

   (c) the sum to infinity of the series.

   (d) Calculate the difference between the sum to infinity of the series and the sum of the first 25 terms of the series.

Edexcel

2 The 3rd term of a geometric series is 6 and the 6th term is 162.
What is the first term of the series?

3 The sequence of terms $u_1, u_2, u_3, \ldots$ is defined by
$$u_n = 5 \times 2^n$$

   (a) Show that the sequence is geometric and write down the common ratio.

   (b) Show that none of the terms in the sequence is a square number.

   (c) Work out the sum of the first 10 terms.

4 Evaluate the sum $\displaystyle\sum_{n=1}^{10} 4 \times 3^{n-1}$

5 A geometric series is $a + ar + ar^2 + \ldots$

   (a) Prove that the sum of the first n terms of this series is given by $S_n = \dfrac{a(1-r^n)}{1-r}$

   The 2nd and 4th terms of the series are 3 and 1.08 respectively.
Given that all the terms in the series are positive, find

   (b) the value of r and the value of a,

   (c) the sum to infinity of the series.

Edexcel

6 A geometric series has first term 1200. Its sum to infinity is 960.

   (a) Show that the common ratio of the series is $-\frac{1}{4}$.

   (b) Find, to three decimal places, the difference between the 9th and 10th terms of the series.

   (c) Write down an expression for the sum of the first n terms of the series.

   Given that n is odd,

   (d) prove that the sum of the first n terms of the series is $960(1 + 0.25^n)$.

Edexcel

7 The first term of a geometric series is 20 and the sum to infinity is 50.
Find the sum of the first 10 terms, correct to 2 d.p.

8 The sum of the first three terms of a geometric series is 950.
The first term is 200 and all the terms are positive.

   (a) If r is the common ratio, show that it satisfies the equation $4r^2 + 4r - 15 = 0$.

   (b) What is the 3rd term of the series?

4 Binomial expansion

In this chapter you will learn how to find any term in the expansion of $(1 + x)^n$.

A Pascal's triangle (answers p 135)

To multiply out or **expand** $(a + b)^2$, you can use a table:

$(a + b)^2 = a^2 + 2ab + b^2$

Similarly you can expand $(a + b)^3$ by multiplying $(a^2 + 2ab + b^2)$ by $(a + b)$:

$(a + b)^3 = a^3 + 3a^2b + 3ab^2 + b^3$

A1 (a) Expand $(a + b)^4$ by multiplying $(a^3 + 3a^2b + 3ab^2 + b^3)$ by $(a + b)$.

 (b) Verify that $(a + b)^5 = a^5 + 5a^4b + 10a^3b^2 + 10a^2b^3 + 5ab^4 + b^5$.

Notice these things about the expansion of $(a + b)^5$:

- The terms start with a^5; in each following term the power of a goes down by 1 and the power of b goes up by 1, until b^5 is reached. The total power is always 5.
- The coefficients are 1, 5, 10, 10, 5, 1; they form a symmetrical pattern.

If you detach the coefficients from the expansions, you get an interesting pattern:

$(a + b)^0 = \mathbf{1}$

$(a + b)^1 = \mathbf{1}a + \mathbf{1}b$

$(a + b)^2 = \mathbf{1}a^2 + \mathbf{2}ab + \mathbf{1}b^2$

$(a + b)^3 = \mathbf{1}a^3 + \mathbf{3}a^2b + \mathbf{3}ab^2 + \mathbf{1}b^3$

$(a + b)^4 = \mathbf{1}a^4 + \mathbf{4}a^3b + \mathbf{6}a^2b^2 + \mathbf{4}ab^3 + \mathbf{1}b^4$

$(a + b)^5 = \mathbf{1}a^5 + \mathbf{5}a^4b + \mathbf{10}a^3b^2 + \mathbf{10}a^2b^3 + \mathbf{5}ab^4 + \mathbf{1}b^5$

```
                1
              1   1
            1   2   1
          1   3   3   1
        1   4   6   4   1
      1   5  10  10   5   1
```

The triangular pattern of numbers is called **Pascal's triangle**, after the French mathematician Blaise Pascal (1623–63).

A2 (a) How are the numbers in each row of Pascal's triangle related to the numbers in the previous row?

 (b) Write down the next row of the triangle and hence expand $(a + b)^6$.

 (c) Can you explain the relationship between the rows of Pascal's triangle? (You might do so using the 'table' method of expansion above.)

Example 1

Expand $(1 + 2x)^4$.

Solution

Use the expansion of $(a + b)^4$, with a replaced by 1, and b by 2x.

The expansion starts with 1^4.

The next term includes 1^3 and $(2x)^1$.

After this comes a term with 1^2 and $(2x)^2$, and so on.

The coefficients, from Pascal's triangle, are 1, 4, 6, 4, 1.

$$\begin{aligned}
\text{The expansion is } (1 + 2x)^4 &= 1^4 + 4 \times 1^3 \times (2x)^1 + 6 \times 1^2 \times (2x)^2 + 4 \times 1^1 \times (2x)^3 + (2x)^4 \\
&= 1 + 4 \times 2x + 6 \times 4x^2 + 4 \times 8x^3 + 16x^4 \\
&= 1 + 8x + 24x^2 + 32x^3 + 16x^4
\end{aligned}$$

Example 2

Expand $(1 - 3x)^3$.

Solution

Use the expansion of $(a + b)^3$, with a replaced by 1, and b by −3x.

$$\begin{aligned}
\text{The expansion is } (1 - 3x)^3 &= 1^3 + 3 \times 1^2 \times (-3x)^1 + 3 \times 1^1 \times (-3x)^2 + (-3x)^3 \\
&= 1 - 9x + 27x^2 - 27x^3
\end{aligned}$$

Exercise A (answers p 135)

Use Pascal's triangle (extended if necessary) to answer these questions.

1 Expand $(1 + x)^3$.

2 Expand each of these.

    (a) $(1 + 2x)^3$ **(b)** $(1 + 2x)^5$ **(c)** $(1 - x)^6$ **(d)** $(1 - 3x)^6$ **(e)** $\left(1 + \frac{1}{2}x\right)^7$

3 Expand   **(a)** $\left(1 - \frac{1}{2}x\right)^5$ **(b)** $(2 + x)^3$ **(c)** $(3 - 2x)^4$

4 (a) Expand $(1 + x)^8$ up to and including the term in x^3.

    (b) By substituting $x = 0.1$ in your result for (a), calculate an approximate value for $(1.1)^8$.

    (c) By means of a suitable substitution, use your result for (a) to calculate an approximate value for $(0.9)^8$.

If n is small, then the expansion of $(a + b)^n$ can be found by extending Pascal's triangle as far as is necessary.

However, for large values of n this method is cumbersome. What is needed is a way of calculating the coefficients for a given value of n. This is provided by the **binomial theorem**. In order to understand it, you need to know something about arrangements.

B Arrangements (answers p 135)

Suppose you have four letters: A, B, C, D. They can be arranged in order in different ways, for example ACDB, CBDA, DBAC, and so on. (Another word for an arrangement in order is 'permutation'.)

The first letter can be A, B, C or D. Each of these 4 choices can be followed by any of the 3 others, so these are the possible choices for the first two letters:

A then B, C or D: AB...   AC...   AD...
B then A, C or D: BA...   BC...   BD...
C then A, B or D: CA...   CB...   CD...
D then A, B or C: DA...   DB...   DC...

There are thus 12 choices for the first two letters. This is because there are 4 ways of choosing the first letter and each choice can be combined with 3 ways of choosing the second letter.

Each of these 12 possibilities can be followed by either of the remaining 2 letters. For example, AB can be followed by either C or D, giving ABC..., ABD... So altogether there are 24 choices for the first three letters.

Finally, for the fourth letter there is only one choice – the last remaining letter. For example, ABD must be followed by C, giving ABDC. So there are also 24 arrangements of all four letters.

B1 (a) How many arrangements are there of the five letters A, B, C, D, E?

(b) How can you work out the number of arrangements without having to list them all and count them?

Suppose you have seven letters to arrange in order. There are 7 choices for the first letter. Each of these can be combined with 6 choices for the second letter, and so on:

	1st		2nd		3rd		4th		5th		6th		7th	
Number of arrangements of 7 letters =	7	×	6	×	5	×	4	×	3	×	2	×	1	= 5040

The number $7 \times 6 \times 5 \times \ldots \times 2 \times 1$ is called **7 factorial** (written 7!).

In general,

$$n! = n(n-1)(n-2)(n-3) \times \ldots \times 3 \times 2 \times 1$$

B2 (a) Calculate the value of 6!.

(b) Given that $9! = 362\,880$, calculate 10!.

So far you have been looking at arrangements of a set of different letters. Now suppose that the letters are not all different, for example A, A, B, C.

Here are some of the arrangements: AACB, BAAC, CABA, ...

B3 (a) How many arrangements are there of the letters A, A, B, C?

(b) Why is the number half the number of arrangements of four different letters?

To see the effect of making some letters identical, first distinguish the identical letters. Think of the set A, A, B, C as A_1, A_2, B, C.

There are 4! = 24 ways of arranging the four letters A_1, A_2, B, C. Here are some of them:

A_1A_2BC A_2A_1BC A_1BA_2C A_2BA_1C BCA_1A_2 BCA_2A_1 ...

Notice that these arrangements come in pairs, for example A_1A_2BC and A_2A_1BC. As the two letter As are really the same, both arrangements in this pair correspond to the same arrangement AABC.

So the number of arrangements when the two As are identical is $\frac{4!}{2} = 12$.

D **B4** Suppose you have the set A, A, A, B, C. First distinguish the As as A_1, A_2, A_3.

  (a) How many arrangements are there of the five different letters A_1, A_2, A_3, B, C?

  (b) Here is one of the arrangements: $A_1BA_3A_2C$.
  How many arrangements (including this one) correspond to the arrangement ABAAC?

  (c) How many arrangements are there of the set A, A, A, B, C?

Suppose three letters in a set of six are identical: A, A, A, B, C, D.
If the three As are distinguished, then the set becomes A_1, A_2, A_3, B, C, D and there are 6! arrangements.

These arrangements can be split up into groups according to the positions occupied by the three As. For example, one group is shown on the right. This group corresponds to the arrangement AABDAC.

$A_1A_2BDA_3C$
$A_1A_3BDA_2C$
$A_2A_1BDA_3C$
$A_2A_3BDA_1C$
$A_3A_1BDA_2C$
$A_3A_2BDA_1C$

There are 3! arrangements in each group because there are 3! ways of arranging the 3 As within the group.

So when the As are identical, the number of arrangements is $\frac{6!}{3!} = 120$.

The general formula is this:

The number of arrangements of a set of n objects when r of them are identical is $\frac{n!}{r!}$.

Arrangements with objects of only two kinds

The special case that will be needed for the binomial theorem is where the set consists of n objects (letters) of which r are of one kind and the remaining $n - r$ are of another.

For example, suppose the set is A, A, A, A, B, B, B.

If all the As and all the Bs are distinguished, then there are 7! arrangements altogether.

Because the four As are identical, you have to divide by 4!. This gives $\frac{7!}{4!}$ arrangements in which the As are identical.

But because the three Bs are identical, you then have to divide this number by 3!.

Number of arrangements of A, A, A, A, B, B, B $= \frac{7!}{4! \times 3!} = \frac{7 \times 6 \times 5 \times 4 \times 3 \times 2 \times 1}{(4 \times 3 \times 2 \times 1) \times (3 \times 2 \times 1)}$

Notice that many of the factors in the numerator and denominator cancel out.

After cancelling out as many as possible, the result is $\frac{7 \times 6 \times 5}{3 \times 2 \times 1} = 35$.

The number of ways of arranging n objects of which r are of one type and $n - r$ of another is denoted by the symbol $\binom{n}{r}$. Its value is given by $\binom{n}{r} = \dfrac{n!}{r!(n-r)!}$.

In practice, many factors in the numerator and denominator cancel out.

For example, $\binom{8}{3} = \dfrac{8!}{3! \times 5!} = \dfrac{8 \times 7 \times 6 \times 5 \times 4 \times 3 \times 2 \times 1}{(3 \times 2 \times 1) \times (5 \times 4 \times 3 \times 2 \times 1)} = \dfrac{8 \times 7 \times 6}{3 \times 2 \times 1}$.

This leads to another formula:

$$\binom{n}{r} = \dfrac{n(n-1)(n-2)\ldots}{r!}$$

> Continue until you have r factors in the numerator.

So $\binom{n}{1} = n$ $\qquad \binom{n}{2} = \dfrac{n(n-1)}{2!} \qquad \binom{n}{3} = \dfrac{n(n-1)(n-2)}{3!}$

Written in this way, the general formula is

$$\binom{n}{r} = \dfrac{n(n-1)(n-2)\ldots(n-r+1)}{r!}$$

> The rth factor here is $n - (r-1)$ or $n - r + 1$.

Your calculator may use a different notation: $_nC_r$ or ^nC_r. To calculate $\binom{7}{3}$, enter 7, press $_nC_r$ and then enter 3 = .

The letter 'C' in this notation stands for 'combination', which arises as follows. Suppose you have 7 people and you want to select a group of 3 from them, where the order of selection does not matter. Each 'combination' of 3 people corresponds to saying 'yes' (Y) to 3 people and 'no' (N) to the other 4 people. Here, for example, is one possible combination:

Person: A B C D E F G
Decision: Y N N Y N Y N

Each combination corresponds to an arrangement of 3 Ys and 4 Ns.

So the number of combinations is $\binom{7}{3}$.

B5 Use one of the formulae above to calculate $\binom{9}{3}$. Then check using a calculator.

B6 Use a calculator to find the value of   (a) $\binom{6}{2}$ (b) $\binom{9}{4}$ (c) $\binom{20}{10}$

B7 (a) $\binom{7}{0}$ is the number of arrangements of 7 objects, of which none are of one type and 7 are of the other. So what is its value?

(b) If you use the factorial formula to work out $\binom{7}{0}$, what value must you give to 0!?

C The binomial theorem (answers p 136)

You should now be in a position to see how the work on arrangements relates to expanding expressions of the form $(a + b)^n$.

Consider $(a + b)^2 = (a + b)(a + b)$.

Normally when you expand this you get $a^2 + 2ab + b^2$.
However, for the time being distinguish between ab and ba.
ab arises from multiplying a in the first bracket by b in the second.
ba arises from multiplying b in the first bracket by a in the second.

$$\overbrace{ab}$$
$$(a + b)(a + b)$$
$$\underbrace{ba}$$

Write a^2 as aa and b^2 as bb.

So $(a + b)^2$ is expanded as $aa + ab + ba + bb$.

C1 $(a + b)^3 = (aa + ab + ba + bb)(a + b)$.
Write out the expansion of $(a + b)^3$ in the form $aaa + aab + \dots$
(In other words, don't simplify, combine terms or use indices.)

The expansion of $(a + b)^4$ is the result of multiplying out $(a + b)(a + b)(a + b)(a + b)$.
Each term arises from multiplying as from some brackets by bs from the others.

For example, this combination $(a + b)(a + b)(a + b)(a + b)$ gives the term $abba$.

The expansion of $(a + b)^4$, written without any simplification or index notation, is as follows:

$(a + b)^4 = \quad aaaa$
$\quad + aaab + aaba + abaa + baaa$
$\quad + aabb + abab + abba + baab + baba + bbaa$
$\quad + abbb + babb + bbab + bbba$
$\quad + bbbb$

The first term is of course a^4.

The second line contains all the terms that correspond to a^3b.
They consist of all the arrangements of 1 b and 3 as, so the coefficient of a^3b is $\binom{4}{1} = 4$.

The next line contains all the terms that correspond to a^2b^2.
They consist of all the arrangements of 2 bs and 2 as, so the coefficient of a^2b^2 is $\binom{4}{2} = 6$.
Similarly for the other two lines.

So $(a + b)^4 = a^4 + \binom{4}{1}a^3b + \binom{4}{2}a^2b^2 + \binom{4}{3}ab^3 + b^4$

This expansion of $(a + b)^4$ is an example of the **binomial theorem**:
$$(a + b)^n = a^n + \binom{n}{1}a^{n-1}b + \binom{n}{2}a^{n-2}b^2 + \binom{n}{3}a^{n-3}b^3 + \dots + b^n$$

An important special case arises by letting $a = 1$ and $b = x$:

K
$$(1+x)^n = 1 + \binom{n}{1}x + \binom{n}{2}x^2 + \binom{n}{3}x^3 + \ldots + x^n$$

which can also be written:

$$(1+x)^n = 1 + nx + \frac{n(n-1)}{2!}x^2 + \frac{n(n-1)(n-2)}{3!}x^3 + \ldots + x^n$$

The values of the binomial coefficients can be found either from a calculator or by using one of the formulae. If the value of n is small, you could also find the coefficients by extending Pascal's triangle.

C2 (a) Write down the first four terms in the expansion of $(1 + x)^{10}$.

   (b) By replacing x by $-x$, write down the first four terms in the expansion of $(1 - x)^{10}$.

Example 3

Find the coefficient of y^4 in the expansion of $(1 + 3y)^9$.

Solution

The term containing y^4 is $\binom{9}{4}(3y)^4 = 126 \times 81 y^4 = 10\,206 y^4$.

So the coefficient of y^4 is $10\,206$.

Example 4

Use the binomial theorem to find the value of $(1.02)^8$ correct to two decimal places.

Solution

Use the expansion of $(1 + x)^n$ with $x = 0.02$ and $n = 8$. Continue the expansion until the terms become so small that they do not affect the second decimal place.

$$(1.02)^8 = 1 + \binom{8}{1} \times (0.02) + \binom{8}{2} \times (0.02)^2 + \binom{8}{3} \times (0.02)^3 + \ldots$$

$$= 1 + 8 \times 0.02 + 28 \times 0.0004 + 56 \times 0.000\,008 + \ldots$$

$$= 1 + 0.16 + 0.0112 + 0.000\,448 + \ldots = 1.17 \text{ (to 2 d.p.)}$$

Example 5

Find the coefficient of x^2 in the expansion of $(1 + 4x)^4(1 - 2x)^6$.

Solution

Expand each factor as far as the x^2 term. $\quad (1 + 4x)^4 = 1 + 16x + 96x^2 + \ldots$
$$(1 - 2x)^6 = 1 - 12x + 60x^2 - \ldots$$

Pick out the terms that will give an x^2 when multiplied.

$(1 + 16x + 96x^2)(1 - 12x + 60x^2)$ Term in x^2 is $60x^2 - 192x^2 + 96x^2 = -36x^2$

So the coefficient of x^2 is -36.

Example 6

Find the term containing x^3 in the expansion of $(3 - 2x)^7$.

Solution

Use the binomial theorem for $(a + b)^n$ with $a = 3$, $b = -2x$ and $n = 7$.

The term containing x^3 is $\binom{7}{3} \times 3^4 \times (-2x)^3 = 35 \times 81 \times (-8x^3) = -22\,680x^3$.

Example 7

The expansion of $(3 + kx)^5$ in ascending powers of x, as far as the term in x^2, is

$$243 + ax + 120x^2$$

Given that $a < 0$, find the value of k and the value of a.

Solution

Pascal's triangle gives the binomial coefficients: 1, 5, 10, ...

So the expansion as far as the term in x^2 is

$$3^5 + 5 \times 3^4 \times kx + 10 \times 3^3 \times (kx)^2$$
$$= 243 + 405kx + 270k^2x^2$$

Equating the coefficients of x^2 gives
$$270k^2 = 120$$
$$\Rightarrow \quad k^2 = \tfrac{120}{270} = \tfrac{4}{9}$$
$$\Rightarrow \quad k = \pm \tfrac{2}{3}$$

As $a < 0$ the value of k is $-\tfrac{2}{3}$.

As $a = 405k$ $\;a = 405 \times -\tfrac{2}{3} = -270$.

Example 8

In the expansion of $(1 + 2x)^n$, the coefficient of x^2 is 6 times the coefficient of x.
Given that $n > 2$, find the value of n.

Solution

The expansion as far as the term in x^2 is
$$1 + n(2x) + \tfrac{1}{2}n(n - 1)(2x)^2$$
$$= 1 + 2nx + 2n(n - 1)x^2$$

The coefficient of x^2 is six times the coefficient of x so $\quad 2n(n - 1) = 2n \times 6$

$n = 0$ is a solution of this equation but we know that $n > 2$ so $\quad n - 1 = 6$

$$\Rightarrow \quad n = 7$$

Exercise C (answers p 136)

1 Write down the first four terms in the expansion of $(1 + x)^{12}$.

2 Find the coefficient of

(a) x^5 in the expansion of $(1 + x)^{10}$ (b) x^3 in the expansion of $(1 + x)^{20}$

3 Use the binomial theorem to find the value of $(1.03)^7$ correct to two decimal places.

4 Find the first four terms in the expansion of

(a) $(1 + 2x)^9$ (b) $(1 - 3x)^8$ (c) $(1 + \frac{1}{2}x)^{15}$ (d) $(1 - \frac{1}{5}x)^7$

5 (a) Expand $(1 - 2x)^5$ as far as the term in x^2.

(b) Hence find the coefficient of x^2 in the expansion of $(3 - 4x - x^2)(1 - 2x)^5$.

6 Find the coefficient of x^3 in the expansion of

(a) $(2 + x)^9$ (b) $(2 - x)^9$ (c) $(2 + 3x)^9$

7 (a) Expand $(1 + x)^8$ in ascending powers of x, as far as the term in x^3.

(b) Use your series, together with a suitable value of x, to calculate an estimate of $(0.98)^8$.

8 (a) Expand and simplify $(3 + x)^6 - (3 - x)^6$.

(b) Hence show that, for all integers x, the value of $(3 + x)^6 - (3 - x)^6$ is divisible by 36.

9 The expansion of $(2 + qx)^6$ in ascending powers of x, as far as the term in x^2, is

$$a + 144x + bx^2$$

Find the values of the constants q, a and b.

10 (a) Write down the first four terms of the binomial expansion, in ascending powers of x, of $(1 + 5x)^n$, where $n > 2$.

(b) Given that the coefficient of x^3 in this expansion is 15 times the coefficient of x^2,

   (i) find the value of n

   (ii) find the coefficient of x in the expansion

11 In the expansion of $(1 + kx)^n$, where k and n are positive integers, the coefficient of x^3 is twice the coefficient of x^2.

(a) Prove that $n = 2 + \dfrac{6}{k}$.

(b) Find all the possible pairs of values of k and n.

12 Find the coefficient of x in the expansion of $\left(2x + \dfrac{1}{x}\right)^9$.

Key points

- $n!$ (n factorial) is $n(n-1)(n-2)(n-3)\times\ldots\times3\times2\times1$ (p 44)

- $(a + b)^n = a^n + \binom{n}{1}a^{n-1}b + \binom{n}{2}a^{n-2}b^2 + \binom{n}{3}a^{n-3}b^3 + \ldots + b^n$ (p 47)

- $(1 + x)^n = 1 + \binom{n}{1}x + \binom{n}{2}x^2 + \binom{n}{3}x^3 + \ldots + x^n$

  The coefficient of x^r in this expansion is $\binom{n}{r} = \dfrac{n!}{r!(n-r)!} = \dfrac{n(n-1)(n-2)\ldots(n-r+1)}{r!}$ (pp 46, 48)

Test yourself (answers p 136)

1 Write down the first four terms in the expansion of $(1 + x)^{20}$.

2 Find the coefficient of x^3 in the expansion of **(a)** $(1 + 4x)^7$ **(b)** $(1 - 2x)^{10}$

3 Expand $(1 + 2x)^5(1 - \frac{1}{2}x)^8$ as far as the term in x^2.

4 Use the binomial theorem to find the value, correct to two decimal places, of
   (a) $(1.04)^6$ **(b)** $(0.99)^8$

5 The expansion of $(2 - px)^6$ in ascending powers of x, as far as the term in x^2, is
$$64 + Ax + 135x^2$$
   Given that $p > 0$, find the value of p and the value of A.

Edexcel

6 **(a)** Write down the first four terms of the binomial expansion, in ascending powers of x, of $(1 + 3x)^n$, where $n > 2$.
   Given that the coefficient of x^3 in this expansion is 10 times the coefficient of x^2,
   (b) find the value of n,
   (c) find the coefficient of x^4 in the expansion.

Edexcel

7 The first three terms in the expansion, in ascending powers of x, of $(1 + px)^n$, are $1 - 18x + 36p^2x^2$.
   Given that n is a positive integer, find the value of n and the value of p.

Edexcel

8 **(a)** Given that $(2 + x)^5 + (2 - x)^5 = A + Bx^2 + Cx^4$,
   find the values of the constants A, B and C.
   (b) Using the substitution $y = x^2$ and your answers to part (a), solve
   $$(2 + x)^5 + (2 - x)^5 = 349.$$

Edexcel

9 **(a)** Expand $\left(2 + \frac{1}{4}x\right)^9$ in ascending powers of x, as far as the term in x^3, simplifying each term.
   (b) Use your series, together with a suitable value of x, to calculate an estimate of $(2.025)^9$.

Edexcel

10 $f(x) = \left(1 + \frac{x}{k}\right)^n$, where k and n are integers and $n > 2$.

   Given that the coefficient of x^3 is twice the coefficient of x^2 in the binomial expansion of $f(x)$,

   (a) prove that $n = 6k + 2$.

   Given also that the coefficients of x^4 and x^5 are equal and non-zero,

   (b) form another equation in n and k and hence show that $k = 2$ and $n = 14$.

   Using these values of k and n,

   (c) expand $f(x)$ in ascending powers of x, up to and including the term in x^5.
   Give each coefficient as an exact fraction in its lowest terms.

Edexcel

5 Trigonometry 1

In this chapter you will
- revise the sine and cosine ratios between 0° and 180°
- find lengths and angles in any triangle, using the sine and cosine rules
- calculate the area of any triangle
- learn about radian measure for angles
- calculate lengths of arcs and areas of sectors of circles

A Sine and cosine: revision (answers p 137)

The diagram shows a circle with radius 1 unit.
This is called the unit circle.

The angle $\theta°$ is measured in an anticlockwise direction
from the positive x-axis.

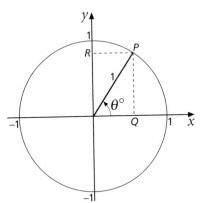

A1 Explain why the coordinates of P are $(\cos\theta°, \sin\theta°)$.

Cos $\theta°$ can be defined as the x-coordinate of P.
Sin $\theta°$ can be defined as the y-coordinate of P.

This allows us to define $\cos\theta°$ and $\sin\theta°$ for any angle $\theta°$.

A2 Without using a calculator, write down each of these.

   (a) $\cos0°$ (b) $\sin0°$ (c) $\sin90°$ (d) $\cos90°$

   (e) $\sin180°$ (f) $\cos270°$ (g) $\sin-90°$ (h) $\cos-90°$

A3 Without using a calculator, write down whether each of these is positive or negative.

   (a) $\cos30°$ (b) $\sin120°$ (c) $\cos120°$ (d) $\cos200°$

   (e) $\sin330°$ (f) $\cos330°$ (g) $\sin220°$ (h) $\cos-120°$

A4 (a) When $90° < \theta° < 180°$, is the x-coordinate of P positive or negative?
      What does this tell you about $\cos\theta°$ when $90° < \theta° < 180°$?

   (b) What can you say about $\sin\theta°$ when $90° < \theta° < 180°$?

A5 Use the unit circle to show that $\sin20° = \sin160°$.

A6 Use the unit circle to show that $\sin(180° - \theta°) = \sin\theta°$ for all values
of $\theta°$ between 0° and 180°.

A7 Draw a sketch graph of $y = \sin\theta°$ for $0° < \theta° < 180°$.

A8 Use the unit circle to show that $\cos20° = -\cos160°$.

A9 Use the unit circle to show that $\cos(180° - \theta°) = -\cos\theta°$ for all values of $\theta°$ between $0°$ and $180°$.

A10 Draw a sketch graph of $y = \cos\theta°$ for $0° < \theta° < 180°$.

A11 Use a calculator to find (to the nearest degree) the acute angle $\theta°$ such that $\sin\theta° = 0.63$. Use your previous results to find another angle (less than $360°$) whose sine is 0.63.

A12 Use a calculator to find (to the nearest degree) the acute angle $\theta°$ such that $\cos\theta° = 0.63$. Use your previous results to find an obtuse angle whose cosine is -0.63.

Example 1

Find two angles (to the nearest degree) in the range $0° < \theta° < 180°$ such that $\sin\theta° = 0.8$.

Solution

Key in $\sin^{-1}0.8$

$\theta° = 53°$ is one angle.

To obtain the other angle think about the unit circle …   *… or the graph of* $\sin\theta°$.

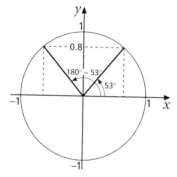   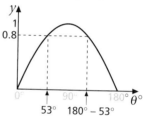

The other angle is $180° - 53° = 127°$.

Exercise A (answers p 138)

1 State whether each of these is positive or negative.

(a) $\sin 95°$ (b) $\cos 95°$ (c) $\sin 170°$ (d) $\cos 170°$

2 (a) Use your calculator to find (to the nearest degree) the angle between $0°$ and $90°$ whose sine is 0.34.

(b) Hence find the two solutions to $\sin\theta° = 0.34$ ($0° < \theta° < 180°$).

3 Solve each of these equations, giving solutions between $0°$ and $180°$ to the nearest degree.

(a) $\sin\theta° = 0.9$ (b) $\cos\theta° = 0.9$ (c) $\sin\theta° = 0.45$ (d) $\cos\theta° = -0.45$

(e) $\sin\theta° = 0.53$ (f) $\cos\theta° = 0.53$ (g) $\sin\theta° = 0.07$ (h) $\cos\theta° = -0.07$

*4 Explain why, if $0° < \theta° < 180°$ and $-1 < k < 1$, $\sin\theta° = k$ has either no solution or two solutions for $\theta°$, but $\cos\theta° = k$ always has one solution.

B Cosine rule (answers p 138)

It is easy to 'solve' a right-angled triangle (find its unknown angles and sides)
by using Pythagoras's theorem and the sine, cosine and tangent ratios.
But if a triangle is not right-angled, we need other methods.

> The side opposite
> angle A is called a,
> the one opposite B
> is b, and so on.

B1 Consider triangle ABC.

    (a) Write PB in terms of c and x.

    (b) Use Pythagoras in triangle CPB to write an
expression for h^2 in terms of a, x and c.

    (c) Use Pythagoras in triangle CPA to write an
expression for h^2 in terms of b and x.

    (d) Put your two expressions for h^2 equal
to each other, and make a^2 the subject.

    (e) Expand brackets and simplify this formula for a^2.

    (f) In triangle CPA, write an expression for x in terms of b and angle A.

    (g) Substitute the expression for x in the formula you obtained in part (e).
Check that you have obtained $a^2 = b^2 + c^2 - 2bc \cos A$.

B2 Prove that the rule you obtained in B1
is still true when angle A is obtuse.

    (Hint: you will need to use the fact
that $\cos(180° - \theta°) = -\cos\theta°$.)

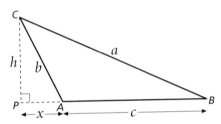

 The **cosine rule** states that $a^2 = b^2 + c^2 - 2bc \cos A$.

Similarly, $b^2 = a^2 + c^2 - 2ac \cos B$ and $c^2 = a^2 + b^2 - 2ab \cos C$.

Example 2

Find the length of side GF in triangle EFG.

Solution

*The triangle is not right-angled. You know two sides
and the enclosed angle, so use the cosine rule.*

In triangle EFG, $e^2 = f^2 + g^2 - 2fg \cos E$

$$e^2 = 6^2 + 8^2 - 2 \times 6 \times 8 \times \cos 75°$$
$$e^2 = 75.153\ldots$$
$$e = 8.67 \text{ (to 2 d.p.)}$$

So the length of GF is 8.67 cm (to 2 d.p.).

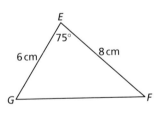

Example 3

Find angle R in triangle PQR.

Solution

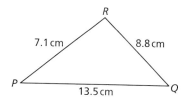

You know all three sides of the triangle, so use the cosine rule.

In triangle PQR, $\quad r^2 = p^2 + q^2 - 2pq \cos R$

$$13.5^2 = 8.8^2 + 7.1^2 - 2 \times 8.8 \times 7.1 \times \cos R$$

$\Rightarrow \quad 2 \times 8.8 \times 7.1 \times \cos R = 8.8^2 + 7.1^2 - 13.5^2$

$\Rightarrow \qquad\qquad \cos R = \dfrac{8.8^2 + 7.1^2 - 13.5^2}{2 \times 8.8 \times 7.1}$

so $\quad \cos R = -0.4353\ldots$

$\qquad\qquad R = 115.8\ldots°$

$\qquad\qquad\quad = 116°$ to the nearest degree

The cosine is negative, so the angle is obtuse.

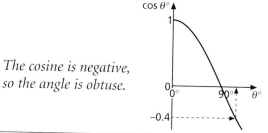

Exercise B (answers p 138)

1 Work out the length marked **?** in each of these triangles.

(a)

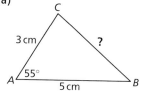

(b)

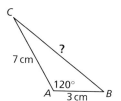

(c)

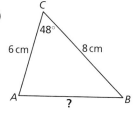

2 Work out the angle marked **?** in each of these triangles.

(a)

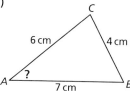

(b)

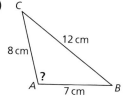

(c)

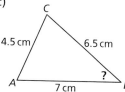

3 The hands of a clock are 10 cm and 7 cm long.
Calculate the distance between their tips when it is exactly 2 o'clock.

4 A triangle has sides 4 cm, 5 cm and 7 cm.
Calculate all its angles.

5 A is 2.1 km due north of B.
C is 3.7 km from B on a bearing of 136°.
Find the distance from C to A.

*6 In the triangle shown, $BC = 8$, $CA = 6$, $AB = 7$
and M is the mid-point of BC. Angle $AMC = \theta°$.

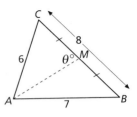

(a) Use the cosine rule to write down an expression
for AC^2 in terms of $\cos \theta°$, CM and AM.

(b) Write an expression for AB^2 in terms of $\cos \theta°$, BM and AM.

(c) Add the expressions you obtained in (a) and (b),
and hence calculate the length of AM.

C Sine rule (answers p 138)

The cosine rule enables you to find a side when you know two sides and the
angle they enclose, or an angle when you know all three sides.

You can solve other triangles using the **sine rule**.

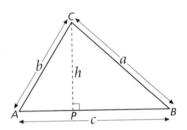

C1 (a) In triangle APC, write h in terms of b and angle A.

(b) In triangle BPC, write h in terms of a and angle B.

(c) Put these two expressions for h equal to each other.

(d) Divide both sides of your equation in (c),
first by $\sin A$, and then by $\sin B$.

(e) Check that your result is $\dfrac{a}{\sin A} = \dfrac{b}{\sin B}$

If we start with sides b and c and angles B and C, we can prove that $\dfrac{b}{\sin B} = \dfrac{c}{\sin C}$.

Combining these two results we have the **sine rule**:

$$\frac{a}{\sin A} = \frac{b}{\sin B} = \frac{c}{\sin C}$$

C2 In triangle ABC, angle A is obtuse.

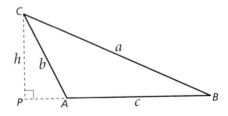

(a) In triangle PAC, express h in
terms of b and angle PAC.

(b) Express angle PAC in terms of
angle A (i.e. angle CAB).
Rewrite the expression for h you
obtained in (a) in terms of angle A.

(c) Use the fact that $\sin(180° - \theta°) = \sin \theta°$ to simplify your expression.

(d) Now write an expression for h in terms of side a and angle B.

(e) Hence show that in this triangle $\dfrac{a}{\sin A} = \dfrac{b}{\sin B}$.

Since angles B and C are acute, $\dfrac{b}{\sin B} = \dfrac{c}{\sin C}$, as before. So $\dfrac{a}{\sin A} = \dfrac{b}{\sin B} = \dfrac{c}{\sin C}$.

Example 4

Find the length of side *ST* in triangle *RST*.

Solution

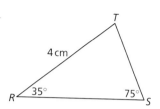

You know side RT and the angle opposite it.
You know the angle opposite side ST, so use the sine rule.

In triangle *RST*, $\dfrac{r}{\sin R} = \dfrac{s}{\sin S} = \dfrac{t}{\sin T}$ *You don't need the* $\dfrac{t}{\sin T}$ *part and could omit it.*

$$\frac{r}{\sin 35°} = \frac{4}{\sin 75°}$$

$$\Rightarrow \quad r = \frac{4 \times \sin 35°}{\sin 75°} = 2.375\ldots$$

so $ST = 2.4\,\text{cm}$ (to 1 d.p.)

Example 5

Find angle *D* in triangle *DEF*.

Solution

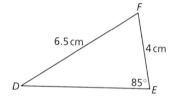

You know side e and angle E.
You know side d, so use the sine rule.

In triangle *DEF*, $\dfrac{d}{\sin D} = \dfrac{e}{\sin E}$

$$\frac{4}{\sin D} = \frac{6.5}{\sin 85°}$$

$$\Rightarrow \quad 4 \times \sin 85° = 6.5 \times \sin D$$

$$\Rightarrow \quad \sin D = \frac{4 \times \sin 85°}{6.5} = 0.613\ldots$$

Use your calculator. $D = 38°$ (to the nearest degree)

Another answer is therefore $D = 180° - 38° = 142°$

But if $D = 142°$, then the angle sum of triangle *DEF* is clearly greater than 180°.

Hence the only possible solution here is $D = 38°$ (to the nearest degree).

$\sin \theta°$ *and* $\sin(180° - \theta°)$ *both have the same value.*

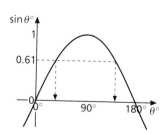

Example 6

Find angle R in triangle PQR.

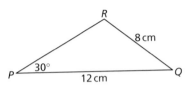

Solution

In triangle PQR, $\dfrac{p}{\sin P} = \dfrac{r}{\sin R}$

$$\dfrac{8}{\sin 30°} = \dfrac{12}{\sin R}$$

$\Rightarrow \quad 8 \sin R = 12 \sin 30°$

$\Rightarrow \quad \sin R = \dfrac{12 \sin 30°}{8} = 0.75$

Use your calculator. $R = 49°$ (to the nearest degree)
Another answer is therefore $R = 180° - 49° = 131°$

$\sin \theta°$ *and* $\sin(180° - \theta°)$
both have the same value.

Check whether both answers are possible.

If $R = 49°$, then $Q = 180° - 30° - 49° = 101°$
If $R = 131°$, then $Q = 180° - 30° - 131° = 19°$

Both answers are possible.

So $R = 49°$ or $131°$ (to the nearest degree).

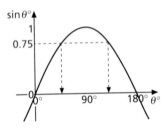

It may be helpful to sketch the two solutions as a further check.

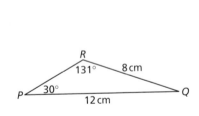
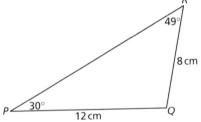

Exercise C (answers p 138)

1 Find the length marked **?** in each of these triangles.

(a)

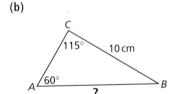

(b)

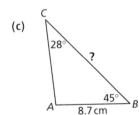

(c)

2 In triangle ABC, $c = 11$ cm, $a = 12$ cm and angle $A = 68°$.

(a) Draw a sketch of triangle ABC.

(b) Use the sine rule to calculate the value of $\sin C$.

(c) Your result in (b) can lead to two different values for angle C. What are these (to the nearest degree)?

(d) For each of your possible values of angle C, find the value of angle B.

(e) Write down the value or values of angle C that are possible. For each possible value of C draw a rough sketch of the triangle.

3 Find the angle marked **?** in each of these triangles. Where there is more than one solution, give both.

(a)

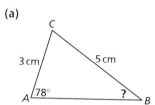

(b)

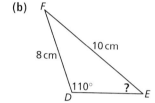

(c)

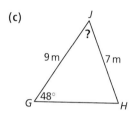

D Both rules

To solve many triangles you will need to use a rule twice, or use the sine rule and the cosine rule.

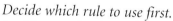

Example 7

Solve triangle DEF.

Solution

'Solve' means find all the unknown angles and sides.

Decide which rule to use first.
In this case, the sine rule is possible.

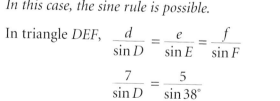

In triangle DEF, $\dfrac{d}{\sin D} = \dfrac{e}{\sin E} = \dfrac{f}{\sin F}$

$$\frac{7}{\sin D} = \frac{5}{\sin 38°} \qquad \frac{f}{\sin F} \text{ is not needed.}$$

$$\Rightarrow 7\sin 38° = 5\sin D$$

$$\Rightarrow \quad \sin D = \frac{7\sin 38°}{5} = 0.8619\ldots$$

Use the calculator. $\quad D = 59.53\ldots° = 59.5°$ (to 1 d.p.)
Another answer is therefore $\quad D = 180° - 59.5° = 120.5°$

Check whether both answers are possible.

$$\text{If } D = 59.5° \text{ then } F = 180° - 38° - 59.5° = 82.5°$$
$$\text{If } D = 120.5° \text{ then } F = 180° - 38° - 120.5° = 21.5°$$

Both answers are possible. So $D = 59.5°$ or $120.5°$ (to 1 d.p.)   (*Solution continues over.*)

Deal with each possible value of D separately.
For each value, draw a sketch showing what you know so far.

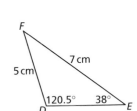

Use the result you obtained before rounding.

If $D = 59.53...°$

then $F = 180° - 38° - 59.53...° = 82.46...°$

Now use the sine rule again.

$$\frac{f}{\sin 82.46...°} = \frac{5}{\sin 38°}$$

$$\Rightarrow \qquad f = \frac{5\sin 82.46...°}{\sin 38°} = 8.05... = 8.1 \text{ (1 d.p.)}$$

So the first solution is $D = 59.5°$, $F = 82.5°$ and $DE = 8.1\,\text{cm}$
(each answer to 1 d.p.).

Alternatively, if $D = 180° - 59.53...° = 120.46...°$
then $F = 180° - 38° - 120.46...° = 21.53...°$

and $\qquad \dfrac{f}{\sin 21.53...°} = \dfrac{5}{\sin 38°}$

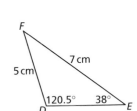

$$\Rightarrow \qquad f = \frac{5\sin 21.53...°}{\sin 38°} = 2.98... = 3.0 \text{ (1 d.p.)}$$

So the second solution is $D = 120.5°$, $F = 21.5°$ and $DE = 3.0\,\text{cm}$ (answers to 1 d.p.).

Exercise D (answers p 139)

1 Use the sine rule to solve (find all the unknown angles and sides in)
each of these triangles.
If there is more than one solution, give both solutions.

(a)

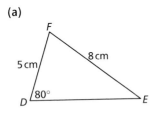

(b)

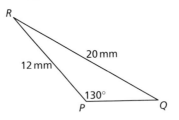

(c)

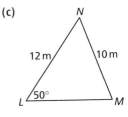

2 Use the cosine rule and then the sine rule to solve these triangles.

(a)

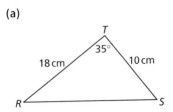

(b)

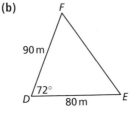

3 Solve these triangles.

(a)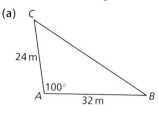

(b)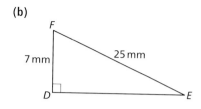

(c)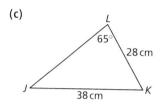

(d)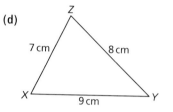

E Area of a triangle

There is a simple formula for the area of a triangle, when you know two sides and the angle between them.

In triangle PBC, $h = a \sin B$.

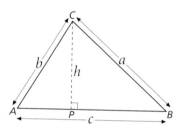

The area of triangle $ABC = \frac{1}{2}$ base$\times$height

$$= \frac{1}{2}c \times h = \frac{1}{2}c \times a \sin B$$

$$= \frac{1}{2}ac \sin B$$

By drawing perpendiculars to the other two sides we can show that:

Area of triangle ABC
$= \frac{1}{2}ab \sin C = \frac{1}{2}bc \sin A = \frac{1}{2}ac \sin B$

This result also holds true for an obtuse-angled triangle.

Example 8

Find the area of triangle RST.

Solution

Area of triangle RST

$= \frac{1}{2}rt \sin S$

$= \frac{1}{2} \times 6 \times 7 \times \sin 40°$

$= 13.498\ldots$

You know S, so the lengths in the formula are r and t.

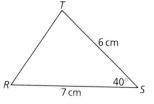

The area of triangle RST is $13.5 \, \text{cm}^2$ (to 1 d.p.).

Example 9

Find the area of triangle PQR.

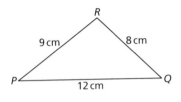

Solution

To find the area you need two sides and the included angle. So first find an angle, using the cosine rule. Any angle will do; here angle P is found.

$$p^2 = q^2 + r^2 - 2qr\cos P$$
$$8^2 = 9^2 + 12^2 - 2\times9\times12\times\cos P$$

$$\cos P = \frac{9^2 + 12^2 - 8^2}{2\times9\times12} = 0.745\ldots$$

$$P = 41.8\ldots°$$ *Don't lose any accuracy at this stage.*

So area of triangle $PQR = \frac{1}{2}qr\sin P$

$$= \frac{1}{2}\times9\times12\times\sin 41.8\ldots°$$
$$= 35.9991\ldots$$

So the area is $36\,\text{cm}^2$ (to the nearest cm^2).

Exercise E (answers p 139)

1 Find the area of each triangle.

(a)

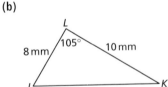

(b)

(c)

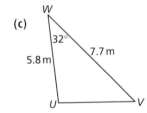

2 Triangle RST has $RS = 8\,\text{cm}$, $ST = 10\,\text{cm}$ and $TR = 11\,\text{cm}$.

(a) Use the cosine rule to find one angle of the triangle.

(b) Use your result to find the area of the triangle.

3 Find the area of each of these triangles.

(a)

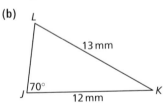

(b)

(c)

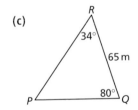

F Radians and arcs (answers p 139)

We measure angles in degrees for historical reasons:
the ancient Babylonians divided their day into 360 units
of time, and their circle into 360 units too.

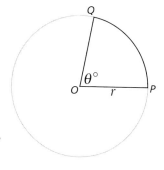

But using the degree as the unit of angle measurement
leads to complicated formulas.

For example, the distance all round the circle shown is $2\pi r$.

The arc PQ, which subtends an angle of θ degrees at the centre,
is therefore $\dfrac{\theta}{360}$ of the whole circle, or $\dfrac{\theta}{360} \times 2\pi r = \dfrac{\pi r \theta}{180}$.

To simplify this formula we use a different measure of angle
in more advanced mathematics.

This measure is called the **radian**.

One radian is defined as the angle subtended at the centre
of a circle radius r by an arc of length r (i.e. equal to the radius).

As an arc of length r subtends an angle of one radian, so the
whole circumference of the circle ($2\pi r$) subtends 2π radians.

So $360° = 2\pi$ radians.

F1 Write the following angles in radians, giving answers in terms of π.

(a) $180°$ (b) $90°$ (c) $60°$ (d) $30°$ (e) $270°$ (f) $1°$

F2 Work out the size of one radian in degrees.

F3 In a circle of radius r, an angle of one radian is subtended by an arc of length r.

(a) What length arc subtends an angle of 2 radians?

(b) What length arc subtends an angle of $\frac{1}{2}$ radian?

(c) What length arc subtends an angle of θ radians?

F4 A circle has a radius of 8 cm.
An arc subtends an angle of 0.25 radians at the centre of the circle.
How long is the arc, in centimetres?

Angles can be measured in radians, where 2π radians $= 360°$.
We can write 2π radians as $2\pi^c$ or 2π rad, but the ^{c} or rad is normally omitted.

Other important equivalents that you should remember are
$$180° = \pi \text{ rad} \quad 90° = \frac{\pi}{2} \text{ rad} \quad 60° = \frac{\pi}{3} \text{ rad} \quad 45° = \frac{\pi}{4} \text{ rad} \quad 30° = \frac{\pi}{6} \text{ rad}$$

If an arc subtends an angle of θ radians at the centre of a circle radius r,
the length of the arc is $r\theta$.

Example 10

A sector with angle 45° is cut from a circle of radius 8 metres.

Find

(a) the arc length RS   (b) the perimeter of the sector

Solution

To use the formula for arc length, you must work in radians.

(a) The arc length $RS = r\theta = 8 \times \dfrac{\pi}{4} = 6.283\ldots$

Arc $RS = 6.3\,\text{m}$ (to 1 d.p.)

(b) Perimeter of sector $= OR + OS + \text{arc } RS = 8 + 8 + 6.283\ldots = 22.283\ldots$

Perimeter $= 22.3\,\text{m}$ (to 1 d.p.)

Some values of sine, cos and tan can be found easily using Pythagoras and symmetry.

A 45° right-angled triangle whose shorter sides are of length 1 unit has (by Pythagoras) a hypotenuse of length $\sqrt{2}$.

Hence $\sin 45° = \cos 45° = \dfrac{1}{\sqrt{2}}$ and $\tan 45° = 1$.

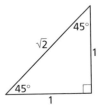

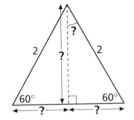

F5 The diagram shows an equilateral triangle with a perpendicular from the apex to the base.

(a) Copy the diagram and fill in the lengths and angle marked with ?.

(b) Hence write down the sine, cos and tan of both 30° and 60°, giving them in surd form.

K You should know or be able to quickly work out that

$$\sin \frac{\pi}{4} = \sin 45° = \frac{1}{\sqrt{2}} \qquad \cos \frac{\pi}{4} = \cos 45° = \frac{1}{\sqrt{2}} \qquad \tan \frac{\pi}{4} = \tan 45° = 1$$

$$\sin \frac{\pi}{6} = \sin 30° = \tfrac{1}{2} \qquad \cos \frac{\pi}{6} = \cos 30° = \frac{\sqrt{3}}{2} \qquad \tan \frac{\pi}{6} = \tan 30° = \frac{1}{\sqrt{3}}$$

$$\sin \frac{\pi}{3} = \sin 60° = \frac{\sqrt{3}}{2} \qquad \cos \frac{\pi}{3} = \cos 60° = \tfrac{1}{2} \qquad \tan \frac{\pi}{3} = \tan 60° = \sqrt{3}$$

Exercise F (answers p 139)

1 Change the following angles into radians, giving answers in terms of π.

(a) $210°$ (b) $135°$ (c) $120°$ (d) $330°$ (e) $300°$

2 Change the following angles into degrees.

(a) $\dfrac{\pi}{8}$ (b) $\dfrac{\pi}{10}$ (c) $\dfrac{\pi}{180}$ (d) $\dfrac{\pi}{4}$ (e) $\dfrac{5\pi}{6}$

(f) $\dfrac{5\pi}{4}$ (g) $\dfrac{5\pi}{12}$ (h) $\dfrac{7\pi}{4}$ (i) $\dfrac{2\pi}{9}$ (j) $\dfrac{4\pi}{3}$

3 Copy this table and complete it, giving exact values for sine, cos and tan. All angles are between 0 and π radians.

Radians	Degrees	$\sin\theta$	$\cos\theta$	$\tan\theta$
$\dfrac{\pi}{6}$		$\dfrac{1}{2}$		$\dfrac{1}{\sqrt{3}}$
$\dfrac{2\pi}{3}$				
	$135°$			
$\dfrac{5\pi}{6}$				

4 The sector OAB is cut from a circle of radius $2\,\text{m}$.

(a) What is the length of arc AB?

(b) What is the perimeter of the sector?

5 The curved edge of the pendant shown shaded in the diagram is an arc of a circle, radius $6\,\text{cm}$, which subtends an angle of $110°$ at the centre of the circle.

(a) Calculate the length of the arc.

(b) Calculate the length of the straight line PQ.

(c) Hence work out, to 3 s.f., the perimeter of the pendant.

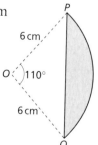

6 A circle has radius $7\,\text{cm}$.
An arc of the circle has length $10\,\text{cm}$.
What angle, in degrees, does the arc subtend at the centre of the circle?

7 A sector of a circle has an angle at the centre of $\dfrac{\pi}{4}$ and a perimeter of $12\,\text{cm}$.
Work out the radius of the circle.

G Area of a sector

The area of a complete circle of radius r is πr^2.

The sector POQ occupies $\dfrac{\theta}{2\pi}$ of the whole circle.

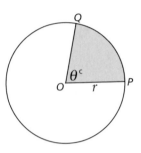

Hence the area of sector POQ is $\dfrac{\theta}{2\pi} \times \pi r^2$ or $\frac{1}{2}r^2\theta$.

 The area of a sector of a circle, radius r, that subtends an angle θ at the centre is $\frac{1}{2}r^2\theta$.

Example 11

A sector with angle $55°$ is cut from a circle of radius 8 metres.
Find the area of the sector.

Solution

To use the formula above, work in radians.

$55° = \dfrac{\pi}{180} \times 55$ radians, so the area of the sector is $\frac{1}{2}r^2\theta = \frac{1}{2} \times 8^2 \times \dfrac{\pi}{180} \times 55$

$$= 30.71\ldots$$

The area is $30.7\,\text{m}^2$ (to 1 d.p.).

Example 12

A circle, centre O, has radius $25\,\text{mm}$. A sector OAB of the circle subtends an angle at O of $40°$.
Find the area of the segment bounded by the arc AB and the chord AB.

Solution

Draw a sketch.
Area of segment (shaded) = area of sector OAB – area of triangle OAB

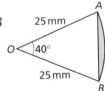

To find the area of the sector OAB, work in radians.

$40° = \dfrac{\pi}{180} \times 40$ radians

So area of sector $OAB = \frac{1}{2} \times 25^2 \times \dfrac{\pi}{180} \times 40 \,\text{mm}^2 = 218.16\ldots\,\text{mm}^2$ *Do not approximate yet.*

Area of triangle $OAB = \frac{1}{2} \times 25 \times 25 \times \sin 40° = 200.87\ldots\,\text{mm}^2$ *You can use radians or degrees here, as long as your calculator is in the corresponding mode.*

Area of segment $= 218.16\ldots\,\text{mm}^2 - 200.87\ldots\,\text{mm}^2$

$$= 17.29\ldots\,\text{mm}^2 = 17.3\,\text{mm}^2 \text{ (to 1 d.p.)}$$

Exercise G (answers p 139)

1 Find the areas to 1 d.p. of sectors with

   (a) angle 115° and radius 9 cm   **(b)** angle 20° and radius 20 m

   (c) angle 200° and radius 5.5 cm   **(d)** angle 19° and radius 45 mm

2 Find the areas of these sectors in terms of π.

   (a) angle $\dfrac{\pi}{4}$, radius 8   **(b)** angle 120°, radius 10

3 A sector has an area of 20 cm² and radius 8 cm.
   What angle, in degrees, does it subtend at the centre?

4 A sector has radius r cm and angle at the centre of θ radians.
   The perimeter of the sector is 18 cm.

   (a) Find an expression for θ in terms of r.

   (b) Find an expression for the area of the sector in terms of r.

5 An area in the shape of a sector is to be fenced off
   for a crowd at a concert. The sector has radius 400 m,
   and angle at the centre of 2^c.

   (a) Calculate the length of fence needed for the perimeter.

   (b) Health and Safety inspectors decide that the crowd
       density should not exceed 1 person per 2 m².
       Calculate the maximum crowd.

6 *OAB* is a sector of a circle, centre *O*, radius r.
   Find these in terms of r and θ.

   (a) The length *BC*

   (b) The area of triangle *OAB*

   (c) The area of the sector *OAB*

   (d) The area of the shaded segment

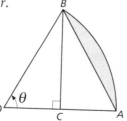

7 A circular cake of diameter 20 cm is cut along *AB*,
   halfway from the centre to the rim.

   (a) Show that the angle θ is 120°.

   (b) Calculate the area of the sector *OAB*, to 1 d.p.

   (c) Work out the area of triangle *OAB*, to 1 d.p.

   (d) Hence find the area of cake cut off, to 1 d.p.

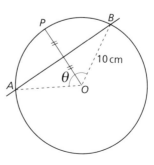

8 The diagram shows a gardener's design for the shape of a flower bed with perimeter $ABCD$.

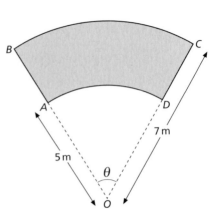

AD is an arc of a circle with centre O and radius $5\,\text{m}$. BC is an arc of a circle with centre O and radius $7\,\text{m}$. OAB and ODC are straight lines and the size of $\angle AOD$ is θ radians.

(a) Find, in terms of θ, an expression for the area of the flower bed.

Given that the area of the flower bed is $15\,\text{m}^2$,

(b) show that $\theta = 1.25$,

(c) calculate, in m, the perimeter of the flower bed.

The gardener now decides to replace arc AD with the straight line AD.

(d) Find, to the nearest cm, the reduction in the perimeter of the flower bed.   Edexcel

---

Key points

- When solving a triangle ABC you can use

  the cosine rule: $\begin{aligned} a^2 &= b^2 + c^2 - 2bc\cos A \\ b^2 &= a^2 + c^2 - 2ac\cos B \\ c^2 &= a^2 + b^2 - 2ab\cos C \end{aligned}$

  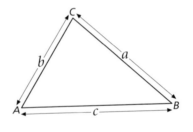

  the sine rule: $\dfrac{a}{\sin A} = \dfrac{b}{\sin B} = \dfrac{c}{\sin C}$ (pp 54, 56)

- The area of any triangle ABC is given by $\frac{1}{2}ab\sin C = \frac{1}{2}bc\sin A = \frac{1}{2}ac\sin B$ (p 61)

- Angles can be measured in radians, where 2π radians $= 360°$.

  Other important equivalents that you should remember are

  $180° = \pi\,\text{rad} \quad 90° = \dfrac{\pi}{2}\,\text{rad} \quad 60° = \dfrac{\pi}{3}\,\text{rad} \quad 45° = \dfrac{\pi}{4}\,\text{rad} \quad 30° = \dfrac{\pi}{6}\,\text{rad}$ (p 63)

- If an arc subtends an angle of θ radians at the centre of a circle radius r, the length of the arc is $r\theta$.   (p 63)

- The area of a sector of a circle, radius r, with angle θ radians at the centre is $\frac{1}{2}r^2\theta$.   (p 66)

Test yourself (answers p 140)

1 Work out the value of **?** in each triangle below.
Where there is more than one value, give both.

(a)
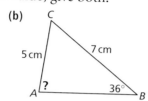

(b)

(c)
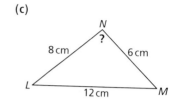

2 Find the area of each triangle in question 1.
Give both answers if there are two.

3 A sector of a circle, radius 5 cm, subtends 78° at the centre.
Calculate the sector's

(a) arc length   (b) perimeter   (c) area

4 A sector of a circle has radius 12 cm and area 90 cm².
What is the perimeter of the sector?

5 The shape of a badge is a sector ABC of a circle with centre A
and radius AB, as shown in the diagram. The triangle ABC is
equilateral and has perpendicular height 3 cm.

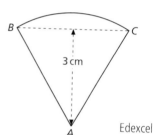

(a) Find, in surd form, the length of AB.

(b) Find, in terms of π, the area of the badge.

(c) Prove that the perimeter of the badge is $\dfrac{2\sqrt{3}}{3}(\pi + 6)$ cm.

Edexcel

6

Shape X
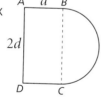

Shape Y
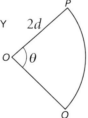

The diagram above shows the cross-sections of two drawer handles.
Shape X is a rectangle $ABCD$ joined to a semicircle with BC as diameter.
The length $AB = d$ cm and $BC = 2d$ cm.
Shape Y is a sector OPQ of a circle with centre O and radius $2d$ cm.
Angle POQ is θ radians.

Given that the areas of shapes X and Y are equal,

(a) prove that $\theta = 1 + \frac{1}{4}\pi$.

Using this value of θ, and given that $d = 3$, find in terms of π,

(b) the perimeter of shape X   (c) the perimeter of shape Y

(d) Hence find the difference, in mm, between the perimeters of shapes X and Y.   *Edexcel*

6 Trigonometry 2

In this chapter you will learn
- about the graphs of the sine, cosine and tangent functions (the 'circular functions')
- about relationships between the circular functions
- how to solve equations involving the circular functions

A Sines and cosines (answers p 140)

In chapter 5 you saw how to define the sine
and cosine of an angle using the unit circle.

$\cos \theta°$ is defined to be the x-coordinate of P.
$\sin \theta°$ is defined to be the y-coordinate of P.

These definitions apply for all values of $\theta°$, both
positive (anticlockwise) and negative (clockwise).

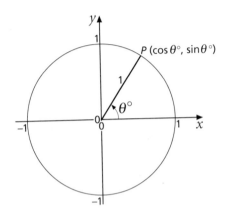

A1 Use the unit circle to decide which of these
are the same as $\sin 50°$.

(a) $\sin 130°$ (b) $\sin 230°$ (c) $\sin -50°$ (d) $\sin 310°$

(e) $\sin 410°$ (f) $\sin 490°$ (g) $\sin -310°$ (h) $\sin -230°$

A2 Use the unit circle to explain why $\sin (-\theta)° = -\sin \theta°$ for all values of $\theta°$.

You saw in chapter 5 that $\sin (180 - \theta)° = \sin \theta°$.
You can also see from the unit circle that the angle $\theta°$ is equivalent to $360° + \theta°$, so

$\sin (360 + \theta)° = \sin \theta°$.

The graph of $y = \sin \theta°$ also shows these equivalences.

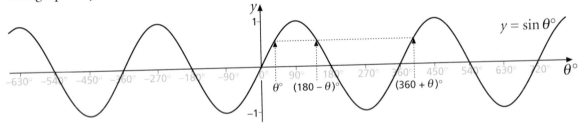

$\sin (-\theta)° = -\sin \theta°$, so the curve has rotation symmetry about $(0, 0)$.
The curve repeats every $360°$, so $y = \sin \theta°$ has a **period** of $360°$.

A3 The sine of each of these angles is equal to either $\sin 20°$ or $-\sin 20°$.
Decide which in each case.

(a) $160°$ (b) $340°$ (c) $200°$ (d) $-20°$ (e) $-160°$

(f) $380°$ (g) $520°$ (h) $560°$ (i) $700°$ (j) $-700°$

D **A4** Use the unit circle to decide which of these are the same as $\cos 50°$.

(a) $\cos 130°$ (b) $\cos 230°$ (c) $\cos -50°$ (d) $\cos 310°$

(e) $\cos 410°$ (f) $\cos 490°$ (g) $\cos -310°$ (h) $\cos -230°$

A5 Use the unit circle to explain why $\cos(-\theta)° = \cos\theta°$ for all values of $\theta°$.

K You can see from the unit circle that $\cos(180 - \theta)° = -\cos\theta°$.
Also $\cos(360 + \theta)° = \cos\theta°$.

You can also see these from the graph of $y = \cos\theta°$.

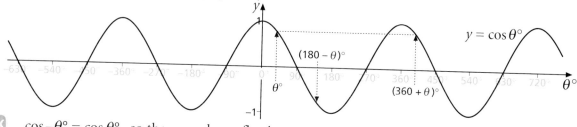

K $\cos-\theta° = \cos\theta°$, so the curve has reflection symmetry about the y-axis.
Like $\sin\theta°$, $\cos\theta°$ has period $360°$.

A6 Given that $\cos 20° = 0.94$ (to 2 s.f.), find each angle $\theta°$ such that

(a) $\cos\theta° = 0.94 \ (-90° \le \theta° \le 0°)$ (b) $\cos\theta° = -0.94 \ (90° \le \theta° \le 180°)$

(c) $\cos\theta° = 0.94 \ (270° \le \theta° \le 360°)$ (d) $\cos\theta° = -0.94 \ (-270° \le \theta° \le -180°)$

A7 (a) If $0° \le \theta° < 360°$, then one solution to $\cos\theta° = 0.73$ is $\theta° = 43°$.
What is the other solution?

(b) If $0° \le \theta° < 360°$, one solution to $\cos\theta° = -0.17$ is $\theta° = 100°$.
What is the other solution?

(c) If $0° \le \theta° < 360°$, and you know one solution to $\cos\theta° = k$,
explain how you find another solution.

K When you solve an equation like $\sin\theta° = k$ or $\cos\theta° = k$ (where $-1 < k < 1$),
there are two solutions for $\theta°$ between $0°$ and $360°$.
Further solutions for $\theta°$ can be found by taking each of these two solutions and
adding or subtracting multiples of $360°$.

Example 1

Find all the angles $\theta°$ (to the nearest degree), where $-360° < \theta° < 360°$, such that $\sin\theta° = 0.96$.

Solution

Key in $\sin^{-1} 0.96$. The solution is $\theta° = 74°$.   *74° is called the **principal value** of the solution.*
Another solution is $\theta° = 180° - 74° = 106°$.

These are the two solutions between $0°$ and $360°$. You can add or subtract
any multiple of $360°$ to get further angles whose sine is 0.96.

The two angles between $0°$ and $-360°$ are $74° - 360° = -286°$ and $106° - 360° = -254°$.

The four solutions in the required interval are therefore $-286°, -254°, 74°$ and $106°$.

Example 2

Find all the angles a, where $0 < a < 4\pi$, such that $\cos a = 0.5$.
Give your answers in radians.

Solution

$\cos a = 0.5 \Rightarrow$ one solution is $a = \dfrac{\pi}{3}$.   *You need to know that $\cos \dfrac{\pi}{3} = 0.5$ (see page 64).*

One way to find the other solutions is to sketch the graph of $y = \cos a$ over the required interval.

From the sketch, another solution is
$$a = 2\pi - \frac{\pi}{3} = \frac{5\pi}{3}.$$

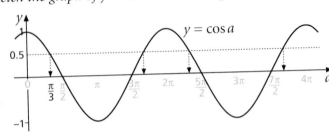

The two solutions marked on the right-hand side of the graph are each 2π radians bigger than the two solutions already found.

So these solutions are $2\pi + \dfrac{\pi}{3} = \dfrac{7\pi}{3}$ and $2\pi + \dfrac{5\pi}{3} = \dfrac{11\pi}{3}$.

The four solutions are therefore $a = \dfrac{\pi}{3}, \dfrac{5\pi}{3}, \dfrac{7\pi}{3}$ and $\dfrac{11\pi}{3}$.

Exercise A (answers p 140)

1 $\sin 70° = 0.94$ (to 2 s.f.).

   (a) Write down another angle between $0°$ and $360°$ whose sine is 0.94.

   (b) Write down two further angles between $360°$ and $720°$ whose sine is 0.94.

2 $\cos 1^c = 0.54$ (to 2 s.f.).   (Remember 1^c means 1 radian.)

   (a) Work out another angle (to 2 d.p.) in radians between 0 and 2π whose cosine is 0.54.

   (b) Work out two further angles in radians between 2π and 4π whose cosine is 0.54.

3 (a) Solve each of these equations, giving all the solutions between $0°$ and $360°$.

     (i) $\sin \theta° = 0.64$ (ii) $\cos \theta° = 0.64$ (iii) $\sin \theta° = -0.29$ (iv) $\cos \theta° = -0.88$

   (b) Write down the solutions to each part of (a) between $360°$ and $720°$.

4 Solve each of these, giving solutions between 0 and 2π in terms of π.

   (a) $\sin \theta = \tfrac{1}{2}$ (b) $\sin \theta = 1$ (c) $\cos \theta = 0$

5 Solve each of these equations, giving all the solutions (in radians) between -2π and 2π.

   (a) $\sin \theta = \dfrac{1}{\sqrt{2}}$ (b) $\sin \theta = -\dfrac{1}{\sqrt{2}}$ (c) $\cos \theta = \dfrac{\sqrt{3}}{2}$ (d) $\cos \theta = -\tfrac{1}{2}$

6 Solve each of these equations, giving answers to the nearest degree in the range specified.

   (a) $\sin \theta° = 0.1$ $(-360° \le \theta° < 360°)$ (b) $\cos \theta° = -0.6$ $(0° \le \theta° < 720°)$

   (c) $4\sin \theta° = 3$ $(0° \le \theta° < 720°)$ (d) $8\cos \theta° + 3 = 0$ $(-360° \le \theta° < 360°)$

B Transforming sine and cosine graphs (answers p 141)

The sine and cosine functions are **periodic**: they repeat themselves after an interval called the **period**.
The period for $y = \sin \theta°$ is 360°.
So $\sin \theta° = \sin (\theta + 360)° = \sin (\theta + 720)°\ldots$ and so on.

For $y = \sin \theta°$, y takes values between −1 and 1.
The **amplitude** of $y = \sin \theta°$ is half this distance, so $y = \sin \theta°$ has an amplitude of 1.

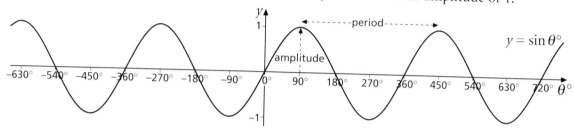

You need to be familiar with the graphs of the circular functions after various transformations.

B1 (a) Sketch the graph of $y = 2 \sin \theta°$ for $-360° \leq \theta° \leq 360°$.

   (b) What is the period of $y = 2 \sin \theta°$?

   (c) What is the amplitude of $y = 2 \sin \theta°$?

   (d) Describe the transformation that maps the graph of $y = \sin \theta°$ on to $y = 2 \sin \theta°$.

B2 (a) Sketch the graph of $y = a \sin \theta°$ for a value of a that you choose yourself (not 1 or 2!).

   (b) What is the period of $y = a \sin \theta°$?

   (c) What is the amplitude of $y = a \sin \theta°$?

   (d) Describe the transformation that maps the graph of $y = \sin \theta°$ on to $y = a \sin \theta°$.

B3 What is the value of $\sin 2\theta°$ when

   (a) $\theta° = 0°$ (b) $\theta° = 22\frac{1}{2}°$ (c) $\theta° = 45°$ (d) $\theta° = 90°$ (e) $\theta° = 135°$

B4 (a) Sketch the graph of $y = \sin 2\theta°$ for $-360° \leq \theta° \leq 360°$.

   (b) Write down the period and amplitude of $y = \sin 2\theta°$.

   (c) Describe the transformation that maps the graph of $y = \sin \theta°$ on to $y = \sin 2\theta°$.

B5 (a) What transformation maps the graph of $y = \sin \theta°$ on to $y = \sin b\theta°$?

   (b) Write down the period and amplitude of $y = \sin b\theta°$.

   (c) Check your answers for a value of b that you choose.

B6 (a) (i) For the graph of $y = \sin(\theta + 30)°$, find a negative value of $\theta°$ that makes $y = 0$.

(ii) Sketch the graph of $y = \sin(\theta + 30)°$.

(b) Describe the transformation that maps $y = \sin\theta°$ on to $y = \sin(\theta + 30)°$.

(c) What transformation maps $y = \sin\theta°$ on to $y = \sin(\theta + c)°$?

B7 (a) Describe the transformation that would map $y = \sin\theta°$ on to $y = (\sin\theta°) + d$.

(b) What is the amplitude of $y = (\sin\theta°) + d$?

B8 (a) Sketch the graph of $y = \sin(-\theta)°$ for $-360° \leq \theta° \leq 360°$.

(b) How is the graph of $y = \sin(-\theta)°$ related to that of $y = \sin\theta°$?

(c) Sketch the graph of $y = -\sin\theta°$ for $-360° \leq \theta° \leq 360°$.

(d) How is the graph of $y = -\sin\theta°$ related to that of $y = \sin\theta°$?

K If you start with the graph of $y = \sin\theta°$ (shown in grey in these diagrams)...

... the graph of $y = a\sin\theta°$ is obtained by a stretch in the y-direction, scale factor a

... the graph of $y = \sin b\theta°$ is obtained by a stretch in the θ-direction, scale factor $\dfrac{1}{b}$

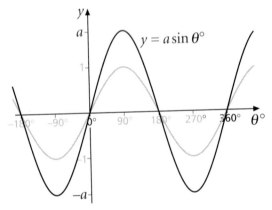

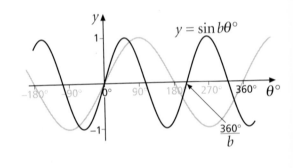

... the graph of $y = \sin(\theta + c)°$ is obtained by a translation of $\begin{bmatrix} -c \\ 0 \end{bmatrix}$

... the graph of $y = (\sin\theta°) + d$ is obtained by a translation of $\begin{bmatrix} 0 \\ d \end{bmatrix}$

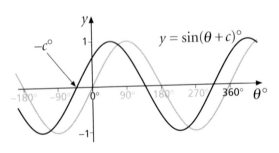

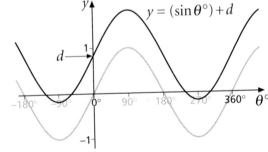

Exercise B (answers p 141)

1 Each of these sketches shows the graph of $y = \sin \theta°$ after a single transformation.
Identify each transformation and give the equation of the transformed graph.

(a)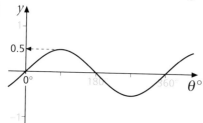

(b)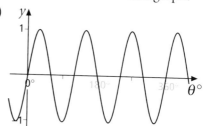

(c)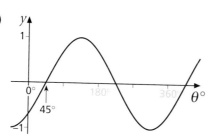

(d)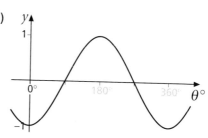

(e)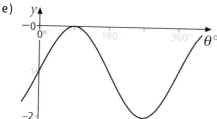

(f)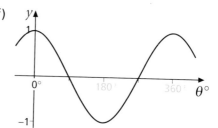

(g)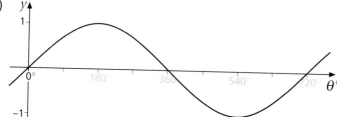

2 (a) By considering graph 1(f), write down a relationship between
the sine and cosine ratios that is true for all $\theta°$.

(b) Write down a similar relationship based on graph 1(d).

3 For each of the following equations, where θ is measured in radians,
• sketch the graph of $y = \sin \theta \ (-2\pi \le \theta \le 2\pi)$
• superimpose the required graph

(a) $y = \sin\left(\theta - \frac{\pi}{3}\right)$ (b) $y = \sin\left(\theta + \frac{\pi}{6}\right)$ (c) $y = \sin\left(\theta - \frac{\pi}{2}\right)$

4 For each of the following graphs, first sketch the graph of $y = \cos\theta$ (where θ is measured in radians), labelling each θ-axis as shown on the right.

Then superimpose the required graph.

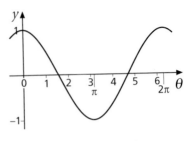

(a) $y = (\cos\theta) + 2$

(b) $y = 2\cos\theta$

(c) $y = \cos 2\theta$

(d) $y = \cos(\theta + 2)$

5 Each of these sketches shows the graph of $y = \cos\theta$ after a single transformation. In the graphs, θ is measured in radians.
Identify each transformation and give the equation of the transformed graph.

(a)

(b)

(c)

(d)

(e)

(f)

6 For each of the following, sketch the graph of $y = \cos\theta°$ for $-360° \le \theta° \le 360°$ and superimpose the required graph.

(a) $y = \cos(\theta + 60)°$

(b) $y = \cos(\theta - 180)°$

(c) $y = \cos(\theta + 180)°$

*7 Sketch each of these graphs for $-360° \le \theta° \le 360°$, labelling your axes carefully.

(a) $y = 2\sin(\theta + 60)°$

(b) $y = -\cos(\theta - 60)°$

*8 (a) For $y = \sin(2\theta + 120)°$ write down   (i) the period   (ii) the amplitude

(b) What value of $\theta°$ makes $\sin(2\theta + 120)° = 0$?

(c) Sketch the graph of $y = \sin(2\theta + 120)°$.

C Tangents (answers p 143)

You have seen how to define $\sin\theta°$ and $\cos\theta°$ in the unit circle shown on the right.

In triangle OQP, $\tan\theta° = \dfrac{QP}{OQ}$, so

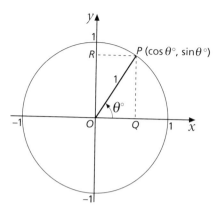

$$\boxed{\tan\theta° = \frac{\sin\theta°}{\cos\theta°}}$$

$\sin\theta°$ and $\cos\theta°$ are already defined for any angle, so you can use this relationship to define $\tan\theta°$ for any angle.

Note, however, that $\tan\theta°$ will not be defined if $\cos\theta° = 0$, that is if $\theta° = 90°$ or $270°$ or $450°$ and so on.

C1 This sketch shows the four quadrants, as $\theta°$ increases from $0°$ to $360°$, and whether $\sin\theta°$ is positive or negative in each of them.

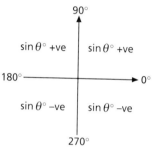

(a) Copy the sketch and write whether $\cos\theta°$ is positive or negative in each quadrant.

(b) Use the fact that $\tan\theta° = \dfrac{\sin\theta°}{\cos\theta°}$ to write in each quadrant whether $\tan\theta°$ is positive or negative.

C2 Show that $\tan(-\theta)° = -\tan\theta°$ by simplifying $\dfrac{\sin(-\theta)°}{\cos(-\theta)°}$.

The graph of $\tan\theta°$, like that of $\sin\theta°$ and $\cos\theta°$, is periodic. Unlike these functions, the period of $\tan\theta°$ is $180°$, so $\tan(180 + \theta)° = \tan\theta°$.

$\tan(-\theta)° = -\tan\theta°$, so the graph has rotation symmetry about $(0, 0)$.

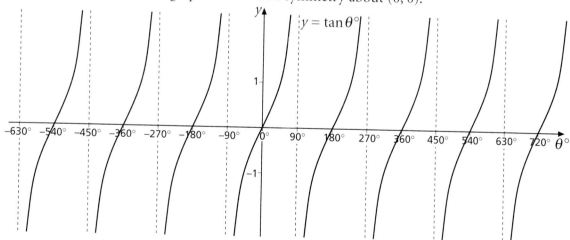

Note also that the graph of $\tan\theta°$ has asymptotes at $-90°, 90°, 270°$, and so on.

When you solve an equation such as $\tan\theta° = k$ (where k can have any value), you can see from the graph that there will always be one solution between $0°$ and $180°$. From this one solution, further solutions for $\theta°$ can be found by adding or subtracting multiples of $180°$.

Example 3

Find, to the nearest degree, all the angles $\theta°$ ($-360° \le \theta° \le 360°$) such that $\tan\theta° = 1.19$.

Solution

Key in $\tan^{-1}1.19$.

Since tan *has period* $180°$, *add or subtract multiples of* $180°$ *to get the other solutions.*

One solution is $\theta° = 50°$.

Other solutions are $50° + 180° = 230°$, $50° - 180° = -130°$, and $50° - 2\times180° = -310°$
The solutions are $\theta° = -310°, -130°, 50°$ and $230°$.

Exercise C (answers p 143)

1 Solve each of these equations, giving all solutions between $0°$ and $360°$, to the nearest degree.

(a) $\tan x° = 3$
(b) $\tan x° = -3$
(c) $2\tan x° = -1$
(d) $5\tan x° = 8$

2 Solve these, giving answers in terms of π in the range specified.

(a) $\tan a = \sqrt{3}$ $(-\pi \le a \le \pi)$
(b) $\tan a = -\dfrac{1}{\sqrt{3}}$ $(-\pi \le a \le \pi)$
(c) $\tan a = -1$ $(-2\pi \le a \le 0)$
(d) $\tan a = 0$ $(\pi \le a \le 5\pi)$

3 The four graphs below show $y = \tan\theta°$ after a single transformation.
The graphs are (not in order) $y = \tan 2\theta°$, $y = \tan\frac{1}{2}\theta°$, $y = \tan(\theta + 45)°$, $y = \tan(\theta - 45)°$.
Identify which graph is which.

(a)

(b)

(c)

(d)

4 Sketch each of these graphs for $-2\pi < x < 2\pi$, labelling the axes clearly.

(a) $\tan\dfrac{x}{3}$
(b) $\tan x + 0.5$
(c) $\tan\left(x + \dfrac{\pi}{2}\right)$
(d) $\tan\left(x - \dfrac{\pi}{6}\right)$

D Solving further equations (answers p 144)

You have solved simple equations such as $\sin \theta° = -0.6$, giving your answers for $\theta°$ within a specific range.

You sometimes need to go outside the given range to find a complete solution to a problem.

D1 Find the values of $\theta°$ to the nearest degree between $0°$ and $360°$ which satisfy the equation $\sin (\theta + 50)° = 0.4$.

Example 4

Solve $\sin (\theta + 70)° = 0.6$ to the nearest degree, for $0° \leq \theta < 360°$.

Solution

$\theta°$ is between $0°$ and $360°$, so $(\theta + 70)°$ is between $70°$ and $430°$.

$$\sin (\theta + 70)° = 0.6 \text{ gives } (\theta + 70)° = 37° \text{ (to the nearest degree)}$$
$$\text{and } (\theta + 70)° = 180° - 37° = \underline{143°}.$$

Since sine has period $360°$, we also have $(\theta + 70)° = 37° + 360° = \underline{397°}$
$$\text{and } (\theta + 70)° = 143° + 360° = 503°.$$

Adding or subtracting further multiples of $360°$ would clearly go outside the required range of $70°$ to $430°$.

The two underlined values above are within the range $70°$ to $430°$, and these lead to

$$(\theta + 70)° = 143° \implies \theta° = 73°$$
$$\text{and } (\theta + 70)° = 397° \implies \theta° = 327°.$$

Example 5

Solve $\tan 2\theta = -\sqrt{3}$, giving answers between 0 and 2π.

Solution

If θ is between 0 and 2π, then 2θ will be between 0 and 4π.

We know that $\tan \dfrac{\pi}{3} = \sqrt{3}$, therefore $\tan\left(-\dfrac{\pi}{3}\right) = -\sqrt{3}$.

So if $\tan 2\theta = -\sqrt{3}$, then one possibility is $2\theta = -\dfrac{\pi}{3}$.

This does not, however, lead to a solution in the range required.

Since tan has period π, other possibilities are $2\theta = -\dfrac{\pi}{3} + \pi = \dfrac{2\pi}{3} \implies \theta = \dfrac{\pi}{3}$

Consider angles for 2θ *from 0 to 4π.*

$$\text{and } 2\theta = -\dfrac{\pi}{3} + 2\pi = \dfrac{5\pi}{3} \implies \theta = \dfrac{5\pi}{6}$$
$$\text{and } 2\theta = -\dfrac{\pi}{3} + 3\pi = \dfrac{8\pi}{3} \implies \theta = \dfrac{4\pi}{3}$$
$$\text{and } 2\theta = -\dfrac{\pi}{3} + 4\pi = \dfrac{11\pi}{3} \implies \theta = \dfrac{11\pi}{6}$$

So the solutions are $\theta = \dfrac{\pi}{3}, \dfrac{5\pi}{6}, \dfrac{4\pi}{3}$ and $\dfrac{11\pi}{6}$.

Example 6

Find all the solutions to $2\sin\theta° - \cos\theta° = 0$ between $-180°$ and $180°$, to the nearest degree.

Solution

Reduce the equation to one just in $\tan\theta$.

$$2\sin\theta° - \cos\theta° = 0$$
$$\Rightarrow \quad 2\sin\theta° = \cos\theta°$$

You can divide by $\cos\theta°$ *because* $\cos\theta° = 0$
is not a solution of the original equation.

$$\Rightarrow \quad 2\frac{\sin\theta°}{\cos\theta°} = 1$$
$$\Rightarrow \quad 2\tan\theta° = 1$$
$$\Rightarrow \quad \tan\theta° = \tfrac{1}{2}$$

So one value of $\theta°$ is $27°$.

Key in $\tan^{-1}0.5$ *on the calculator.*

tan has period $180°$.

Another value is $27° - 180° = -153°$.

So the two solutions are $\theta° = -153°$ and $27°$.
Other solutions are outside the required range

Example 7

Find the solutions to $2\sin 3t = 1$ for $-\pi \le t \le \pi$.

Solution

If $-\pi \le t \le \pi$, *then* $-3\pi \le 3t \le 3\pi$, *and so you need to find values of* $3t$ *from* -3π *to* 3π.

If $2\sin 3t = 1$, then $\sin 3t = \tfrac{1}{2}$.

One possibility is $3t = \dfrac{\pi}{6}$ $\left(\text{since }\sin\dfrac{\pi}{6} = \tfrac{1}{2}\right)$

$\sin\theta = \sin(\pi - \theta)$

Another possibility is $3t = \pi - \dfrac{\pi}{6} = \dfrac{5\pi}{6}$

$\sin\theta$ *has period* 2π.

Other possibilities are $3t = \dfrac{\pi}{6} + 2\pi$

Add or subtract as many multiples of 2π
as you need to be sure of including all the
required solutions. Discard any solutions
outside the required range at the end.

$$3t = \dfrac{5\pi}{6} + 2\pi$$
$$3t = \dfrac{\pi}{6} - 2\pi$$
$$3t = \dfrac{5\pi}{6} - 2\pi$$

If $3t = \dfrac{\pi}{6}$, $t = \dfrac{\pi}{18}$

If $3t = \dfrac{5\pi}{6}$, $t = \dfrac{5\pi}{18}$

$3t = \dfrac{\pi}{6} + 2\pi \Rightarrow 3t = \dfrac{13\pi}{6} \Rightarrow t = \dfrac{13\pi}{18}$

$3t = \dfrac{5\pi}{6} + 2\pi \Rightarrow 3t = \dfrac{17\pi}{6} \Rightarrow t = \dfrac{17\pi}{18}$

$3t = \dfrac{\pi}{6} - 2\pi \Rightarrow 3t = -\dfrac{11\pi}{6} \Rightarrow t = -\dfrac{11\pi}{18}$

$3t = \dfrac{5\pi}{6} - 2\pi \Rightarrow 3t = -\dfrac{7\pi}{6} \Rightarrow t = -\dfrac{7\pi}{18}$

So the solutions for t are $-\dfrac{11\pi}{18}, -\dfrac{7\pi}{18}, \dfrac{\pi}{18}, \dfrac{5\pi}{18}, \dfrac{13\pi}{18}$ and $\dfrac{17\pi}{18}$.

Exercise D (answers p 144)

1 Solve each of these equations to the nearest degree, giving all solutions between 0° and 360°.

(a) $\cos(\theta + 80)° = 0.66$ (b) $\sin(\theta - 50)° = -0.9$ (c) $\tan(\theta + 120)° = 1.5$

(d) $\sin 2t° = 0.7$ (e) $\cos 3t° = 0.4$ (f) $5\tan 2t° = 1$

2 Solve each of these, giving all answers between 0 and 2π.

(a) $\sin 2h = \frac{1}{2}$ (b) $\cos 4t = 1$ (c) $\tan 3f = 1$

3 Find the values of $t°$ in the range $0° \leq t° \leq 60°$ which satisfy

(a) $8\sin 10t° = 5$ (b) $10\cos\frac{1}{2}t° = 9$ (c) $5\tan 5t° - 1 = 0$

4 Solve each of these, giving solutions to the nearest 0.1° in the range indicated.

(a) $\sin 3\theta° = 0.6 \ (-180° \leq \theta° \leq 180°)$ (b) $\cos 2\theta° = -0.38 \ (-360° \leq \theta° \leq 0°)$

(c) $\tan 5\theta° = -2 \ (-180° \leq \theta° \leq 180°)$ (d) $\sin\frac{\theta°}{2} = 0.76 \ (-360° \leq \theta° \leq 360°)$

5 Find the solutions to these, giving answers in radians between 0 and 2π.

(a) $\sin\theta - \sqrt{3}\cos\theta = 0$ (b) $\sqrt{3}\sin\theta + \cos\theta = 0$ (c) $\sin\theta + \sqrt{3}\cos\theta = 0$

*6 Find the values of $t°$ in the range $0° \leq t° \leq 360°$ which satisfy

(a) $4 - 7\cos(2t + 35)° = 0$ (b) $3 + 4\sin(4t - 21)° = 0$

(c) $3\cos(0.5t + 20)° = 2$ (d) $\sin(2t + 20)° - 3\cos(2t + 20)° = 0$

E Further equations and identities (answers p 144)

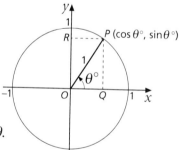

Using Pythagoras in the unit circle gives $OQ^2 + QP^2 = OP^2 = 1$.
Hence $(\cos\theta°)^2 + (\sin\theta°)^2 = 1$.

Writing $(\cos\theta°)^2$ as $\cos^2\theta°$ and $(\sin\theta°)^2$ as $\sin^2\theta°$ gives

$$\cos^2\theta° + \sin^2\theta° = 1$$

This important relationship is true for all values of the angle θ.

Example 8

Given that θ is an acute angle and $\sin\theta = \frac{1}{3}$, find   (a) $\cos\theta$ (b) $\tan\theta$

Solution

(a) Using $\cos^2\theta + \sin^2\theta = 1$,

$$\cos^2\theta + \left(\tfrac{1}{3}\right)^2 = 1, \ \cos^2\theta = 1 - \tfrac{1}{9} = \tfrac{8}{9}$$

$$\Rightarrow \ \cos\theta = \sqrt{\frac{8}{9}} = \frac{\sqrt{8}}{\sqrt{9}} = \frac{\sqrt{8}}{3} = \frac{2\sqrt{2}}{3}$$

Take the positive root because θ is acute.

Note that the results are true whether θ is measured in degrees or radians.

(b) $\tan\theta = \dfrac{\sin\theta}{\cos\theta} = \dfrac{\frac{1}{3}}{\frac{2\sqrt{2}}{3}} = \dfrac{1}{2\sqrt{2}}$

D **E1** If θ is in the second quadrant and $\sin \theta = \frac{1}{3}$, find **(a)** $\cos \theta$ **(b)** $\tan \theta$

You can also solve equations involving the squares of the circular functions.

E2 Consider the equation $2 \cos^2 \theta° - 3 \cos \theta° + 1 = 0$.

(a) Think of $\cos \theta°$ as a single letter, say c. Rewrite the equation replacing $\cos \theta°$ with c.

(b) You now have a quadratic equation in c. The equation factorises. Factorise it.

(c) Check that one of your factors is $(c - 1)$.

(d) If $c - 1 = 0$, then $c = 1$, that is, $\cos \theta° = 1$.
For what value of $\theta°$ ($0° \le \theta° \le 90°$) is $\cos \theta° = 1$?

(e) Similarly, use your second factor to find a solution for $\theta°$ between $0°$ and $90°$.

(f) Check that both solutions you have found work in the original equation.

D **E3** (a) Use the fact that $\cos^2 \theta° + \sin^2 \theta° = 1$ to rewrite the equation
$\sin^2 \theta° - \cos \theta° - 1 = 0$ in terms of $\cos \theta°$ only.

(b) Factorise your new equation and thus solve $\sin^2 \theta° - \cos \theta° - 1 = 0$ ($0 \le \theta° < 360°$).

Example 9

Solve the equation $\cos^2 \theta° + \cos \theta° - 1 = 0$, giving solutions between $-90°$ and $90°$ to the nearest $0.1°$.

Solution

The quadratic will not factorise so use the formula.

$$\cos^2 \theta° + \cos \theta° - 1 = 0 \Rightarrow \cos \theta° = \frac{-1 \pm \sqrt{1^2 - 4 \times 1 \times -1}}{2 \times 1}$$

$$\cos \theta° = 0.618\ldots \text{ or } -1.618\ldots$$

$$\cos \theta° = -1.618\ldots \text{ has no solution.}$$

$$\cos \theta° = 0.618\ldots \Rightarrow \theta° = 51.8° \text{ or } -51.8° \text{ (to } 0.1°)$$

Example 10

Solve the equation $2 \sin^2 x = 3 \cos x$ for $0 \le x \le 2\pi$.

Solution

The range shows you are expected to give the solutions in radians.

$$2 \sin^2 x = 3 \cos x$$

$\cos^2 x + \sin^2 x = 1 \Rightarrow \sin^2 x = 1 - \cos^2 x$ so substitute for $\sin^2 x$.

$$2(1 - \cos^2 x) = 3 \cos x$$
$$\Rightarrow \quad 2 - 2 \cos^2 x = 3 \cos x$$

Rearrange.
Think of $\cos x$ as c and factorise.

$$2 \cos^2 x + 3 \cos x - 2 = 0$$
$$(2 \cos x - 1)(\cos x + 2) = 0$$

$$\Rightarrow \cos x = \frac{1}{2} \text{ or } \cos x = -2$$

$\cos x = -2$ has no solution, so the only solutions are given by $\cos x = \frac{1}{2}$.

$$\cos x = \frac{1}{2} \Rightarrow x = \frac{\pi}{3} \text{ or } 2\pi - \frac{\pi}{3} = \frac{5\pi}{3} \text{ in the required range}$$

so the solutions are $\dfrac{\pi}{3}$ and $\dfrac{5\pi}{3}$.

Example 11

Solve the equation $2\sin^2 x = 3\cos^2 x$ for $0 \leq x \leq 2\pi$, giving solutions to 2 d.p.

Solution

The range indicates you are expected to give the solutions in radians.

$$2\sin^2 x = 3\cos^2 x$$

You could write $2\sin^2 x = 2(1 - \cos^2 x)$ and solve for $\cos^2 x$ instead.

$$\Rightarrow \quad \frac{\sin^2 x}{\cos^2 x} = \frac{3}{2}$$

$$\Rightarrow \quad \tan^2 x = 1.5$$

$$\Rightarrow \quad \tan x = \pm\sqrt{1.5} = \pm 1.224\ldots$$

Set the calculator to radians, and use $\tan^{-1} 1.224\ldots$ $x = 0.886\ldots$

$$= 0.89 \text{ (2 d.p.)}$$

tan has period π.   Another solution is $x = 0.886\ldots + \pi$

$$= 4.03 \text{ (2 d.p.)}$$

If $\tan x = -1.224\ldots$, then $x = -0.886\ldots$ *Not within the required range*

and $-0.886\ldots + \pi = 2.26$ (2 d.p.)

and $-0.886\ldots + 2\pi = 5.40$ (2 d.p.)

So the required solutions are 0.89, 2.26, 4.03 and 5.40 (radians).
Check these by substituting back into the original equation.

Example 12

Prove that $\dfrac{2 - \sin^2 \theta}{\cos^2 \theta + 1} = 1$.   *Note that this is not an equation; you have to prove it is true for all θ. Start with the more complex side and show it is equal to the other side.*

Solution

$$\frac{2 - \sin^2 \theta}{\cos^2 \theta + 1} = \frac{2 - \left(1 - \cos^2 \theta\right)}{\cos^2 \theta + 1} = \frac{2 - 1 + \cos^2 \theta}{\cos^2 \theta + 1} = \frac{1 + \cos^2 \theta}{\cos^2 \theta + 1} = 1$$

Example 13

Show that $(x - 1)$ is a factor of $x^3 - 2x^2 - x + 2$, and hence factorise $x^3 - 2x^2 - x + 2$.
Hence find all the values of θ (where $0 \leq \theta < 2\pi$) such that $\sin^3 \theta - 2\sin^2 \theta - \sin \theta + 2 = 0$.

Solution

Use the factor theorem.   When $x = 1$, $x^3 - 2x^2 - x + 2 = 1 - 2 - 1 + 2 = 0$.
Hence $(x - 1)$ is a factor of $x^3 - 2x^2 - x + 2$.

$$x^3 - 2x^2 - x + 2 = (x - 1)(x^2 - x - 2)$$
$$= (x - 1)(x + 1)(x - 2)$$

To solve $\sin^3 \theta - 2\sin^2 \theta - \sin \theta + 2 = 0$, let $x = \sin \theta$.

$$\text{So } x^3 - 2x^2 - x + 2 = 0$$
$$\Rightarrow \quad (x - 1)(x + 1)(x - 2) = 0$$

Hence $x = \sin \theta = 1, -1$ or 2.

If $\sin \theta = 1, \theta = \dfrac{\pi}{2}$. If $\sin \theta = -1, \theta = \dfrac{3\pi}{2}$. $\sin \theta = -2$ has no solutions.

So the solutions are $\theta = \dfrac{\pi}{2}$ and $\theta = \dfrac{3\pi}{2}$.

Exercise E (answers p 144)

1 If $\sin \theta = \frac{1}{4}$, find $\cos \theta$ and $\tan \theta$ if **(a)** θ is acute **(b)** θ is in the second quadrant

2 (a) By replacing $\sin^2 x°$ by $1 - \cos^2 x°$, show that the equation
$1 + \cos x° = 3 \sin^2 x°$ is equivalent to $3 \cos^2 x° + \cos x° - 2 = 0$.

(b) Factorise the left-hand side of this equation.

(c) Solve the equation to find all values of $x°$ between $0°$ and $360°$.

3 Solve the following equations for $0 \le \theta \le 2\pi$.

(a) $2 \cos^2 \theta = \cos \theta + 1$ **(b)** $\sqrt{3} \sin \theta - \cos \theta = 0$ **(c)** $2 \sin^2 \theta = 7 \cos \theta - 2$

4 Solve the following equations for $0 \le x \le 2\pi$.

(a) $\sin^2 x = 0.25$ **(b)** $\cos^2 x - \sin^2 x = 1$ **(c)** $\tan^2 x = 3$

(d) $\cos^2 x - 4 \sin^2 x = 0$ **(e)** $\cos^2 x - 4 \sin^2 x = 1$ **(f)** $\cos^2 x = 2 + 2 \sin x$

5 (a) Show that $(x - 1)$ is a factor of $x^3 - x^2 - 3x + 3$, and hence factorise $x^3 - x^2 - 3x + 3$.

(b) Hence find all the values of θ $(0 \le \theta < 2\pi)$ such that $\tan^3 \theta - \tan^2 \theta - 3 \tan \theta + 3 = 0$.

6 Show that **(a)** $(\sin x + \cos x)^2 = 1 + 2 \sin x \cos x$ **(b)** $\dfrac{6 - \cos^2 \theta}{\sin^2 \theta + 5} = 1$

*7 Show that $(1 + \sin \theta + \cos \theta)^2 = 2(1 + \sin \theta)(1 + \cos \theta)$.

*8 Find the relationship between y and x, given that $x = 3 \cos \theta$ and $y = 2 \sin \theta$.

Key points

- $\sin(-\theta) = -\sin \theta$, $\sin(180 - \theta)° = \sin \theta°$ (in radians, $\sin(\pi - \theta) = \sin \theta$) (p 70)
- $\cos(-\theta) = \cos \theta$, $\cos(180 - \theta)° = -\cos \theta°$ (in radians, $\cos(\pi - \theta) = -\cos \theta$) (p 71)
- The graphs of the sine and cosine functions are periodic, with period $360°$ or 2π. (pp 70–72)
- The graph of $y = a \sin \theta$ is obtained from that of $y = \sin \theta$ by a stretch in the y-direction, scale factor a. $y = -\sin \theta$ is obtained by a reflection in the θ-axis. The same applies for cos and tan. (p 74)
- The graph of $y = \sin b\theta$ is obtained from that of $y = \sin \theta$ by a stretch in the θ-direction, scale factor $\frac{1}{b}$. $y = \sin(-\theta)$ is obtained by a reflection in the y-axis. The same applies for cos and tan. (p 74)
- The graph of $y = \sin(\theta + c)$ is obtained from $y = \sin \theta$ by a translation of $\begin{bmatrix} -c \\ 0 \end{bmatrix}$. The same applies for cos and tan. (p 74)
- The graph of $y = (\sin \theta) + d$ is obtained from $y = \sin \theta$ by a translation of $\begin{bmatrix} 0 \\ d \end{bmatrix}$. The same applies for cos and tan. (p 74)
- $\tan \theta = \dfrac{\sin \theta}{\cos \theta}$ (p 77)
- $\tan(-\theta) = -\tan \theta$; the tangent function is periodic, with period $180°$ or π. (p 77)
- $\cos^2 \theta + \sin^2 \theta = 1$ (p 81)

Test yourself (answers p 145)

1 (a) Sketch, for $0° \leq x° \leq 360°$, the graph of $y = \sin(x + 30)°$.

    (b) Write down the coordinates of the points at which the graph meets the axes.

    (c) Solve, for $0° \leq x° < 360°$, the equation $\sin(x + 30)° = -\frac{1}{2}$.

Edexcel

2 Find all the values of $\theta°$ in the interval $0° \leq \theta° < 360°$ for which

    (a) $\cos(\theta + 75)° = 0.5$

    (b) $\sin 2\theta° = 0.7$, giving your answers to one decimal place.

Edexcel

3 (a) Write down the exact values of

    (i) $\sin \dfrac{\pi}{3}$ (ii) $\cos \dfrac{\pi}{4}$ (iii) $\tan \dfrac{\pi}{6}$

    $f(x) = \sin 2x$, where $0 \leq x < 2\pi$.

    (b) Sketch the graph of $f(x)$, showing the value of x at each point where the graph crosses the x-axis.

    (c) Write down the coordinates of each of the stationary points of $f(x)$ within the given range.

    (d) Calculate, in terms of π, all the values of x for which $f(x) = \frac{1}{2}$.

4 Solve the following equations, giving solutions between $0°$ and $360°$ to the nearest $0.1°$.

    (a) $\sin(x + 60)° = 0.2$ (b) $\cos(x - 40)° = 0.78$ (c) $\tan(x + 70)° = -1.2$

5 Solve the following, giving solutions in radians between 0 and 2π to 2 d.p.

    (a) $\sin 2x = 0.2$ (b) $\cos 3x = -0.78$ (c) $\tan \frac{1}{2}x = 1.2$

6 (a) Given that $2 \sin 2\theta = \cos 2\theta$, show that $\tan 2\theta = 0.5$.

    (b) Hence find the values of $\theta°$, to one decimal place, in the interval $0° \leq \theta° < 360°$ for which $2 \sin 2\theta° = \cos 2\theta°$.

Edexcel

7 Sketch the following graphs for $0° \leq \theta° \leq 720°$, labelling your axes clearly.

    (a) $y = \sin(\theta + 45)°$ (b) $y = \frac{1}{3} \cos \theta°$ (c) $y = 2 + \sin \theta°$ (d) $y = \tan 2\theta°$

8 Show that   (a) $\dfrac{3 - 2\cos^2 \theta}{2 \sin^2 \theta + 1} = 1$ (b) $\tan \theta \sin \theta = \dfrac{1}{\cos \theta} - \cos \theta$

9 (a) Given that $2 \sin^2 \theta = 2 + \cos \theta$, show that $2 \cos^2 \theta + \cos \theta = 0$.

    (b) Hence find exactly all the values of θ, where $0 \leq \theta < 2\pi$, such that $2 \sin^2 \theta = 2 + \cos \theta$.

10 Find, in degrees, the values of $\theta°$ in the interval $0° \leq \theta° < 360°$, for which $2 \cos^2 \theta° - \cos \theta° - 1 = \sin^2 \theta°$.

    Give your answers to one decimal place where appropriate.

Edexcel

11 Find the values of $\theta°$, to one decimal place, in the interval $-180° \leq \theta° < 180°$ for which $2 \sin^2 \theta° - 2 \sin \theta° = \cos^2 \theta°$.

Edexcel

7 Exponentials and logarithms

In this chapter you will learn how to
- sketch the graphs of exponential functions
- use logarithmic notation
- use the laws of logarithms
- solve equations of the form $a^x = b$

A Graphs of exponential functions (answers p 146)

A1 Aquatic plants are growing on the surface of a pond.
Initially the plants cover an area of $1\,\text{m}^2$.

Each week the area covered by plants is doubled.

(a) Complete this table showing the area of pond, $A\,\text{m}^2$, covered by the plants
t weeks after measurements were started.

t (weeks)	0	1	2	3	4
A (m²)	1				

(b) Plot the values of t and A on a graph with axes as shown.
Join the points with a curve.

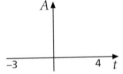

(c) Write down a formula connecting the surface area, A, with the time, t.

(d) Use your formula and a calculator to find the value of A when $t = 0.5$.
Check that your graph gives the same result.

(e) Use your formula to calculate the value of A when $t = 1.7$.

(f) Assuming that the same rule for growth applied before the measurements
were started, extend your graph back to $t = -3$.

The type of growth shown by these plants is called **exponential growth**.

A function of the form $y = a^x$ is called an **exponential function** ('exponential' is
another word for 'power').

The variable, x, is the index.

A2 Use a graph plotter to plot the graph of $y = 2^x$.
(a) What is the value of y when $x = 0$?
(b) What happens to y when x is large and positive?
(c) What happens to y when x is large and negative?

A3 (a) Investigate the shape of the graph of $y = a^x$ for positive values of a.
(b) Through which point do all graphs of the form $y = a^x$ pass?

K For all values of a, the graph of $y = a^x$ passes through the point $(0, 1)$.

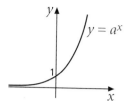

A4 Use a graph plotter to plot the graph of $y = (\frac{1}{2})^x$.

(a) What happens to y when x is large and positive?

(b) What happens to y when x is large and negative?

(c) Use the laws of indices to show that the graph of $y = (\frac{1}{2})^x$ is the same as the graph of $y = 2^{-x}$.

(d) What transformation maps the graph of $y = 2^x$ onto the graph of $y = (\frac{1}{2})^x$?

The type of growth shown by the function $y = a^x$, where $0 \leq a \leq 1$ is known as **exponential decay**.

A5 The graph of $y = 2^x$ is translated by $\begin{bmatrix} 0 \\ 1 \end{bmatrix}$.

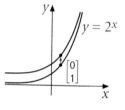

(a) Show that the point $(3, 8)$ is on the graph of $y = 2^x$.

(b) What is the image of the point $(3, 8)$ on the translated curve?

(c) What is the y-intercept on the translated curve?

(d) What is the equation of the translated curve?

D

A6 The graph of $y = 2^x$ is translated by $\begin{bmatrix} 3 \\ 0 \end{bmatrix}$.

What is the equation of the translated curve?

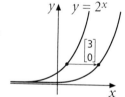

A7 The graph of $y = 2^x$ is translated by $\begin{bmatrix} -1 \\ 0 \end{bmatrix}$.

What is the equation of the translated curve?

A8 The graph of $y = 2^x$ is transformed by a stretch of scale factor 3 in the direction of the y-axis.

(a) Sketch the two graphs on the same set of axes, showing where each cuts the y-axis.

(b) What is the equation of the transformed curve?

A9 The graph of $y = 2^x$ is transformed by a stretch of scale factor 3 in the direction of the x-axis.

What is the equation of the transformed curve?

A10 (a) Use the laws of indices to show that the graph of $y = 16 \times 2^x$ is the same as the graph of $y = 2^{x+4}$.

(b) State two possible transformations which map the graph of $y = 2^x$ on to the graph of $y = 2^{x+4}$.

A11 State two possible transformations which map the graph of $y = 2^x$ on to the graph of $y = 2^{x+5}$.

Example 1

(a) Describe the transformation that maps the graph of $y = 3^x$ on to the graph of $y = 3^{x+2}$.

(b) On the same set of axes, sketch the graphs of $y = 3^x$ and $y = 3^{x+2}$.

Solution

(a) *In the transformed equation, x has been replaced by (x + 2), which is equivalent to a translation of 2 to the left.*

The graph of $y = 3^{x+2}$ is a translation of $\begin{bmatrix} -2 \\ 0 \end{bmatrix}$ of $y = 3^x$.

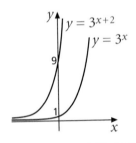

(b) The graph of $y = 3^x$ passes through $(0, 1)$.
The graph of $y = 3^{x+2}$ passes through $(0, 9)$.

Exercise A (answers p 146)

1 On the same set of axes, sketch the graphs of $y = 2^x$, $y = 4^x$ and $y = (\frac{1}{2})^x$.

2 (a) Describe the transformation which maps the graph of $y = 5^x$ on to the graph of $y = 5^{x+1}$.

(b) On the same set of axes, sketch the graphs of $y = 5^x$ and $y = 5^{x+1}$.

3 (a) What is the equation of the image of the graph of $y = 6^x$ after a translation of $\begin{bmatrix} 3 \\ 0 \end{bmatrix}$?

(b) What is the equation of the image of the graph of $y = 6^x$ after a translation of $\begin{bmatrix} 0 \\ 3 \end{bmatrix}$?

4 The function f is defined by $f(x) = 4^x$.

(a) Write down $f(x - 2)$.

(b) What transformation maps the graph of $y = f(x)$ on to the graph of $y = f(x - 2)$?

5 The function g is defined by $g(x) = 7^x$.

(a) Write down $g(3x)$.

(b) What transformation maps the graph of $y = g(x)$ on to the graph of $y = g(3x)$?

6 Describe the transformation which maps the graph of $y = 3^x$ on to

(a) $y = 3^{-x}$ (b) $y = 3^x - 5$ (c) $y = 2 \times 3^x$ (d) $y = 3^{x+4}$

7 (a) Use the laws of indices to show that the graph of $y = 16 \times 4^x$ is the same as the graph of $y = 4^{x+2}$.

(b) State two possible transformations which map the graph of $y = 4^x$ on to the graph of $y = 4^{x+2}$.

8 State two possible transformations which map the graph of $y = 5^x$ on to the graph of $y = 5^{x-1}$.

B Logarithms (answers p 147)

B1 Use your graph from question A1 to find after how long the area of the pond covered by plants will be $10\,\text{m}^2$.

In order to be able to solve problems like this exactly, we need to be able to find the inverse of an exponential function.

B2 Consider the function $y = 2^x$.

(a) Find the value of y when

(i) $x = 2$ (ii) $x = 5$ (iii) $x = -1$

(b) Find the value of x when

(i) $y = 1$ (ii) $y = 8$ (iii) $y = \frac{1}{4}$

The exponential function $y = 2^x$ expresses y in terms of x.
To find x given the value of y, we need to find the inverse function, x in terms of y.
For example, if $2^x = 8$, then $x = 3$ because $2^3 = 8$.

The index, 3, is known as the **logarithm** of 8 to base 2 or the log-to-base-2 of 8, written as $\log_2 8$.
Similarly, $\log_2 32 = 5$ because $2^5 = 32$.

The 'log$_2$' of a number is the power to which you have to raise 2 in order to get the number.
In symbols,
$y = 2^x$ and $x = \log_2 y$ are equivalent statements.

B3 (a) Rewrite $2^6 = 64$ in logarithmic form.

(b) Rewrite $\log_2 128 = 7$ in exponential form.

B4 (a) Given that $y = 5^x$, find the value of x when

    (i) $y = 5$ (ii) $y = 125$ (iii) $y = 0.2$

  (b) Given that $y = 10^x$, find the value of x when

    (i) $y = 1000$ (ii) $y = \frac{1}{100}$ (iii) $y = 0.001$

A logarithm can be defined with any positive base.

For example, log-to-base-5 of 25, or $\log_5 25$ is equal to 2 because $5^2 = 25$

If a number is expressed in exponential form as $y = a^x$,
then the index x is known as $\log_a y$.

$y = a^x$ and $x = \log_a y$ are equivalent statements.

> $\log_{\text{base}}$ number $=$ index
>
> is equivalent to
>
> base^{index} = number

This can also be written as

$$y = a^x \iff x = \log_a y$$

where the symbol $\iff$ means 'implies and is implied by'.

B5 (a) Rewrite $5^4 = 625$ in logarithmic form.

  (b) Rewrite $\log_{10} 100 = 2$ in exponential form.

B6 Write the following in logarithmic form.

  (a) $3^4 = 81$ (b) $7^3 = 343$ (c) $8^{-1} = 0.125$

B7 Write the following in exponential form.

  (a) $\log_3 9 = 2$ (b) $\log_4 64 = 3$ (c) $\log_9 \frac{1}{9} = -1$

B8 (a) Write $\log_2 2 = x$ in index form.

  (b) What is the value of x?

B9 (a) Write $\log_2 1 = x$ in index form.

  (b) What is the value of x?

B10 (a) Write $\log_2 \frac{1}{2} = x$ in index form.

  (b) What is the value of x?

B11 Write down the values of the following.

  (a) $\log_a a$ (b) $\log_a 1$ (c) $\log_a \left(\dfrac{1}{a} \right)$

B12 (a) (i) Write $\log_5 5^2 = x$ in index form.

       (ii) What is the value of x?

  (b) What is the value of $\log_3 3^4$?

  (c) What is the value of $\log_a a^x$?

B13 (a) (i) Write $2^{\log_2 8} = x$ in log form.

(ii) What is the value of x?

(b) What is the value of $3^{\log_3 9}$?

(c) What is the value of $a^{\log_a x}$?

You have now obtained the following properties of logarithms.

$y = a^x \iff x = \log_a y$

$\log_a a = 1 \qquad\qquad \log_a 1 = 0$

$\log_a \left(\dfrac{1}{a} \right) = -1$

$\log_a a^x = x$

$a^{\log_a x} = x$

Example 2

Write down these values.

(a) $\log_4 16$ **(b)** $\log_3 81$ **(c)** $\log_9 3$

Solution

(a) Since $4^2 = 16$, $\log_4 16 = 2$

(b) Since $3^4 = 81$, $\log_3 81 = 4$

(c) Since $9^{\frac{1}{2}} = 3$, $\log_9 3 = \frac{1}{2}$

Example 3

Find the value of x in $\log_x 625 = 4$.

Solution

First write $\log_x 625 = 4$ *in exponential form.* $\log_x 625 = 4$ is the same as $x^4 = 625$

$$5^4 = 625, \text{ so } x = 5$$

Exercise B (answers p 147)

1 (a) Write the following as powers of 2.

    (i) 64   **(ii)** $\sqrt{2}$ **(iii)** $\frac{1}{8}$ **(iv)** 0.25   **(v)** 1

(b) Hence write down the values of the following.

    (i) $\log_2 64$ **(ii)** $\log_2 \sqrt{2}$ **(iii)** $\log_2 \frac{1}{8}$ **(iv)** $\log_2 0.25$ **(v)** $\log_2 1$

2 Write the following in index form.

    (a) $\log_3 \frac{1}{9} = -2$ **(b)** $\log_8 1 = 0$ **(c)** $\log_4 32 = 2.5$ **(d)** $\log_8 4 = \frac{2}{3}$

3 Write the following in logarithmic form.

(a) $6^3 = 216$ (b) $3^5 = 243$ (c) $4^{-3} = \frac{1}{64}$ (d) $27^{\frac{2}{3}} = 9$

4 Write down the values of the following.

(a) $\log_3 9$ (b) $\log_5 125$ (c) $\log_5 \frac{1}{25}$ (d) $\log_7 1$

(e) $\log_3 {}^4\sqrt{3}$ (f) $\log_4 2$ (g) $\log_{11} 11$ (h) $\log_{10} 0.1$

5 Find the values of the following.

(a) $\log_a a^2$ (b) $\log_a \left(\frac{1}{a^2} \right)$ (c) $\log_a \sqrt{a}$ (d) $\log_a (a^3 \times a^4)$

6 Write $\log_3 p = 4$ in index form and hence find the value of p.

7 Write $\log_t 3 = \frac{1}{2}$ in index form and hence find the value of t.

8 Find the value of x in each of the following.

(a) $\log_4 64 = x$ (b) $\log_x 8 = 3$ (c) $\log_3 x = 3$ (d) $\log_x 216 = 3$

(e) $\log_x 0.04 = -2$ (f) $\log_4 x = -\frac{1}{2}$ (g) $\log_5 0.2 = x$ (h) $\log_3 x = \frac{1}{2}$

9 Here is a table of values and sketch of the graph of the function $y = 2^x$.

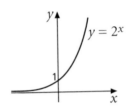

x	-2	-1	0	1	2	3
$y = 2^x$	0.25	0.5	1	2	4	8

The table can be inverted to find values of the function $y = \log_2 x$.

(a) Complete this table of values for $y = \log_2 x$.

x	0.25	0.5	1	2	4	8
$y = \log_2 x$			0			

(b) Use the values in the table to draw the graph of $y = \log_2 x$.

(c) What is the relationship between the graph of $y = 2^x$ and the graph of $y = \log_2 x$?

C Laws of logarithms (answers p 148)

C1 (a) Write down the values of

(i) $\log_2 8$ (ii) $\log_2 16$ (iii) $\log_2 128$

(b) $8 \times 16 = 128$ can be written as $2^a \times 2^b = 2^c$.
What are a, b and c? How is c related to a and b?

(c) Use this to explain why $\log_2 8 + \log_2 16 = \log_2 (8 \times 16)$.

C2 $3^2 \times 3^3 = 3^5$.
Show how this explains that $\log_3 9 + \log_3 27 = \log_3 (9 \times 27)$.

These results suggest that logs are related by the law

$$\log_a m + \log_a n = \log_a mn$$

In fact, it is possible to prove that this result is true for any positive base a.

Let $m = a^x$ so $x = \log_a m$ and let $n = a^y$ so $y = \log_a n$

Then $\log_a mn = \log_a(a^x \times a^y)$

$\Rightarrow \quad \log_a mn = \log_a(a^{x+y})$

$\Rightarrow \quad \log_a mn = x + y$

$\Rightarrow \log_a m + \log_a n = \log_a mn$

C3 Given that $\log_5 3 = 0.6826$ and $\log_5 4 = 0.8614$ (to 4 d.p.), use the law found above to find the value of $\log_5 12$.

C4 Using a similar method to that shown above, prove the result

$$\log_a m - \log_a n = \log_a\left(\frac{m}{n}\right)$$

C5 Given that $\log_8 3 = 0.5283$ and $\log_8 21 = 1.4641$, use the law found above to find the value of $\log_8 7$.

C6 Prove the result that $-\log_a m = \log_a\left(\frac{1}{m}\right)$.

C7 Use the index law $(a^x)^2 = a^{2x}$ to prove the result

$$2\log_a m = \log_a m^2$$

(Hint: start by letting $m = a^x$ and consider $\log_a m^2$.)

C8 Use the index law $(a^x)^k = a^{kx}$ to prove the result

$$k\log_a m = \log_a m^k$$

C9 Given that $\log_3 2 = 0.6309$ to 4 d.p., find the values of

(a) $\log_3 \frac{1}{2}$ (b) $\log_3 16$ (c) $\log_3 4$ (d) $\log_3 \sqrt{2}$

K In summary, the laws of logarithms are

$$\log_a m + \log_a n = \log_a mn$$

$$\log_a m - \log_a n = \log_a\left(\frac{m}{n}\right)$$

$$-\log_a m = \log_a\left(\frac{1}{m}\right)$$

$$k\log_a m = \log_a m^k$$

C10 Given that $\log_{10} 2 = 0.3010$ and $\log_{10} 3 = 0.4771$, use the laws of logs and the result that $\log_{10} 10 = 1$ to find the following.

(a) $\log_{10} \frac{1}{2}$ (b) $\log_{10} 1.5$ (c) $\log_{10} 4$ (d) $\log_{10} 5$

(e) $\log_{10} 6$ (f) $\log_{10} 9$ (g) $\log_{10} 16$ (h) $\log_{10} 20$

Example 4

Write $\log_a 3 + \log_a 8 - \log_a 2$ as a single logarithm.

Solution

Use the laws of logs to combine $\log_a 3$ and $\log_a 8$.

Now combine with $\log_a 2$.

$$\log_a 3 + \log_a 8 - \log_a 2 = \log_a 3 \times 8 - \log_a 2$$
$$= \log_a \frac{3 \times 8}{2}$$
$$= \log_a 12$$

Example 5

Express $\log_a \dfrac{x^2}{yz}$ in terms of $\log_a x$, $\log_a y$ and $\log_a z$.

Solution

Use $\log_a m - \log_a n$.

Use $k \log_a m$.

Use $\log_a m + \log_a n$.

$$\log_a \frac{x^2}{yz} = \log_a x^2 - \log_a yz$$
$$= 2 \log_a x - \log_a yz$$
$$= 2 \log_a x - (\log_a y + \log_a z)$$
$$\text{so } \log_a \frac{x^2}{yz} = 2 \log_a x - \log_a y - \log_a z$$

Exercise C (answers p 148)

1 Write each of the following as a single logarithm.

(a) $\log_a 5 + \log_a 2$ (b) $\log_a 12 - \log_a 3$ (c) $2 \log_a 3$

(d) $1 + \log_a 8$ (e) $3 \log_a 4 - \log_a 2$ (f) $\log_a 6 + 2 \log_a 2 - \log_a 3$

2 Given that $\log_5 3 = 0.6826$ to 4 d.p., use the laws of logs to find the values of the following.

(a) $\log_5 5$ (b) $\log_5 9$ (c) $\log_5 \frac{1}{3}$ (d) $\log_5 \sqrt{3}$

(e) $\log_5 15$ (f) $\log_5 25$ (g) $\log_5 0.6$ (h) $\log_5 \frac{9}{25}$

3 Express the following in terms of $\log_a x$ and $\log_a y$.

(a) $\log_a \dfrac{x}{y}$ (b) $\log_a xy$ (c) $\log_a \dfrac{x^2}{y}$ (d) $\log_a \dfrac{\sqrt[a]{y}}{x}$

4 The notation 4! means $4 \times 3 \times 2 \times 1$ and is read as '4 factorial'.

Given that $\log_5 4! = 1.9746$, write down the value of $\log_5 5!$.

5 Write each of the following as a single logarithm.

(a) $2 \log_a p + \log_a q$ (b) $1 + 3 \log_a p$ (c) $\frac{1}{2} \log_a p - 4 \log_a q$

6 A colony of bacteria doubles in size every hour.

  (a) Explain why the time t hours for the colony to increase in size 1000-fold is given by $2^t = 1000$.

  (b) Express t as a logarithm to base 2 and explain why $9 < t < 10$.

  (c) By using trial and improvement and the power key on your calculator, find an approximate value of t to two decimal places.

7 Solve these equations for x.

  (a) $\log_x 4 + \log_x 16 = 3$
          (b) $\log_2 96 - \log_2 6 = x$

  (c) $\log_6 4 + \log_6 x = 2$
          (d) $\log_4 (x + 1) - \log_4 3 = 1$

  (e) $\log_2 2x - \log_2 (3x - 4) = 1$
      (f) $\log_2 x^2 = 2 + \log_2 (x + 3)$

D Equations of the form $a^x = b$ (answers p 148)

Logarithms are useful for a variety of purposes, one of which is met in this section. Originally, however, they were used as a way of easing multiplication and division, by replacing them with addition and subtraction.
In 1615, the Scottish mathematician John Napier discussed the idea of using logarithms with the Oxford professor Henry Briggs. Two years later, Briggs published his first table of logarithms (to 14 decimal places!) and after much further work published his *Arithmetica Logarithmica* in 1624.

Logarithms can now be found directly from a calculator. 'Log' is usually taken to mean $\log_{10}$, and you will find that the $\boxed{\log}$ key on calculators evaluates logarithms to the base 10.

  D1 Use the log key on your calculator to check your answers to C10.

In answering question 6 in Exercise C about a colony of bacteria you used trial and improvement to solve the equation $2^t = 1000$.

Problems concerning growth often lead to such equations, in which the unknown appears as an index. These equations can be solved using logarithms.

  D2 (a) What is the relationship between $\log 2^t$ and $\log 2$?

  (b) Solve the equation $2^t = 1000$ by first taking logs to base 10 of both sides and then using the relationship you stated in (a). Compare your answer with the answer you obtained using trial and improvement.

  D3 £1000 is invested in an account which earns 1% interest per month, all interest being reinvested.

  (a) Explain why the number m of months taken for the total investment to reach £2000 is given by the equation $1.01^m = 2$.

  (b) Use logs to find m.

D4 The population of a village is decreasing at a rate of 5% each year.

(a) By what factor is the population multiplied each year? (This is known as the growth factor.)

(b) After t years, the population of the village is $\frac{3}{5}$ of its original value. Show that $0.6 = 0.95^t$.

(c) Find the value of t.

Example 6

Solve $4^x = 28$.

Solution

$$4^x = 28$$

Take logs of both sides.

$$\log 4^x = \log 28$$

Use the laws of logs.

$$x \log 4 = \log 28$$

$$\Rightarrow \quad x = \frac{\log 28}{\log 4} = 2.4036...$$

$$\Rightarrow \quad x = 2.40 \text{ to 3 s.f.}$$

Example 7

Solve $5^{2x+1} = 8$.

Solution

$$5^{2x+1} = 8$$

Take logs of both sides.

$$\log 5^{2x+1} = \log 8$$

Use the laws of logs.

$$(2x+1) \log 5 = \log 8$$

$$\Rightarrow \quad 2x + 1 = \frac{\log 8}{\log 5}$$

$$\Rightarrow \quad x = \frac{1}{2}\left(\frac{\log 8}{\log 5} - 1\right)$$

$$\Rightarrow \quad x = 0.146 \text{ to 3 s.f.}$$

Example 8

Solve $5^{2x} - 3(5^x) + 2 = 0$.

Solution

As $5^{2x} = (5^x)^2$, this is a quadratic expression.

This quadratic factorises.

Either $(5^x - 1) = 0$ or $(5^x - 2) = 0$.

Use the result $a^0 = 1$.

$$5^{2x} - 3(5^x) + 2 = 0$$

$$(5^x - 1)(5^x - 2) = 0$$

giving $5^x = 1$ and $5^x = 2$

When $5^x = 1$, then $x = 0$

When $5^x = 2$,

Take logs of both sides.

Use the laws of logs.

then $\log 5^x = \log 2$

$$x \log 5 = \log 2$$

$$\Rightarrow \quad x = \frac{\log 2}{\log 5} = 0.4306...$$

so the solutions are $x = 0$ and $x = 0.431$ to 3 s.f.

Exercise D (answers p 149)

1 Solve these equations for x.

(a) $2^x = 32$

(b) $9^x = 243$

(c) $8^x = 256$

(d) $3^x = 10.05$

(e) $5^x = 9.2$

(f) $2.073^x = 7.218$

2 The number, n, of years needed for an investment of £4000 to grow to £5000 at 8% per annum compound interest is given by $1.08^n = 1.25$. Find n using logarithms.

3 The half-life, t days, of bismuth-210 is given approximately by the equation $10 \times (0.87)^t = 5$. Find its half-life in days, correct to two significant figures.

4 A colony of bacteria has a growth factor of 3.7 per hour and initially there are 250 bacteria.

(a) Write down an expression for the number of bacteria, n, after t hours.

(b) Find the time (to the nearest minute) after which there are 10 000 bacteria.

5 The charge of a capacitor has a growth factor of 0.9 per second. After how long will there be $\frac{1}{5}$ of the original charge? Give your answer in seconds to 2 d.p.

6 Find the smallest possible integer satisfying the inequality $2^n > 50^{132}$.

7 The population of a city is predicted to rise at a rate of 6% per year. In 2003 the population was 250 000.

(a) What is the growth factor for the population?

(b) Write down an expression for the population, P, after t years.

(c) Use this model to predict the number of years it will take for the population to reach 400 000.

8 A radioactive isotope is decaying at a rate of 7.5% per year.

(a) After t years, the amount of isotope present has decayed by a half. Show that $0.5 = 0.925^t$.

(b) Find the value of t.

9 A savings account has an interest rate of 3.25% per annum. After how long will an investment have increased by $\frac{1}{4}$ of its original value?

10 Solve these equations for x.

(a) $3^{x-1} = 5$

(b) $7^{2x+1} = 5$

(c) $5(3^x) + 1 = 3$

(d) $4^{x+2} = 5^x$

(e) $4(7^x) - 2 = 3$

(f) $6^{x-4} = 2^{x+3}$

11 (a) Solve the equation $y^2 - 5y + 6 = 0$.

(b) Hence solve the equation $2^{2x} - 5(2^x) + 6 = 0$.

12 Solve these equations.

(a) $3^{2x} - 4(3^x) + 3 = 0$ (b) $5^{2x} - 6(5^x) + 8 = 0$ (c) $2^{2x} + 3(2^x) - 10 = 0$

13 A population of deer is introduced into a park. The population P at a time t years after the deer have been introduced is modelled by

$$P = \frac{2000a^t}{4 + a^t}$$

where a is a constant. Given that there are 800 deer in the park after 6 years,

(a) calculate, to four decimal places, the value of a,

(b) use the model to predict the number of years needed for the population of deer to increase from 800 to 1800.

(c) With reference to this model, give a reason why the population of deer cannot exceed 2000.

Edexcel

*14 (a) The formula $\log_a x = \dfrac{\log_b x}{\log_b a}$, known as the change of base formula, can be used to change a logarithm from one base to another.

Given that $p = \log_a x \Rightarrow a^p = x$, prove the change of base formula.
(Hint: start by taking logarithms to base b of both sides.)

(b) Given that $5^x = 8$,

(i) write x as a single logarithm

(ii) use the change of base formula to find x to three significant figures

---

Key points

- A function of the form $y = a^x$ is an exponential function.

(p 86)

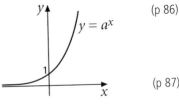

- The graph of $y = a^x$ is positive for all values of x and passes through the point $(0, 1)$.

(p 87)

- A logarithm is the inverse of an exponential function.
  $y = a^x \Leftrightarrow x = \log_a y$

(p 90)

- $\log_a a = 1$ $\qquad\qquad$ $\log_a 1 = 0$
  $\log_a a^x = x$ $\qquad\qquad$ $a^{\log_a x} = x$

(pp 90–91)

- The laws of logarithms are

$$\log_a m + \log_a n = \log_a mn$$
$$\log_a m - \log_a n = \log_a \left(\frac{m}{n}\right)$$
$$-\log_a m = \log_a \left(\frac{1}{m}\right)$$
$$k \log_a m = \log_a m^k$$

(p 93)

- An equation of the form $a^x = b$ can be solved by taking logs of both sides.

(pp 95–96)

Test yourself (answers p 150)

1 Describe, in each of the following cases, a single transformation which maps the graph of $y = 3^x$ on to the graph of the function given.

(a) $y = 3^{x+2}$ (b) $y = 3^{-x}$ (c) $y = 4 \times 3^x$ (d) $y = 3^x - 1$

2 (a) Show that $\log_5 125 = 3$.

(b) Find the value of

(i) $\log_5 (125^4)$ (ii) $\log_5 \left(\dfrac{1}{\sqrt{125}} \right)$

3 (a) Describe a geometrical transformation by which the graph of $y = 2^{x+3}$ can be obtained from that of $y = 2^x$.

(b) The graph of $y = 2^{x+3}$ passes through the point $(0, p)$. What is the value of p?

4 (a) Using $p = \frac{1}{2}$ write down the value of $\log_2 p$.

(b) Given also that $\log_2 q = t$, express $\log_2 \dfrac{p^3}{\sqrt{q}}$ in terms of t.   Edexcel

5 Given that $p = \log_q 16$, express in terms of p

(a) $\log_q 2$ (b) $\log_q (8q)$ Edexcel

6 Given that $\log_a x = \log_a 7 + 3 \log_a 2$, where a is a positive constant, show that $x = 56$.

7 (a) Given that $3 + 2\log_2 x = \log_2 y$, show that $y = 8x^2$.

(b) Hence, or otherwise, find the roots α and β, where $\alpha < \beta$, of the equation $3 + 2\log_2 x = \log_2 (14x - 3)$.   Edexcel

8 (a) Simplify $\dfrac{x^2 + 4x + 3}{x^2 + x}$.

(b) Find the value of x for which $\log_2 (x^2 + 4x + 3) - \log_2 (x^2 + x) = 4$.   Edexcel

9 Solve these equations for x.

(a) $4^x = 24$ (b) $2^{x-3} = 9$ (c) $3^{2x+1} = 12$

10 A radioactive isotope decays at a rate of 12% per year.
After t years the amount of isotope has decreased to half of its original value. This is the half-life of the isotope.

Form and solve an equation to find the value of t.

11 Find the possible values of x for which $3^{2x} - 5(3^x) + 4 = 0$.

8 Differentiation

In this chapter you will learn how to
- tell whether a function is increasing or decreasing
- find stationary points on a graph and use these to help sketch the graph
- use the second order derivative to distinguish between types of stationary point
- solve optimisation problems

Key points from Core 1

- The derivative of y with respect to x is denoted by $\dfrac{dy}{dx}$.

- The derivative of the sum of two or more functions is the sum of the separate derivatives.

- The derivative of $f(x)$ is denoted by $f'(x)$.

- The derivative of x^n is nx^{n-1}.

- The value of the derivative at a point P on a graph tells you the gradient of the tangent at P.

- The second order derivative of y with respect to x is the derivative of $\dfrac{dy}{dx}$ and is denoted by $\dfrac{d^2y}{dx^2}$.

A Increasing and decreasing functions

This is the graph of a function $f(x)$.

At point A, where $x = a$, the gradient is positive.

In symbols, $f'(a) > 0$.

f is **increasing** at A.

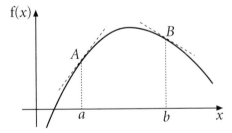

At point B, where $x = b$, the gradient is negative.

In symbols, $f'(b) < 0$.

f is **decreasing** at B.

Example 1

The function f is defined by $f(x) = 2x - 10\sqrt{x}$.

Is f increasing or decreasing at the point where $x = 4$?

Solution

$f(x) = 2x - 10x^{\frac{1}{2}}$

$f'(x) = 2 - 5x^{-\frac{1}{2}}$

$f'(4) = 2 - 5 \times \frac{1}{2} = -\frac{1}{2}.$ $f'(4) < 0$, so f is decreasing.

Testing whether a function is increasing or decreasing at a given point is straightforward. Simply calculate the derivative and see whether it is positive or negative.

The reverse process of finding the range of points for which a given function is increasing or decreasing is not so easy. It involves solving an inequality.

Example 2

The function f(x) given by $f(x) = 2x^3 - 3x^2 - 36x$ is decreasing over the interval $a < x < b$. Calculate the values of a and b.

Solution

$f'(x) = 6x^2 - 6x - 36$

For f(x) to be decreasing, $f'(x) < 0$, so $6x^2 - 6x - 36 < 0$

$\Rightarrow \qquad x^2 - x - 6 < 0$

$\Rightarrow \qquad (x + 2)(x - 3) < 0$

Use a 'sign diagram' to solve this inequality.

```
                        -2              3
        _____|_____|_____
x + 2     -  -  -  0  +  +  +  +  +  +  +  +
x - 3     -  -  -  -  -  -  -  -  -  0  +  +  +
        _____
(x + 2)(x - 3)   +  +  +  0  -  -  -  -  -  0  +  +  +
```

$(x + 2)(x - 3) < 0$ for $-2 < x < 3$.

So $a = -2$ and $b = 3$.

Exercise A (answers p 151)

1 The function f is defined by $f(x) = x^3 - 5x^2 + 1$.
   Is the function increasing or decreasing at the point where $x = 3$?

2 Determine whether each of these functions is increasing or decreasing at the given point.
   (a) $f(x) = (x^2 + 3)(x^2 - 5)$ where $x = \frac{1}{2}$ (b) $y = x(\sqrt{x} - 1)$ where $x = 4$

3 The function f(x) defined by $f(x) = x^3 - 6x^2$ is decreasing over the interval $p < x < q$. Calculate the values of p and q.

4 The function g(x) is given by $g(x) = x^3 - 27x + 20$.
   Find the range of values of x for which $g(x)$ is an increasing function.

5 The function s(x) is defined by $s(x) = x(75 - x^2)$.
   Find the range of values of x for which $s(x)$ is an increasing function.

6 The population of an animal colony is modelled by the equation
   $$P = 500 + 150t - \tfrac{1}{2}t^3 \quad (t \geq 0)$$
   where t is the time in years since the population was first counted.
   For what range of values of t will P be increasing?

B Stationary points (answers p 151)

Here is the graph of the function

$$f(x) = \tfrac{1}{3}x^3 - 2x^2 + 3x + 1$$

At each of the points A and B, the value of the gradient $f'(x)$ is 0.

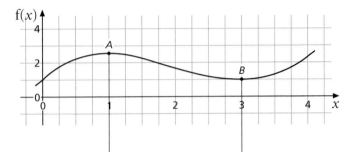

A and B are called **stationary points** of the graph.

A is a **local maximum**.
B is a **local minimum**.

This is the graph of the derivative

$$f'(x) = x^2 - 4x + 3$$

$f'(x)$ is zero at $x = 1$ and $x = 3$, the values corresponding to the stationary points A and B of $f(x)$.

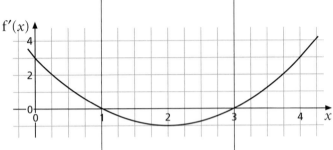

The function $f'(x)$ can also be differentiated. This is the graph that is obtained.

The derivative of $f'(x)$ is denoted by $\mathbf{f''(x)}$. It is the **second order derivative** of $f(x)$.

$$f''(x) = 2x - 4$$

$f''(x)$ gives the gradient of $f'(x)$.

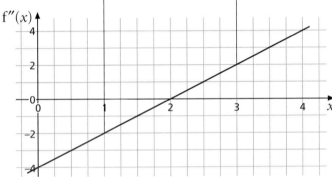

B1 (a) Point A, where $x = 1$, is a maximum point on the graph of $f(x)$.

Look at the graph of $f'(x)$ at the point where $x = 1$.
The value of $f'(x)$ goes from positive on the left to negative on the right.
Is $f'(x)$ increasing or decreasing at $x = 1$?

(b) What feature of the graph of $f''(x)$ at $x = 1$ tells you that $f'(x)$ must be decreasing at $x = 1$?

(c) What feature of the graph of $f''(x)$ tells you that $f'(x)$ must be increasing at $x = 3$?

The second derivative can be used to test whether a stationary point is a maximum or a minimum.

If the value of $f''(x)$ is positive at the stationary point, the point is a minimum.

If the value of $f''(x)$ is negative, the point is a maximum.

(Note. If the value of $f''(x)$ is zero, no conclusion can be drawn. In this case you will have to look at the sign of $f'(x)$ either side of the stationary point.)

In the other notation for derivatives, the second derivative of y with respect to x is denoted by $\dfrac{d^2y}{dx^2}$.

Finding stationary points is useful when sketching the graph of a function.

Example 3

(a) Find the stationary points on the graph of $y = x^3 - 3x^2 - 9x + 5$ and determine their types.

(b) Sketch the graph.

Solution

(a) $\dfrac{dy}{dx} = 3x^2 - 6x - 9$. At stationary points $\dfrac{dy}{dx} = 0$, so $3x^2 - 6x - 9 = 0$

$$\Rightarrow \quad 3(x^2 - 2x - 3) = 0$$
$$\Rightarrow \quad (x + 1)(x - 3) = 0$$
$$\Rightarrow \quad x = -1 \text{ or } x = 3$$

Find the value of y at each of these values of x.

When $x = -1$, $y = (-1)^3 - 3 \times (-1)^2 - 9 \times -1 + 5 = 10$

When $x = 3$, $y = 3^3 - 3 \times 3^2 - 9 \times 3 + 5 = -22$

So the stationary points are $(-1, 10)$ and $(3, -22)$.

Differentiate $\dfrac{dy}{dx}$ to get the second derivative. Then find its value at each stationary point.

$$\dfrac{d^2y}{dx^2} = 6x - 6$$

When $x = -1$, $\dfrac{d^2y}{dx^2} = 6 \times -1 - 6 = -12$. This is negative, so $x = 1$ gives a maximum.

When $x = 3$, $\dfrac{d^2y}{dx^2} = 6 \times 3 - 6 = 12$. This is positive, so $x = 3$ gives a minimum.

So $(-1, 10)$ is a maximum and $(3, -22)$ is a minimum.

(b) When $x = 0$, $y = 5$.

When x is large and positive, so is y.
When x is large and negative, so is y.

$(-1, 10)$ is a maximum and $(3, -22)$ is a minimum.

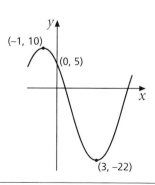

Exercise B (answers p 151)

1 Given that $f(x) = 5x^3 - 3x^2 + 7x - 2$, find   (a) $f'(x)$ (b) $f''(x)$

2 Given that $y = 3x^4 + 2x^3$, find   (a) $\dfrac{dy}{dx}$ (b) $\dfrac{d^2y}{dx^2}$

3 Find the stationary points on the graph of $y = x^3 - 6x^2 + 9x + 4$ and use the second derivative to determine their types.

4 For each of the following graphs

    (i) find the stationary points and determine their types

    (ii) sketch the graph

  (a) $y = x^3 + 3x^2 - 45x + 8$ **(b)** $y = 4x^3 - 15x^2 + 12x + 1$ **(c)** $y = x^3 + 12x^2 + 36x - 5$

  (d) $y = 9x + 6x^2 - 4x^3$ **(e)** $y = 4x^3 - 9x^2 - 30x + 1$ **(f)** $y = (x - 6)(x + 6)^2$

5 Find the x-coordinate(s) of the stationary points on each of these graphs and determine the type of each stationary point.

  (a) $y = x - 6\sqrt{x}$ **(b)** $y = \dfrac{x^3}{3} + \dfrac{16}{x}$

6 (a) Find the coordinates of the stationary point on the graph of

$$y = x^2 + \frac{16}{x} \quad (x > 0)$$

  (b) What happens to the value of y as x

    (i) approaches 0   **(ii)** becomes larger and larger

  (c) Sketch the graph for $x > 0$.

C Stationary points of inflexion (answers p 152)

Here is the graph of the function

    $f(x) = x^3 - 9x^2 + 27x$

At the point A, where $x = 3$, the gradient is 0.

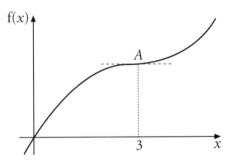

A is a stationary point, but neither a maximum nor a minimum.

A is called a **stationary point of inflexion**. At such a point the gradient is either positive on both sides of the point or negative on both sides.

By differentiating, $f'(x) = 3x^2 - 18x + 27$
                    $f''(x) = 6x - 18$

Notice that $f''(3) = 0$.

It can be shown that for any function $f(x)$, if there is a stationary point of inflexion at $x = a$, then $f'(a) = 0$ and $f''(a) = 0$.
However, the converse statement is not true. If $f'(a)$ and $f''(a)$ are both zero, it does not follow that there is a stationary point of inflexion at $x = a$.

  C1 (a) Sketch the graph of $y = f(x)$ where $f(x) = x^4$.

     (b) Calculate the values of $f'(0)$ and $f''(0)$.

     (c) What type of stationary point is $(0, 0)$?

     (d) What happens in the case of the function $f(x) = -x^4$?

D Optimisation

Optimisation means getting the best result. This might mean **minimising** the amount of material used in a design or the amount of pollution caused by an industrial process, or **maximising** the number of customers served in an hour or the number of vaccinations during an epidemic.

A problem of this kind arises in marketing when deciding on the price to charge for a product. If the price is very low, a large number of the product may be sold but the total income from sales may not amount to much. If the price is very high, very few may be sold and again the income will be small. Somewhere in between there might be a price that will give the largest income.

Example 4

The owner of a castle wants to know how much to charge for admission.

The relationship between the number N of tickets sold per day and the price £P is believed to be as shown in the graph, whose equation is

$$N = 800 - 80P$$

What price should the owner charge in order to get the maximum possible income?

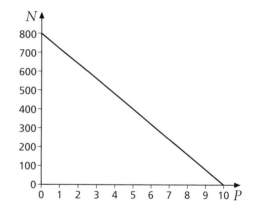

Solution

The income I gained from selling N tickets is N times P, so

$I = P(800 - 80P)$
  $= 800P - 80P^2$

For the income I to be a maximum, $\dfrac{dI}{dP} = 0$.

So $\dfrac{dI}{dP} = 800 - 160P = 0$

From which $P = \dfrac{800}{160} = 5$.

Check that $P = 5$ gives a maximum by using $\dfrac{d^2I}{dP^2}$.

$\dfrac{d^2I}{dP^2} = -160$, which is negative at every value of P, including $P = 5$.

So $P = 5$ gives a maximum. The owner should charge £5.

Exercise D (answers p 152)

1 For a speed of v m.p.h., the fuel economy, F miles per gallon, of a new car is found to be roughly modelled, for $30 \leq v \leq 80$, by the formula

$$F = 25 + v - 0.01v^2$$

What speed is most economical for this car?

2 A new housing estate started with a population of approximately 500 people.

  (a) It was planned that it should grow by roughly 100 inhabitants each year.

  (i) Find an expression for the intended population P of the estate t years after its opening.

  (ii) Find $\dfrac{\mathrm{d}P}{\mathrm{d}t}$ and explain what it represents.

  (b) For various reasons, the new estate did not grow as planned and the population was better modelled by the quadratic expression

$$P = 100(5 + t - 0.25t^2)$$

  (i) What was the rate of change of the population at the end of the first, second and third years?

  (ii) What was the maximum population of the estate?

  (iii) According to the model, what would happen to the population?

3 A farmer has 60 m of fencing. She wants to use it for three sides of a rectangular sheep pen with an existing hedge used for the fourth side.

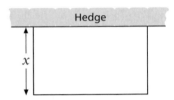

  (a) Let x metres be the length of the side shown. Write an expression for the area, $A\,\mathrm{m}^2$, in terms of x.

  (b) Calculate the value of x for which A is a maximum.

  (c) Calculate the maximum area.

4

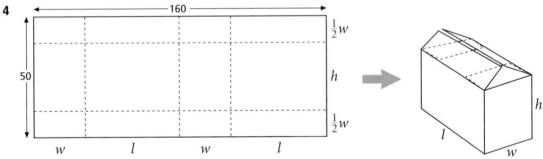

A box is to be made from a rectangular piece of card, 160 cm by 50 cm, by cutting and folding as necessary along the dotted lines shown in the left-hand diagram. The problem is to find the values of l, w and h which maximise the volume, $V\,\mathrm{cm}^3$.

  (a) Explain why $2l + 2w = 160$. Hence express l in terms of w.

  (b) Similarly, find h in terms of w.

  (c) The volume of the box is given by $V = whl$. Use your answers to (a) and (b) to show that $V = w(50 - w)(80 - w)$.

  (d) Find the value of w corresponding to the maximum possible volume. What dimensions will the box then have?

5 An open-topped tray is made from a rectangular piece of metal 8 cm by 5 cm. A square is cut from each corner, as shown below, and the remainder made into the tray by bending along the dotted lines and welding.

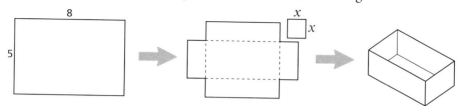

(a) If the squares cut out have side x cm, show that the volume of the tray is V cm³, where $V = x(8 - 2x)(5 - 2x)$.

(b) What should the dimensions be if the volume is to be as large as possible?

6 A box with a lid has a square base of side x cm and a height of h cm.

(a) Find an expression for the total surface area of the box in terms of x and h.

(b) The total surface area of the box is 384 cm².

(i) Find a formula for h in terms of x.

(ii) Hence show that, if the volume of the box is V cm³, then $V = 96x - \frac{1}{2}x^3$.

(iii) Find the value of x for which the volume is a maximum and the corresponding value of h.

(iv) Calculate the maximum volume of the box.

7 The end faces of a prism are in the shape of a right-angled triangle with sides $3x$ cm, $4x$ cm and $5x$ cm. The length of the prism is l cm. The total surface area of the prism is 64 cm².

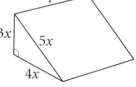

(a) Show that $l = \dfrac{16}{3x} - x$.

(b) Show that the volume V cm³ of the prism is given by $V = 32x - 6x^3$.

(c) Calculate the maximum possible volume of the prism.

*8 A bicycle manufacturer has designed a new model and wishes to fix the price so that profits are maximised. After an initial cost of £50 000 to set up the production line, it will cost £85 in labour, raw materials and components to produce each bike.

Market research suggests that the firm can hope to sell 5000 bikes if the price is fixed at £100 per bike, but they can only expect to sell 1000 if the price is £200. They assume that the relationship between price and demand is linear between these two extremes.

How many bikes would you advise the company to manufacture and at what price should they be sold?

Key points

- If $f'(a) > 0$, then $f(x)$ is increasing at $x = a$.
  If $f'(a) < 0$, then $f(x)$ is decreasing at $x = a$. (p 100)

- Points where $f'(x) = 0$ are called stationary points. (p 102)

- The second order derivative of $f(x)$ is the derivative of $f'(x)$.
  It is denoted by $f''(x)$.
  (In the other notation, the second order derivative is denoted by $\dfrac{d^2 y}{dx^2}$.) (pp 102–103)

- If $f'(a) = 0$ and $f''(a) > 0$, the point where $x = a$ is a local minimum of $f(x)$.
  If $f'(a) = 0$ and $f''(a) < 0$, the point where $x = a$ is a local maximum of $f(x)$. (p 102)

Mixed questions (answers p 153)

1 Find the coordinates of the stationary points on the graph of $y = x^3 - 3x$ and determine their types.

2 Given that $y = (x - 5)(2x^2 + 1)$, find

(a) $\dfrac{dy}{dx}$ (b) $\dfrac{d^2 y}{dx^2}$

3 Given that $f(x) = 3 + 5x - 2x^2$,

(a) find the coordinates of all the points at which the graph of $y = f(x)$ crosses the coordinate axes

(b) sketch the graph of $y = f(x)$

(c) calculate the coordinates of the stationary point of $f(x)$

4 For the curve C with equation $y = x^4 - 2x^2 + 4$,

(a) find $\dfrac{dy}{dx}$

(b) find the coordinates of each of the stationary points

(c) determine the nature of each stationary point

(d) sketch the curve C

5 The function $f(x)$ is defined by $f(x) = x^2(8x - 3)$.

(a) Find $f'(x)$.

(b) Find $f''(x)$.

(c) Determine whether the function is increasing or decreasing at the point where $x = 1$.

(d) Find the x-coordinates of the stationary points on the curve $y = x^2(8x - 3)$.

(e) Determine whether each stationary point is a maximum point or a minimum point.

6 On a journey, the average speed of a car is v ms^{-1}. For $v \geq 5$, the cost per kilometre, C pence, of the journey is modelled by

$$C = \frac{160}{v} + \frac{v^2}{100}$$

Using this model,

(a) show, by calculus, that there is a value of v for which C has a stationary value, and find this value of v.

(b) Justify that this value of v gives a minimum value of C.

(c) Find the minimum value of C and hence find the minimum cost of a 250 km car journey.

Edexcel

7 The function given by $f(x) = 7 + 15x - 6x^2 - x^3$ is increasing over the interval $a < x < b$. Calculate the values of a and b.

8 A simple shelter is made from a rectangular piece of sheet metal 4 m by 2 m by cutting and bending as shown below.

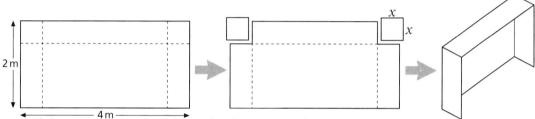

(a) If the squares removed from the sheet are each x m by x m, show that the volume, V m^3, of the shelter is given by

$$V = 2x^3 - 8x^2 + 8x$$

(b) Find the value of x for which the volume is as large as possible.

(c) Calculate the largest possible volume of the shelter.

9 A box made from sheet metal is in the shape of a square-based prism open at the top.

The volume of the box is 256 cm^3.

The base is a square of side x cm.

(a) Find an expression in terms of x for the height of the box.

(b) Show that the area, A cm^2, of the metal is given by

$$A = x^2 + \frac{1024}{x}$$

(c) Find the value of x for which A is a minimum.

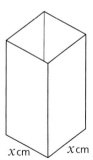

10 For the curve C with equation $y = x^4 - 8x^2 + 3$,

(a) find $\dfrac{dy}{dx}$

(b) find the coordinates of each of the stationary points

(c) determine the nature of each stationary point

The point A, on the curve C, has x-coordinate 1.

(d) Find an equation for the normal to C at A, giving your answer in the form $ax + by + c = 0$, where a, b and c are integers.

Edexcel

11 A manufacturer produces cartons for fruit juice. Each is in the shape of a closed cuboid with base dimensions $2x$ cm by x cm and height h cm, as shown in the diagram.

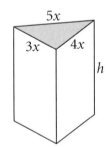

Given that the capacity of a carton has to be $1030\,\text{cm}^3$,

(a) express h in terms of x

(b) show that the surface area, $A\,\text{cm}^2$, of a carton is given by

$$A = 4x^2 + \frac{3090}{x}$$

The manufacturer needs to minimise the surface area of a carton.

(c) Use calculus to find the value of x for which A is a minimum.

(d) Calculate the minimum value of A.

(e) Prove that this value of A is a minimum.

Edexcel

12 The diagram shows a prism whose cross-section is a right-angled triangle with sides $3x$, $4x$ and $5x$ cm. The height is h cm.

(a) (i) Show that the volume, $V\,\text{cm}^3$, is given by $V = 6x^2 h$.

(ii) Show that the surface area, $S\,\text{cm}^2$, is given by $S = 12x^2 + 12xh$.

(b) Given the the volume of the prism is $100\,\text{cm}^3$, show that

$$S = 12x^2 + \frac{200}{x}$$

(c) Find, correct to three significant figures, the value of x for which S is a minimum, showing that this value does give a minimum for S.

*13 (a) The graph of the function $y = x^2(x - a)$ has a stationary point where $x = 6$. Find the value of a.

(b) The graph of the function $y = (x - 3)^2(x - b)$ has a stationary point where $x = 6$. Find the value of b.

(c) The graph of the function $y = x(x - c)^2$ has a stationary point where $x = 6$. Find the two possible values of c.

Test yourself (answers p 154)

1 Given that $f(x) = 15 - 7x - 2x^2$,

(a) find the coordinates of all the points at which the graph of $y = f(x)$ crosses the coordinate axes

(b) sketch the graph of $y = f(x)$

(c) calculate the coordinates of the stationary point of $f(x)$

Edexcel

2

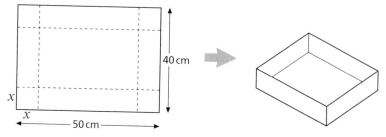

A rectangular sheet of metal measures 50 cm by 40 cm. Squares of side x cm are cut from each corner of the sheet and the remainder is folded along the dotted lines to make an open tray.

(a) Show that the volume, V cm^3, of the tray is given by $V = 4x(x^2 - 45x + 500)$.

(b) State the range of possible values of x.

(c) Find the value of x for which V is a maximum.

(d) Hence find the maximum value of V.

(e) Justify that the value of V you have found in part (c) is a maximum.

Edexcel

3 The graph of the function $y = x^3 - 3x^2 - 9x$ has two stationary points.

(a) Find $\dfrac{dy}{dx}$.

(b) Is the function increasing or decreasing at the point where $x = 0$?

(c) Find the coordinates of the stationary points.

(d) Find the value of $\dfrac{d^2y}{dx^2}$ at the stationary points, and hence determine whether the stationary points are maxima or minima.

4 An open box is made of sheet metal.
The base of the box is a rectangle x cm by $2x$ cm.
The height of the box is h cm.

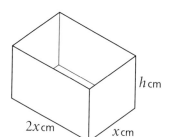

(a) Find an expression, in terms of x and h, for

    (i) the volume, V cm^3, of the box

    (ii) the area, A cm^2, of the metal

(b) Given that the volume of the box is 288 cm^3, show that $A = 2x^2 + \dfrac{864}{x}$.

(c) Find the value of x for which A is a minimum, showing that it is a minimum.

9 Integration

In this chapter you will learn how to
- calculate the area under a graph
- evaluate definite integrals
- use the trapezium rule to find an approximate value for a definite integral

---

Key points from Core 1

- If $\dfrac{dy}{dx} = f(x)$, then $y = \int f(x)dx$.

- $\int x^n \, dx = \dfrac{x^{n+1}}{n+1} + c.$

A Linear graphs: area function (answers p 155)

The first diagram below shows the area under the graph of $y = x$ between $x = 0$ and $x = 1$.
This area will be denoted by A(1). The other diagrams show A(2), A(3) and A(4).

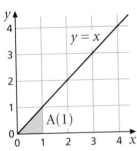 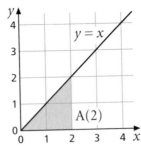 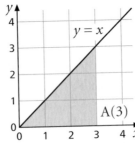 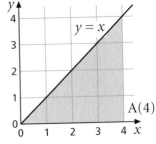

A1 (a) Copy and complete this table of
values for the function A(x).

x	0	1	2	3	4
A(x)					

(b) Plot the values of x and A(x) on a graph.

(c) What is the formula for A(x) in terms of x?

A2 Repeat for the graph of $y = 2x$.

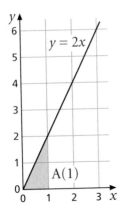 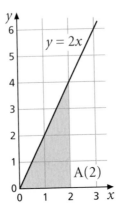 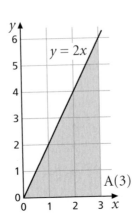 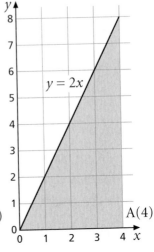

A3 Repeat for the graph of $y = x + 1$.

The last of the diagrams below should help you work out the formula for A(x).

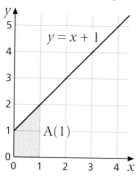 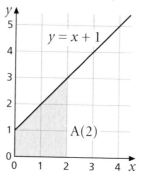 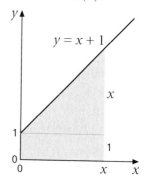

A4 The area function for the graph of $y = 3$ is simpler than any of those you have worked out so far.

What is it?

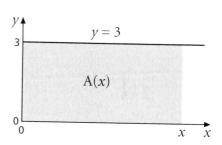

A5 Use this diagram to help you find the area function for the graph of $y = 2x + 3$.

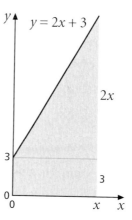

A6 **(a)** Make a table of the area functions you have found so far.

(b) What do you notice?

(c) What would you guess to be the area function for the graph of $y = x^2$?

Graph	Area function A(x)
$y = 3$	
$y = x$	
$y = 2x$	
$y = x + 1$	
$y = 2x + 3$	

It appears from the results in A6 that the area function is the indefinite integral of the given function (but without the constant of integration). In the next section we test whether this is true for the graph of $y = x^2$.

B Area function for y = x² (answers p 155)

The area under a linear graph is made up of rectangles and triangles, whose areas can easily be calculated.

The situation is different with a curved graph, but approximation is possible.

Here is the graph of $y = x^2$.
It is split up into strips, each of which is roughly a triangle or a trapezium.

A(1) is the area of the first strip,
A(2) the total area of the first two strips,
A(3) the total area of the first three strips,
and so on.

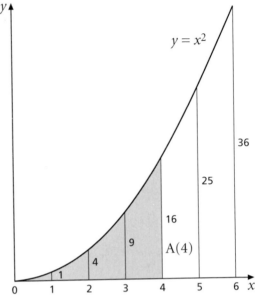

B1 (a) Calculate, approximately, the area of each strip by treating it as a trapezium. (Treat the first strip as a triangle.)

(b) Does the use of the trapezium overestimate or underestimate the true area?

(c) Work out the approximate values of A(1), A(2), A(3), and so on, and enter them in a table.

x	0	1	2	3	4	5	6
A(x)							

(d) From question A6, a guess for the actual area function is $\frac{1}{3}x^3$. Work out the values of $\frac{1}{3}x^3$ and compare them with the approximate values of A(x). Does there appear to be any agreement?

A better approximation for the area can be found by using narrower strips (and correspondingly more of them).

Here is the start of a table in which strips of width 0.1 are used. This calculation can be set up in a spreadsheet.

Strip from ... to ...		Value of y		Area of strip	x	Approximation to A(x)	$\frac{1}{3}x^3$
		left	right				
0	0.1	0	0.01	0.0005	0.1	0.0005	0.000333
0.1	0.2	0.01	0.04	0.0025	0.2	0.003	0.002667
0.2	0.3	0.04	0.09	0.0065	0.3	0.0095	0.009
0.3	0.4	0.09	0.16	0.0125	0.4	0.022	0.021333

There is close agreement between the approximate value of A(x) and $\frac{1}{3}x^3$.

C Definite integrals

The results of sections A and B suggest that the area under a graph is related to integration. We will assume that this is true. An explanation is given at the end of the chapter.

The area function $A(x)$ for the graph of $y = x^2$ is the integral of x^2, which is $\frac{1}{3}x^3$. (In this case there is no need to include the constant of integration; the reason will appear soon.)

The diagram shows the area under the graph of $y = x^2$ between $x = 3$ and $x = 6$.

This area is denoted by

$$\int_3^6 x^2 \, dx$$

(read as 'integral 3 to 6 of $x^2 \, dx$').

The area is the difference between $A(6)$ and $A(3)$:

$$\text{Area} = \tfrac{1}{3} \times 6^3 - \tfrac{1}{3} \times 3^3 = 72 - 9 = 63$$

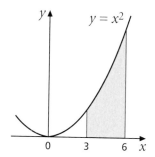

A special notation is used for calculations like this:

$\left[\tfrac{1}{3}x^3\right]_3^6$ means 'work out $\tfrac{1}{3}x^3$ when $x = 6$ and when $x = 3$; then subtract'.

The following example shows how the calculation above is set out in practice.

Example 1

Calculate the area under the graph of $y = x^2$ between $x = 3$ and $x = 6$.

Solution

$$\text{Area} = \int_3^6 x^2 \, dx = \left[\tfrac{1}{3}x^3\right]_3^6 = \left(\tfrac{1}{3} \times 6^3\right) - \left(\tfrac{1}{3} \times 3^3\right) = 72 - 9 = 63$$

The expression $\int_3^6 x^2 \, dx$ is called a **definite integral**. It works out to a numerical value.

The constant of integration is not included because it cancels out when the subtraction is done:

$$\text{Area} = \int_3^6 x^2 \, dx = \left[\tfrac{1}{3}x^3 + c\right]_3^6 = \left(\tfrac{1}{3} \times 6^3 + c\right) - \left(\tfrac{1}{3} \times 3^3 + c\right) = 72 + c - 9 - c = 63$$

Historical note

The notation $\int \ldots$ was introduced by Leibniz. '$\int$' is a long 's' for 'sum'. Leibniz thought of integration as summing a large number of strips of very small width ('dx').

Example 2

Evaluate the integral $\int_2^3 (x+2)(2x+3)(2x-1)\,dx$.

Solution

$$\int_2^3 (x+2)(2x+3)(2x-1)\,dx = \int_2^3 (4x^3 + 12x^2 + 5x - 6)\,dx$$
$$= \left[x^4 + 4x^3 + \tfrac{5}{2}x^2 - 6x \right]_2^3$$
$$= \left(3^4 + 4\times 3^3 + \tfrac{5}{2}\times 3^2 - 6\times 3 \right) - \left(2^4 + 4\times 2^3 + \tfrac{5}{2}\times 2^2 - 6\times 2 \right)$$
$$= 193\tfrac{1}{2} - 46 = 147\tfrac{1}{2}$$

Example 3

Evaluate $\int_1^4 \left(\dfrac{x^2+1}{\sqrt{x}} \right)\,dx$.

Solution

$$\int_1^4 \left(\frac{x^2+1}{\sqrt{x}} \right)\,dx = \int_1^4 \left(\frac{x^2}{\sqrt{x}} + \frac{1}{\sqrt{x}} \right)\,dx = \int_1^4 \left(x^{\frac{3}{2}} + x^{-\frac{1}{2}} \right)\,dx$$
$$= \left[\tfrac{2}{5}x^{\frac{5}{2}} + 2x^{\frac{1}{2}} \right]_1^4 = \left(\tfrac{2}{5}\times 4^{\frac{5}{2}} + 2\times 4^{\frac{1}{2}} \right) - \left(\tfrac{2}{5}\times 1^{\frac{5}{2}} + 2\times 1^{\frac{1}{2}} \right) = 14.4$$

Exercise C (answers p 156)

1 (a) Write down the integral which represents the shaded area.

(b) Calculate this area.

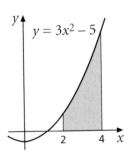

$y = 3x^2 - 5$

2 Evaluate $\int_1^3 (t^3 + t^2 + t + 1)\,dt$.

3 Evaluate these integrals.

(a) $\int_0^1 (x - x^2)\,dx$ 　　　　(b) $\int_2^4 (x+1)\,dx$ 　　　　(c) $\int_{-2}^{-1} x^2\,dx$

(d) $\int_0^1 (x+1)(x+2)\,dx$ 　(e) $\int_0^3 (x-2)^2\,dx$ 　(f) $\int_4^9 (1+\sqrt{x})\,dx$

4 Find the value of a (> 1) for which $\int_1^a (2x+3)\,dx = 24$.

5 (a) Evaluate the following integrals.

(i) $\int_2^4 x^2\,dx$ 　　　　　　(ii) $\int_{-4}^{-2} x^2\,dx$

(b) Sketch the graph of $y = x^2$ and use it to explain your results in (a).

6 Calculate the area under the graph of $y = x^3 + 2x - 3$ between $x = 1$ and $x = 4$.

7 Evaluate these integrals.

(a) $\int_0^4 x(1 + \sqrt{x})\, dx$　　　(b) $\int_0^9 \sqrt{x}(1 + x)\, dx$　　　(c) $\int_0^4 \left(\dfrac{x+1}{\sqrt{x}}\right) dx$

8 (a) Sketch the graph of $y = (x - 3)(6 - x)$, showing clearly where the curve cuts the x-axis.

(b) Calculate the area enclosed between the graph and the x-axis.

9 Evaluate $\int_1^4 \left(\dfrac{x}{2} + \dfrac{1}{x^2}\right) dx$

Edexcel

10 The diagram shows part of the graph of $y = x^2(x - 1)^2$. Calculate the shaded area.

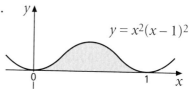

11 Evaluate　　(a) $\int_1^3 \dfrac{1}{x^3}\, dx$　　(b) $\int_{16}^{25} \dfrac{1}{x\sqrt{x}}\, dx$　　(c) $\int_1^4 (x + \sqrt{x})^2\, dx$

*12 The area under the graph of $y = x^2 + k$ between $x = 0$ and $x = 9$ is divided into two equal parts by the line $x = 6$. Calculate the value of k.

D Areas below the x-axis (answers p 156)

D1 The diagram shows the graph of $y = 3x^2 - 12x$.

(a) Calculate the area between the graph and the x-axis between $x = 1$ and $x = 3$.

(b) Why is the result negative?

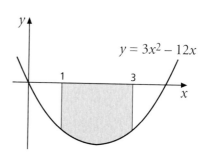

Exercise D (answers p 156)

1 (a) Evaluate $\int_0^3 (x^2 - 9)\, dx$.

(b) Draw a sketch to explain why the result is negative.

2 (a) Find the values of x at the points where the graph of $y = (x + 1)(x - 5)$ cuts the x-axis.

(b) Find the area enclosed between the graph and the x-axis between these points.

3 Repeat question 2 for the graph of $y = 3x^2 - 9x$.

4 (a) Sketch the graph of $y = 4x(x + 5)(x - 2)$ showing where it cuts the x-axis.

(b) Find the area enclosed between the graph and the x-axis between

(i) $x = -5$ and $x = 0$ **(ii)** $x = 0$ and $x = 2$

*5 Evaluate $\int_{-2}^{2} x(x^2 - 4)\, dx$ and draw a sketch to explain the result.

E Area between a curve and a line

Example 4

The curve with equation $y = 6x - x^2$ intersects the line $y = 2x$ at the points O and A.

(a) Find the coordinates of A.

(b) Calculate the shaded area enclosed between the curve and the line.

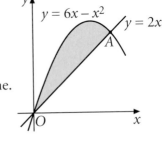

Solution

(a) At points of intersection, $\quad 6x - x^2 = 2x \implies \quad x^2 - 4x = 0$

$$\implies x(x - 4) = 0$$
$$\implies \qquad x = 0 \text{ or } 4$$

When $x = 4$, $2x = 8$ so the coordinates of A are $(4, 8)$.

(b) *The shaded area is the difference between the area under the curve and the area under the line.*

$$\text{Area under curve} = \int_{0}^{4}\left(6x - x^2\right) dx = \left[3x^2 - \tfrac{1}{3}x^3\right]_{0}^{4} = \left(48 - \tfrac{1}{3} \times 64\right) - 0 = 26\tfrac{2}{3}$$

$$\text{Area under line} = \int_{0}^{4} 2x\, dx = \left[x^2\right]_{0}^{4} = 16 - 0 = 16$$

$$\text{Shaded area} = 26\tfrac{2}{3} - 16 = 10\tfrac{2}{3}$$

Two other methods are as follows:

(1) Use the formula for the area of a triangle to find the area under the line.

Base $= 4$, height $= 8$, so area $= \tfrac{1}{2} \times 4 \times 8 = 16$

(2) Form the function that gives the difference between the value of y on the curve and the value of y on the line. This function is $(6x - x^2) - 2x$, or $4x - x^2$. Integrate this function between the limits 0 and 4.

$$\int_{0}^{4}\left(4x - x^2\right) dx = \left[2x^2 - \tfrac{1}{3}x^3\right]_{0}^{4} = \left(32 - \tfrac{1}{3} \times 64\right) - 0 = 10\tfrac{2}{3}$$

Exercise E (answers p 156)

1 The curve with equation $y = 8x - x^2$ intersects the line $y = 12$
at the points A and B.

(a) Find the coordinates of A and B.

(b) Find the area enclosed between the curve and the line.

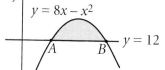

2 The curve whose equation is $y = x^2 - 2x + 5$ crosses the line
$y = x + 5$ at the points A $(0, 5)$ and B.

(a) Find the coordinates of B.

(b) Find the area enclosed between the line and the curve.

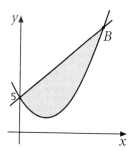

3 The curve $y = x^2 - 6x + 10$ intersects the line $y = 2$ at the points A and B.

(a) Sketch the curve and the line.

(b) Find the area enclosed between the curve and the line.

4 The diagram shows the curve with equation $y = 5 + 2x - x^2$
and the line with equation $y = 2$.

The curve and the line intersect at the points A and B.

(a) Find the x-coordinates of A and B.

The shaded region R is bounded by the curve and the line.

(b) Find the area of R.

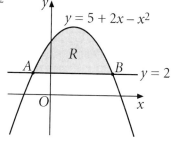

Edexcel

5 The diagram shows the line with equation $y = 9 - x$
and the curve with equation $y = x^2 - 2x + 3$.

The line and the curve intersect at the points A and B,
and O is the origin.

(a) Calculate the coordinates of A and the coordinates of B.

The shaded region R is bounded by the line and the curve.

(b) Calculate the area of R.

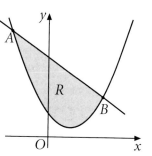

Edexcel

F Numerical integration: the trapezium rule (answers p 157)

The shaded area is the area under the graph of $y = \dfrac{5x-7}{x-1}$ from $x = 1.5$ to $x = 3.5$.

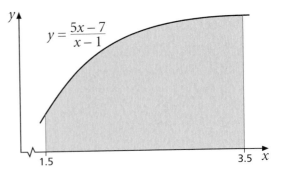

$$\text{Area} = \int_{1.5}^{3.5} \left(\frac{5x-7}{x-1} \right) dx$$

The function $\dfrac{5x-7}{x-1}$ is one that cannot be integrated by the methods you have met so far.

However, it is possible to get a good numerical approximation to the area. One of the simplest methods is called the **trapezium rule.**

The area is divided into vertical strips of equal width. The heights of the vertical lines are called **ordinates.** In the diagram on the right there are five ordinates at $x = 1.5$, 2.0, 2.5, 3.0 and 3.5.

To get an approximation to the area, the curve is replaced by straight line segments and each strip becomes a trapezium. The total area of the trapezia is an estimate of the area under the curve.

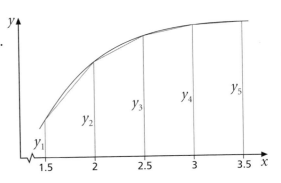

F1 Will the estimate obtained in this way be too large or too small? How can you tell from the diagram?

The first ordinate, labelled y_1, is $\dfrac{5 \times 1.5 - 7}{1.5 - 1} = \dfrac{7.5 - 7}{1.5 - 1} = 1$.

Similarly, y_2 is $\dfrac{10 - 7}{2 - 1} = 3$.

The area of a trapezium is found by using the formula $\frac{1}{2}h(a + b)$, where a and b are the parallel sides and h is the distance between them.

F2 (a) Calculate the area of the first trapezium.

(b) Calculate the area of each of the other four trapezia (rounding to 2 d.p. where necessary) and hence find an estimate of the area under the curve between $x = 1.5$ and $x = 3.5$.

When the area calculation is set out using the symbols h, y_1, y_2 and so on, a pattern appears that leads to a short cut.

$$\begin{aligned} \text{Total area} &= \tfrac{1}{2}h(y_1 + y_2) + \tfrac{1}{2}h(y_2 + y_3) + \tfrac{1}{2}h(y_3 + y_4) + \tfrac{1}{2}h(y_4 + y_5) \\ &= \tfrac{1}{2}h(y_1 + y_2 + y_2 + y_3 + y_3 + y_4 + y_4 + y_5) \\ &= \tfrac{1}{2}h(y_1 + y_5 + 2[y_2 + y_3 + y_4]) \\ &= \tfrac{1}{2}h(\textbf{end ordinates} + \textbf{twice sum of 'interior' ordinates}) \end{aligned}$$

There is nothing special about using five ordinates – any number may be used.

F3 (a) Use the formula in bold type to estimate the area under the curve.
Check that you get the same result as before.

(b) How could you improve on the estimate of the area, still using the trapezium rule?

Example 5

(a) Sketch the graph of $y = \dfrac{12}{x}$ for $0.5 \le x \le 3$.

(b) Use the trapezium rule with six ordinates to calculate an approximation to $\displaystyle\int_{0.5}^{3} \dfrac{12}{x}\,dx$, stating, with a reason, whether your result is an overestimate or underestimate.

Solution

(a) The sketch is shown on the right.

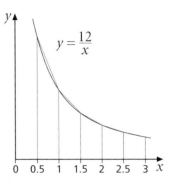

(b) Using six ordinates means five trapezia.
The width of each trapezium is 0.5.
The values of x and y are shown in this table.

x	0.5	1	1.5	2	2.5	3
y	24	12	8	6	4.8	4

Estimate of area $= \dfrac{0.5}{2}(24 + 4 + 2[12 + 8 + 6 + 4.8]) = 22.4$

As the curve is below the line segments, this is an overestimate.

The trapezium rule can easily be set up in a spreadsheet.
The estimate will be improved if you use a larger number of narrower strips.

Exercise F (answers p 157)

1 The diagram shows part of the graph of $y = \sqrt{2x+1}$.

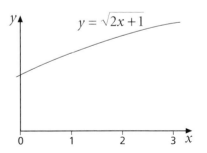

 (a) Use the trapezium rule with four ordinates to calculate an approximation to $\displaystyle\int_{0}^{3} \sqrt{2x+1}\,dx$.

 (b) State, with a reason, whether your result is an overestimate or underestimate.

2 (a) Use the trapezium rule, with ordinates spaced at intervals of 0.5, to estimate the area under the graph of $y = \sqrt{1+x^2}$ from $x = 0$ to $x = 2$.

 (b) By reducing the interval between ordinates to 0.25, calculate a better estimate.

3 (a) Use the trapezium rule with four ordinates to calculate an approximate value for $\int_{1}^{4} \sqrt{x} \, dx$.

(b) Find the exact value of the same integral.

4 (a) Copy and complete this table of values for the function $y = \sqrt{x + \dfrac{1}{x}}$, giving y to 2 d.p.

x	2	2.2	2.4	2.6	2.8	3
y	1.58					

(b) Use the trapezium rule, with the values in the table, to estimate $\int_{2}^{3} \sqrt{x + \dfrac{1}{x}} \, dx$.

G The fundamental theorem of calculus

The fact that the area under the graph of $y = f(x)$ is found by integrating f(x) is known as the 'fundamental theorem of calculus'.

Put another way, the theorem says that if A is the area under the graph of $y = f(x)$ (measured from some starting value of x), then $\dfrac{dA}{dx} = f(x)$.

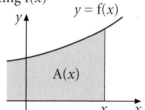

To get an idea of why the theorem is true, think what happens when the value of x is increased by a small amount δx.

Let δy be the corresponding increase in y, and δA the increase in the area (shaded lighter).

The extra area is very close to being a trapezium whose parallel sides are y and $(y + \delta y)$.

So $\delta A = \frac{1}{2}(y + y + \delta y)\delta x = (y + \frac{1}{2}\delta y)\delta x$

So $\dfrac{\delta A}{\delta x} = y + \frac{1}{2}\delta y$

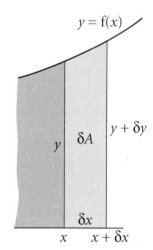

Now think what happens as δx gets smaller and smaller: δy also gets smaller and smaller, $y + \frac{1}{2}\delta y$ gets closer to y, and the ratio $\dfrac{\delta A}{\delta x}$ gets closer to $\dfrac{dA}{dx}$.

So $\dfrac{dA}{dx} = y = f(x)$.

Mixed questions (answers p 157)

1 Evaluate these integrals.

(a) $\displaystyle\int_0^2 \left(4x - x^3\right) dx$

(b) $\displaystyle\int_{-1}^1 \left(x^2 - 1\right)(x - 2)\,dx$

2 The diagram shows the graph of $y = x^2 - \sqrt{x}$. Find the shaded area.

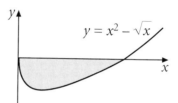

3 The diagram shows part of the curve with equation

$$y = x^3 - 6x^2 + 9x$$

The curve touches the x-axis at A and has a maximum turning point at B.

(a) Show that the equation of the curve may be written as

$$y = x(x - 3)^2$$

and hence write down the coordinates of A.

(b) Find the coordinates of B.

The shaded region R is bounded by the curve and the x-axis.

(c) Find the area of R.

Edexcel

4 (a) Use the trapezium rule with five ordinates to find an approximate value for $\displaystyle\int_0^2 \frac{2}{1+x}\,dx$.

(b) By sketching a graph, determine whether the result in (a) is an overestimate or underestimate.

5 The diagram shows part of the graph of the function $y = \sqrt{x} - x$.

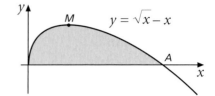

(a) Find the gradient of the curve at the point A.

(b) M is the maximum point on the graph. Find the coordinates of M.

(c) Show that to the right of the point M the function is always decreasing .

(d) Calculate the shaded area.

6 Find the area under the graph of $y = \dfrac{x-1}{x^3}$ between $x = 1$ and $x = 3$.

7 (a) Find $\int (x+1)(x-2)(x-4)\, \mathrm{d}x$.

(b) Hence find the area of the region enclosed between the graph of $y = (x+1)(x-2)(x-4)$ and the x-axis for $2 \le x \le 4$.

8 (a) The graphs of $y = 4x^2$ and $y = (x-6)^2$ intersect where $x = a$ $(a > 0)$. Find the value of a.

(b) Find the shaded area.

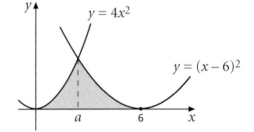

9 A measure of the effective voltage, M volts, in an electrical circuit is given by

$$M^2 = \int_0^1 V^2\, \mathrm{d}t$$

where V volts is the voltage at time t seconds.
Pairs of values of V and t are given in the following table.

t	0	0.25	0.5	0.75	1
V	−48	207	37	−161	−29
V^2					

Use the trapezium rule with five values of V^2 to estimate the value of M.   Edexcel

*10 The diagram shows part of the curve with equation $y = \dfrac{1}{x^2} - 9$ $\quad (x > 0)$

(a) Find the x-coordinate of the point where the curve crosses the x-axis.

(b) Given that the shaded area is 4, find the value of k.

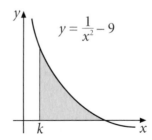

Test yourself (answers p 157)

1 Find the following integrals.

(a) $\int_0^2 \left(x^4 - 3x\right) dx$

(b) $\int_1^4 (x-1)\left(x^2 + 2\right) dx$

2 The curve with equation $y = 3 + 5x - x^2$ intersects the line $y = 3$ at $(0, 3)$ and at another point A.

(a) Find the x-coordinate of A.

(b) Find the shaded area enclosed between the curve and the line.

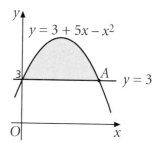

3

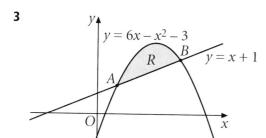

The diagram shows the line with equation $y = x + 1$ and the curve with equation $y = 6x - x^2 - 3$.

The line and the curve intersect at the points A and B, and O is the origin.

(a) Calculate the coordinates of A and the coordinates of B.

The shaded region R is bounded by the line and the curve.

(b) Calculate the area of R.

Edexcel

4 The following is a table of values for $y = \sqrt{1 + \sin x}$, where x is in radians.

x	0	0.5	1	1.5	2
y	1	1.216	p	1.413	q

(a) Find the value of p and the value of q.

(b) Use the trapezium rule and all the values of y in the completed table to obtain an estimate of I, where

$$I = \int_0^2 \sqrt{1 + \sin x}\, dx$$

Edexcel

Answers

1 Dividing polynomials

A Polynomials: revision

Exercise A (p 6)

1 (a) 3 **(b)** −1 **(c)** 9 **(d)** −3 **(e)** $1\frac{5}{16}$

2 (a) $3x^3 - 4x^2 - 12x + 5$ **(b)** $4x^4 + 12x^2 + 9$

(c) $x^3 - 8$ **(d)** $-2x^4 - x + 3$

3 (a) $2x^5 + 2x^4 - 3x^3 - 11x^2 + 12$

(b) $4x^4 - 12x^2 + 9$

(c) $x^6 + 2x^5 + x^4 - 8x^3 - 8x^2 + 16$

4 (a) (i) 6 **(ii)** −12 **(iii)** 0 **(iv)** 0 **(v)** 0

(b)

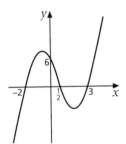

B Division (p 7)

B1 (a) $x + 4$ **(b)** $x + 4$

B2 (a) $3x + 1$ **(b)** $2x + 3$

B3 (a) $x^2 + 2x + 5$ **(b)** $x^2 - 5x - 2$ **(c)** $x^2 + 2x + 3$

B4 (a) $x + 2$ **(b)** $x + 3$ **(c)** $x - 5$

B5 (a) $(x + 5)(x + 1) + 2$ **(b)** 2

B6 (a) $(x - 3)(x - 7) + 10$ **(b)** 10

B7 (a) $(x - 3)(x - 7) - 10$ **(b)** −10

B8 (a) $(2x + 1)(4x + 1) + 2$ **(b)** 2

Exercise B (p 9)

1 (a) $x^2 + 3x + 4$ remainder 5

(b) $x^2 + 4x - 1$

(c) $x^2 - x + 6$ remainder −1

(d) $2x^2 + x + 3$ remainder 3

(e) $3x^2 + 2x - 5$

(f) $5x^2 - 2x - 1$ remainder −2

(g) $x^2 - 1$

2 $x^2 - x - 1$

3 (a) $x^2 + x - 12$

(b) $x^2 - 2x + 5$ remainder 2

(c) $2x^2 + x - 3$

(d) $3x^2 + 6x + 7$ remainder 15

(e) $4x^2 - 5x + 5$ remainder −2

4 $x^2 + x + 1$

5 (a) A demonstration that f(x) divided by ($x + 5$) is $x^2 + 2x - 3$

(b) $f(x) = (x + 5)(x^2 + 2x - 3)$

(c) $f(x) = (x + 5)(x + 3)(x - 1)$

6 (a) (i) 6 **(ii)** 12 **(iii)** 12 **(iv)** 0 **(v)** −30

(b) $(x + 1)$

(c) $(x + 1)(x^2 - 7x + 12)$

(d) $(x^2 - 7x + 12) = (x - 3)(x - 4)$ so $p(x) = (x + 1)(x - 3)(x - 4)$

(e) $x = -1, 3, 4$

7 (a) $2x^2 - 6x - 9$ remainder 1

(b) $x^2 - 3$

(c) $x^2 - \frac{1}{2}x + \frac{1}{4}$ remainder $12\frac{3}{4}$

C Remainders and factors (p 10)

C1 (a) (i) $x^2 + 4x - 1$ remainder 8

(ii) 8

(iii) The value of p(2) is the remainder after division by ($x - 2$).

(b) (i) $x^2 + x - 10$ remainder 20

(ii) 20

(iii) The value of p(−1) is the remainder after division by ($x + 1$).

(c) The value of p(a) is always the remainder aft division by ($x - a$). See the explanation on page 11.

C2 (a) 2 **(b)** $x^2 + 6x + 4$ remainder 2

C3 f(3) = 0 so we know that ($x - 3$) divides f(x) exactly.

C4 (a) (i) −30 **(ii)** −24 **(iii)** −12 **(iv)** 0 **(v)** 6

(b) $(x + 2)$

(c) $(x + 2)(x^2 + x − 12)$

(d) $(x + 2)(x + 4)(x − 3)$

(e) $x = −2, −4, 3$

(f)

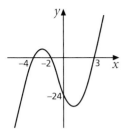

C5 $p(3) = 0$ so $(x − 3)$ is a factor.

Exercise C (p 13)

1 10

2 (a) $p(3) = 0$ so $(x − 3)$ is a factor.

(b) $(x − 3)(x + 1)(x + 7)$

3 (a) $f(−2) = 0$ so $(x + 2)$ is a factor.

(b) $(x + 2)(x − 1)(x − 5)$

4 (a) $q(−7) = 0$ so $(x + 7)$ is a factor.

(b) $(x + 7)(x + 2)(x − 3)$

(c) $x = −7, −2, 3$

5 (a) $(x − 1)(x − 1)(x + 6)$

(b) $x = 1, −6$

(c)

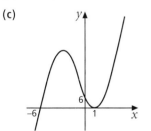

6 (a) $p(1) = 0$ so $(x − 1)$ is a factor

(b) $(x − 1)(x^2 + 2x + 5)$

(c) (i) −16

(ii) $p(x) = 0$ when
$(x − 1)(x^2 + 2x + 5) = 0$,
i.e. when $(x − 1) = 0$ or $(x^2 + 2x + 5) = 0$.
Since the discriminant of $x^2 + 2x + 5$ is
negative, $(x^2 + 2x + 5) = 0$ has no real
solutions. So $p(x) = 0$ has just one real
solution, $x = 1$.

7 (a) $p(−1) = 0$ so $(x + 1)$ is a factor.

(b) $(x + 1)(x^2 − 7)$

(c) $x = −1, \sqrt{7}, −\sqrt{7}$

8 (a) $(x − 2)(x + 1)(x + 5)$

(b) $(x − 1)(x + 2)(2x + 3)$

(c) $(x − 2)(x^2 + x − 1)$

(d) $(x + 1)(x + 2)(x + 4)$

(e) $(x + 1)(2x^2 − 5)$

(f) $(x + 2)(x + 3)^2$

9 (a) $x(x + 8)(x − 8)$ **(b)** $(x + 4)(x^2 − 4x + 16)$

D Dividing by ($bx − c$) (p 14)

D1 (a) $f(2) = 4 \times 2^3 − 6 \times 2^2 + 2 \times 2 − 7 = 5$
so the remainder is 5.

(b) (i) The student's conjecture (which may be 10)

(ii) 5

(c) The remainders are the same.
A possible proof is:
Let R_1 be the remainder after division by
$(x − 2)$. Hence, by the remainder theorem
$f(2) = R_1$. Now let R_2 be the remainder after
division by $(2x − 4)$. Hence we can write
$f(x) = (2x − 4)q(x) + R_2$ where $q(x)$ is a
polynomial in x. Hence,
$f(2) = 0 \times q(x) + R_2 = R_2$. So $R_1 = R_2$ and the
remainders must be the same.
(Clearly, this argument will be valid for any
expression that is a 'multiple' of $(x − 2)$.)

D2 (a) −6

(b) (i) The student's conjecture   **(ii)** −6

(c) The remainders are the same.
A possible proof is:
Let R_1 be the remainder after division by
$(x − \frac{1}{2})$. Hence, by the remainder theorem
$g(\frac{1}{2}) = R_1$. Now let R_2 be the remainder after
division by $(2x − 1)$. Hence we can write
$g(x) = (2x − 1)q(x) + R_2$ where $q(x)$ is a
polynomial in x. Hence,
$g(\frac{1}{2}) = 0 \times q(x) + R_2 = R_2$. So $R_1 = R_2$ and the
remainders must be the same.
(Clearly, this argument will be valid for any
expression that is a 'multiple' of $(x − \frac{1}{2})$.)

D3 (a) 1

   (b) (i) The student's conjecture   **(ii)** 1

   (c) The remainders are the same.
A proof can be constructed on the lines of those in D1 (c) and D2 (c).

D4 (a) $\frac{3}{4}$ **(b)** 6   **(c)** -3

D5 (a) -2 **(b)** $\frac{1}{4}$ **(c)** 0   **(d)** 0

Exercise D (p 15)

1 (a) 4   **(b)** $\frac{1}{2}$ **(c)** $-\frac{2}{3}$

2 (a) 0   **(b)** $(2x-1)(x^2+4x-3)$

3 (a) 0   **(b)** $(3x+2)(2x-1)(x+5)$

4 (a) $(2x-1)(3x+1)(2x+1)$

   (b) $(3x-1)(3x^2+x-1)$

   (c) $(2x-1)(4x^2+2x+1)$

E Further problems

Exercise E (p 17)

1 $k=1$

2 $a=-10$

3 $b=4$

4 $a=1$

5 $k=5$

6 $p=4, q=-37$

7 $a=0, b=-7$

8 $p=1, q=6$

9 $h=2, k=-1$

10 $a=5, b=9$

11 $h=-8, k=3$

12 $y=4x^3+9x^2+\frac{3}{2}x-1$

Mixed questions (p 18)

1 x^2-x+6 remainder 2

2 (a) $(-3)^3-3\times(-3)^2-10\times(-3)+24$
    $=-27-27+30+24$
    $=0$
    So $(x+3)$ is a factor of $x^3-3x^2-10x+24$.

   (b) $(x+3)(x-2)(x-4)$

3 (a) $p(2)=2^3-12\times2+16$
    $=8-24+16$
    $=0$
    So $(x-2)$ is a factor of $x^3-12x+16$.

   (b)

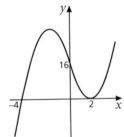

4 2

5 (a) $a+b=2$ **(b)** $a=3, b=-1$

6 (a) $(x-2)$ **(b)** $x=2, 1.73, -1.73$ (to 2 d.p.)

7 $p=2, q=-25$

8 (a) $k=-15$

   (b) $f(n)=(n-3)(n^2+4n+5)$

   (c) One method is to note that the discriminant of n^2+4n+5 is $4^2-4\times1\times5=-4$ which is negative. Hence $n^2+4n+5=0$ has no real solutions and so $f(n)=0$ has only one real solution i.e. $n=3$.

Test yourself (p 19)

1 (a) $(-2)^3-2\times(-2)^2-5\times-2+6$
    $=-8-8+10+6$
    $=0$
    So $(x+2)$ is a factor of x^3-2x^2-5x+6.

   (b) $(x+2)(x-1)(x-3)$

2 (a) $(x-1)(x-2)(x-4)$

   (b)

3 $-4\frac{3}{4}$

4 (a) $f(-3) = 2 \times (-3)^3 + 5 \times (-3)^2 - 8 \times -3 - 15$
$$= -54 + 45 + 24 - 15$$
$$= 0$$
So $(x + 3)$ is a factor of $2x^3 + 5x^2 - 8x - 15$.

(b) $(x + 3)(2x^2 - x - 5)$

(c) $1.85, -1.35$

5 (a) $a = -2, b = 5$

(b) $f(x) = x^3 - 2x^2 + 5x - 10$
so $f(2) = 2^3 - 2 \times 2^2 + 5 \times 2 - 10$
$$= 8 - 8 + 10 - 10$$
$$= 0$$
So $(x - 2)$ is a factor of $f(x)$.

6 (a) -20

(b) $(x - 4)(x^2 + 3x + 5)$

(c) One method is to note that the discriminant of $x^2 + 3x + 5$ is $3^2 - 4 \times 1 \times 5 = -11$ which is negative. Hence $x^2 + 3x + 5 = 0$ has no real solutions and so $f(x) = 0$ has only one real solution, when $x = 4$.

7 (a) -20 **(b)** 1

8 (a) $f(-2) = 3$ by the remainder theorem so
$(-2)^3 + p \times (-2)^2 + 11 \times -2 + 9 = 3$
$\Rightarrow$ $-8 + 4p - 22 + 9 = 3$
$\Rightarrow$ $4p = 24$
$\Rightarrow$ $p = 6$ as required

(b) $f(n) = n^3 + 6n^2 + 11n + 9$
$$= (n + 2)(n^2 + 4n + 3) + 3$$
$$= (n + 2)(n + 1)(n + 3) + 3$$

(c) When n is an integer $(n + 1)(n + 2)(n + 3)$ is the product of three consecutive integers. Hence one of these integers must be a multiple of 3 and so $(n + 1)(n + 2)(n + 3)$ must be a multiple of 3. Hence $f(n) = (n + 1)(n + 2)(n + 3) + 3$ is divisible by 3.

2 Equation of a circle

A A circle as a graph (p 20)

A1 (a) 17   **(b)** 10   **(c)** 12.5   **(d)** 14.5

A2 (a) (i) On the circle   **(ii)** On the circle

        (iii) Inside   **(iv)** Outside

        (v) On the circle

    (b) $x^2 + y^2 = 13^2$

A3 A plot of the graph of $x^2 + y^2 = 13$

A4 Centre $(0, 0)$, radius 7

A5 5

A6 (a) (i) On the circle   **(ii)** On the circle

        (iii) On the circle   **(iv)** On the circle

        (v) Outside   **(vi)** On the circle

        (vii) Inside

    (b) Three other points that satisfy the condition $(x - 2)^2 + (y - 1)^2 = 25$, for example:
$(6, 4), (5, 5), (2, 6), (-1, 5), (-3, 1), (-2, -2), (-1, -3)$

A7 In the case shown in the diagram, the base of the right-angled triangle is $2 - x$, which is $-(x - 2)$.

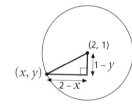

So $(2 - x)^2 = (-(x - 2))^2 = (x - 2)^2$.
The height of the triangle is $1 - y$ but, as above, $(1 - y)^2 = (y - 1)^2$.
So $(x - 2)^2 + (y - 1)^2$ still works as the equation of the circle in this case and similarly all round the circle.

A8 A plot of the graph of $(x - 2)^2 + (y - 1)^2 = 5^2$

A9 $(x - 5)^2 + (y + 2)^2 = 16$

A10 Centre $(-4, 7)$, radius 6

A11 $x^2 - 10x + y^2 + 4y + 13 = 0$

Exercise A (p 22)

1 (a) $(x - 6)^2 + (y - 3)^2 = 4^2$

(b) $(x + 2)^2 + y^2 = 5^2$

(c) $(x-1)^2 + (y+6)^2 = 3^2$

(d) $(x+2)^2 + (y+2)^2 = 7^2$

2 (a) (i) $(2, 6), 4$

(ii) $x^2 - 4x + y^2 - 12y + 24 = 0$

(b) (i) $(-3, 4), 5$

(ii) $x^2 + 6x + y^2 - 8y = 0$

(c) (i) $(4, 0), \sqrt{7}$

(ii) $x^2 - 8x + y^2 + 9 = 0$

(d) (i) $(-1.5, 0.5), 2$

(ii) $x^2 + 3x + y^2 - y - 1.5 = 0$

3 Radius $= \sqrt{3^2 + 4^2} = 5$
Equation is $(x+2)^2 + (y+3)^2 = 5^2$
(or an equivalent equation)

4 The centre is the mid-point of the diameter, $(3, -5)$.
By Pythagoras the radius is $\sqrt{194}$.
The equation is $(x-3)^2 + (y+5)^2 = 194$ or
$x^2 - 6x + y^2 + 10y - 160 = 0$.

5 $(x+4)^2 + (y+2)^2 = 10$ or
$x^2 + 8x + y^2 + 4y + 10 = 0$

6 The centre is $(1, 4)$ and the radius is 3 (or $\sqrt{9}$).
By Pythagoras the distance from the centre to
$(-1, 2)$ is $\sqrt{2^2 + 2^2}$, which is $\sqrt{8}$, which is less
than $\sqrt{9}$. So $(-1, 2)$ lies inside the circle.

7 (a) $2, (2, 1)$ **(b)** $3, (1, -3)$ **(c)** $\sqrt{11}, (-5, 2)$

(d) $7, (0, 5)$ **(e)** $6, (-4, 3)$ **(f)** $2, (0.5, 3.5)$

8 B could not be a circle, because the x^2 and y^2 terms
have different coefficients.

9 $(x-6)^2 + y^2 = 16$

10 (a) Substituting $x = 0$ and $y = 0$ into the LHS gives
0, which is the RHS. So the circle goes through
the point $(0, 0)$.

(b) $(-6, 4)$

11 (a) From the equation of the circle, its centre is $(2, 3)$.
The mid-point of PQ is $(2, 3)$.
So PQ is a diameter.

(b) $a = 7$

(c) PR: -3, RQ: $\frac{1}{3}$; PR and RQ are perpendicular.

(d) An angle in a semicircle is 90°.

12 By completing the square, the equation becomes
$(x+1)^2 + (y-3)^2 = -4$
But the negative value -4 cannot be the square of
the radius, so this cannot be a circle.

B Tangent and normal to a circle

Exercise B (p 24)

1 (a) $y = \frac{2}{3}x + 3$ **(b)** $y = -\frac{3}{2}x + 16$

2 (a) Radius $\sqrt{8}$, centre $(2, 2)$

(b) It could touch at $(0, 0)$ and $(4, 4)$

(c) $y = -x$ or $y = -x + 8$

3 (a) $a = 4, b = 5$

(b) $(x-4)^2 + (y-5)^2 = 25$

(c) 11.6

4 (a) $y = 2x - 3$ **(b)** $(3, 3)$

(c) $(x-2)^2 + (y-1)^2 = 5$

5 Equation of normal is $y = -3x - 5$.
Solving this and the given equation
simultaneously gives the contact point $(-3, 4)$.
By Pythagoras the radius is $\sqrt{10}$.
So the circle's equation is $(x+2)^2 + (y-1)^2 = 10$

6 (a) $(4, 2)$

(b) (i) $\dfrac{b-2}{a-4}$ **(ii)** $\dfrac{4-a}{b-2}$

7 (a)

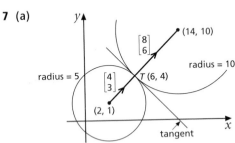

The line segments are on the same line,
because they are both perpendicular to a
tangent where the two circles touch.

(b) $(14, 10)$

(c) A: $(x-2)^2 + (y-1)^2 = 25$
B: $(x-14)^2 + (y-10)^2 = 100$

C Intersection of a straight line and a circle
(p 25)

C1 At $(1, 2)$ and $(7, 8)$

C2 (a) There is only one point, $(3, 6)$.

(b) There are no solutions to the quadratic in x.

Exercise C (p 27)

1 (a) Intersects   **(b)** Is a tangent

(c) Intersects   **(d)** Does not meet

2 (a) Intersects at $(1, 3)$ and $(3, 7)$

(b) Does not meet circle

(c) Touches at $(6, 2)$

(d) Intersects at $(1, 3)$ and $(2, 2)$

3 (a) $(5, -1)$ **(b)** $(12, 0), (-2, 0), (0, -6), (0, 4)$

(c)

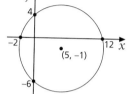

4 (a) $x = -2$, $y = -3$

(b) The line is a tangent to the circle at the point $(-2, -3)$ because the quadratic equation obtained in solving simultaneously the equations for the line and the circle has a single (repeated) root.

5 (a) $(x - 3)^2 + (y - 4)^2 = 18$

(b) $(2 + 2\sqrt{2}, 5 + 2\sqrt{2}), (2 - 2\sqrt{2}, 5 - 2\sqrt{2})$

(c) 8

6 $(x - 9)^2 + (y - 7)^2 = 74$

7 (a) $a = 3$, $b = 6$

(b) The line through the centre perpendicular to PQ has the equation $y = \frac{3}{5}x + 1$.

PQ has the equation $y = -\frac{5}{3}x + 18$.

Solving these simultaneously gives the point of intersection $(7.5, 5.5)$, which by considering the coordinates of P and Q is the mid-point of PQ.

8 $a = 4$

9 Centre $(-2, 2)$, radius $\sqrt{50}$

$(x + 2)^2 + (y - 2)^2 = 50$

10 $(-4, 2)$

Test yourself (p 29)

1 (a) $x^2 + y^2 - 8x - 2y + 13 = 0$

(b) $x^2 + y^2 + 4x + 6y + 4 = 0$

(c) $x^2 + y^2 - 5x - 8y + 18\frac{1}{4} = 0$

(d) $x^2 + y^2 - 2x + 14y + 43 = 0$

2 (a) $6, (2, 1)$ **(b)** $5, (0, -3)$

(c) $\sqrt{3}, (-2, -4)$ **(d)** $3, (1.5, 2.5)$

3 (a) Equation of circle is $(x + 1)^2 + (y + 2)^2 = 13$.
Substituting 1 for x, $2^2 + (y + 2)^2 = 13$
$\Rightarrow y + 2 = 3$ or -3
$\Rightarrow y = 1$ or -5, the first value being that of the point to be verified.

(b) $y = \frac{3}{2}x - \frac{1}{2}$

4 (a) $(5, -3)$ **(b)** 7

5 (a) $y = 2x - 1$

(b) $x = 2$ (repeated root), $y = 3$
The repeated root indicates that the line l touches circle C rather than cuts it.

(c) $\sqrt{45}$ or $3\sqrt{5}$

3 Sequences and series

A Geometric sequences (p 30)

A1 (a) £6553.60 (b) $5 \times 2^{n-1}$ pence

A2 A, C, D and E are geometric sequences.
The common ratios are $3, 0.4, \frac{4}{3}$ and -2 respectively.

A3 $40\frac{1}{2}, 60\frac{3}{4}$

A4 0.419 904

A5 $\frac{3}{32}$

A6 1 572 864

A7 12

A8 (a) $16, 4, 1, \frac{1}{4}, \frac{1}{16}$ (b) $2, \mathbf{10}, 50, \mathbf{250}, \mathbf{1250}$
  (c) $\mathbf{9}, 18, \mathbf{36}, 72, \mathbf{144}$ (d) $2, \mathbf{8}, \mathbf{32}, 128, \mathbf{512}$

A9 -8

Exercise A (p 32)

1 (a) 57 344 (b) $3\frac{1}{2} \times 2^{n-1}$

2 (a) 2, 10, 50, 250 (b) 5

3 0.002 44

4 $\frac{1}{2}$

5 (a) 2nd term $\times (-3)^3 = -12 \times -27 = 324$
    = 5th term, so -3 is the common ratio.
  (b) 4

6 $\frac{2}{3}$

7 $2, -2$

8 (a) 743 hedgehogs (b) 2%

9 (a) To increase an amount by 3%, multiply by 1.03. So on Ken's 5th birthday he will have $1000 \times (1.03)^4 = £1125.51$ (to the nearest 1p)
  (b) £1304.77
  (c) $1000 \times (1.03)^{n-1}$

10 1.2

11 $6, -7$

12 With a as the first term and r as the common ratio, we have
$$\frac{ar^3}{a} = \frac{3}{81} = \frac{1}{27}$$
$$\Rightarrow r^3 = \frac{1}{27} \Rightarrow r = \frac{1}{3}$$
So the nth term is $81 \times \left(\frac{1}{3}\right)^{n-1} = 3^4 \times \frac{1}{3^{n-1}}$
$= 3^{4-(n-1)} = 3^{5-n}$

B Geometric series (p 33)

B1 (a) An estimate of the total on the board
  (b) £327.68
  (c) £655.35

B2 (a) Let $S = 1 + 3 + 3^2 + \ldots + 3^{10}$
    Then $3S = 3 + 3^2 + \ldots + 3^{10} + 3^{11}$
    So $3S - S = (3 + 3^2 + \ldots + 3^{10} + 3^{11})$
    $- (1 + 3 + 3^2 + \ldots + 3^{10}) = 3^{11} - 1$
    Hence $2S = 3^{11} - 1$ and finally $S = \dfrac{3^{11} - 1}{2}$
  (b) 88 573

B3 $\dfrac{3^{13} - 1}{2} = 797\,161$

B4 9

B5 n

Exercise B (p 35)

1 357 913 941

2 20 475

3 12 093 235

4 The first term is 8 and the common ratio is $\frac{1}{2}$ so the sum of the first 10 terms is
$$\frac{8\left(\left(\frac{1}{2}\right)^{10} - 1\right)}{\frac{1}{2} - 1} = 15.98 \text{ (to 2 d.p.)}$$

5 The first term is 1 and the common ratio is -3 so the sum of the first 12 terms is
$$\frac{(-3)^{12} - 1}{-3 - 1} = \frac{531\,440}{-4} = -132\,860$$

6 (a) 47.9985 (b) 32 769
  (c) 17.9589 (d) 28.8000

7 2.286

8 7 174 453

9 (a) 1.845×10^{19} (to 4 s.f.)

  (b) 3.689×10^{14} kg (to 4 s.f.)

10 6141

11 9.333

12 (a) £2.19   **(b)** £438.22

13 $x = 9$

C Sum to infinity (p 36)

C1 (a) $S_{10} = 1023$, $S_{11} = 2047$, $S_{12} = 4095$

  (b) As n gets larger and larger, S_n gets larger and larger without limit.

C2 (a) $S_{10} = -14762$, $S_{11} = 44287$, $S_{12} = -132860$

  (b) As n gets larger and larger, S_n alternates between positive and negative values but gets larger and larger in size without limit.

C3 (a) To four decimal places, $S_{10} = 11.9883$, $S_{11} = 11.9941$, $S_{12} = 11.9971$, $S_{13} = 11.9985$, $S_{14} = 11.9993$

  (b) As n gets larger and larger, S_n increases but gets closer and closer to 12.

C4 (a) To four decimal places, $S_{10} = 0.5896$, $S_{11} = 0.6069$, $S_{12} = 0.5954$, $S_{13} = 0.6031$, $S_{14} = 0.5979$

  (b) As n gets larger and larger, S_n gets closer and closer to 0.6, alternating above and below it.

Exercise C (p 37)

1 (a) The common ratio is $\frac{1}{2}$.
  The sum to infinity is 28.

  (b) The common ratio is $\frac{1}{10}$.
  The sum to infinity is 10.

  (c) The common ratio is -2 which is less than -1 so no sum to infinity exists.

  (d) The common ratio is $-\frac{3}{4}$.
  The sum to infinity is $2\frac{2}{7}$ or $\frac{16}{7}$.

2 $6\frac{1}{4}$ or $\frac{25}{4}$

3 $\frac{1}{6}$

4 27

5 12

6 $9 + 6$

Mixed questions (p 38)

1 (a) $\frac{1}{2}$ **(b)** 832   **(c)** 1664

2 (a) $\frac{3}{5}$ or 0.6   **(b)** $\frac{3}{5} \times 5^{n-1}$

  (c) 46875   **(d)** $58593\frac{3}{5}$ or 58593.6

3 (a) 8737.88 (to 2 d.p.)   **(b)** -29524

4 (a) 3rd term $\times \left(\frac{2}{3}\right)^3 = 54 \times \frac{8}{27} = 16$
  $= $ 6th term, so $\frac{2}{3}$ is the common ratio.

  (b) $364\frac{1}{2}$

5 The common ratio is $\frac{2}{5}$ and the sum to infinity is $\frac{125}{3}$ or $41\frac{2}{3}$.

6 (a) (i) £65900   **(ii)** £78700

  (b) £819700 to the nearest £100

7 (a) (i) 2 min 43 seconds   **(ii)** 18 min 21 seconds

  (b) 3 hours 10 minutes (to the nearest minute)

8 524287.75

9 (a) The common ratio is 0.4 or $\frac{2}{5}$.
  The first term is 200.

  (b) $\frac{1000}{3}$ or $333\frac{1}{3}$

  (c) 8.95×10^{-4} (to 3 s.f.)

10 $\frac{250}{3}$ or $83\frac{1}{3}$

11 (a) 0.05

  (b) $600\left(1 - \left(-\frac{1}{3}\right)^n\right)$

  (c) When n is even $0 < \left(-\frac{1}{3}\right)^n < 1$
  So $0 < 1 - \left(-\frac{1}{3}\right)^n < 1$
  As $1 - \left(-\frac{1}{3}\right)^n$ is less than 1, $600\left(1 - \left(-\frac{1}{3}\right)^n\right)$ is less than 600.

12 -24

13 (a) Let S_n be the number of black squares in B_n.
  So $S_0 = 1$. At each stage, each black square is transformed into 5 black squares so $S_n = 5^n$.
  Let A_n be the total black area in B_n.
  So $A_0 = 1$.
  $A_1 = S_1 \times \frac{1}{9}$ (as the area of each smaller square is $\frac{1}{9}$ of the larger one) $= 5 \times \frac{1}{9}$.
  $A_2 = S_2 \times \left(\frac{1}{9}\right)^2$ (as the area of each smaller square is $\frac{1}{9}$ of $\frac{1}{9}$ now) $= 5^2 \times \left(\frac{1}{9}\right)^2 = \left(\frac{5}{9}\right)^2$.

$A_3 = S_3 \times \left(\frac{1}{9}\right)^3 = 5^3 \times \left(\frac{1}{9}\right)^3 = \left(\frac{5}{9}\right)^3$ and so on giving

$A_n = S_n \times \left(\frac{1}{9}\right)^n = 5^n \times \left(\frac{1}{9}\right)^n = \left(\frac{5}{9}\right)^n$

Now as $\left|\frac{5}{9}\right| < 1$ then, as n tends to infinity, $\left(\frac{5}{9}\right)^n$ tends to 0.

(b) (i) The area of B_0 is 1 square unit so the length of one side of B_0 is $\sqrt{1} = 1$ unit.

(ii) The length of one side of B_0 is 1. At each stage the length of each side is divided by 3 so the length of each side in B_n is $\left(\frac{1}{3}\right)^n$.

Hence the perimeter of each black square in B_n is $4 \times \left(\frac{1}{3}\right)^n$.

So the total perimeter of B_n is

$S_n \times 4 \times \left(\frac{1}{3}\right)^n = 5^n \times 4 \times \left(\frac{1}{3}\right)^n = 4 \times \left(\frac{5}{3}\right)^n$.

Now as $\left|\frac{5}{3}\right| > 1$ then, as n tends to infinity, $\left(\frac{5}{3}\right)^n$ tends to infinity.

14 (a) Let E_n be the number of edges in F_n.

So $E_0 = 3$. At each stage, each edge is transformed into 4 edges so $E_n = 3 \times 4^n$.

Let A_n be the total area of F_n.

$A_1 = A_0 + E_0 \times \frac{1}{9}$ (as each smaller triangle is $\frac{1}{9}$ of the larger one) $= 1 + 3 \times \frac{1}{9}$.

$A_2 = A_1 + E_1 \times \left(\frac{1}{9}\right)^2$ (as each smaller triangle is $\frac{1}{9}$ of $\frac{1}{9}$ now) $= 1 + 3 \times \frac{1}{9} + 3 \times 4^1 \times \left(\frac{1}{9}\right)^2$

$A_3 = A_2 + E_2 \times \left(\frac{1}{9}\right)^3$
$= 1 + 3 \times \frac{1}{9} + 3 \times 4^1 \times \left(\frac{1}{9}\right)^2 + 3 \times 4^2 \times \left(\frac{1}{9}\right)^3$

and so on giving

$A_n = 1 + 3 \times \frac{1}{9} + 3 \times 4^1 \times \left(\frac{1}{9}\right)^2 + 3 \times 4^2 \times \left(\frac{1}{9}\right)^3 + 3 \times 4^3 \times \left(\frac{1}{9}\right)^4 + \ldots + 3 \times 4^{n-1} \times \left(\frac{1}{9}\right)^n$

$= 1 + \frac{3}{4}\left(\frac{4}{9} + \left(\frac{4}{9}\right)^2 + \left(\frac{4}{9}\right)^3 + \left(\frac{4}{9}\right)^4 + \ldots + \left(\frac{4}{9}\right)^n\right)$

Now $\left(\frac{4}{9} + \left(\frac{4}{9}\right)^2 + \left(\frac{4}{9}\right)^3 + \left(\frac{4}{9}\right)^4 + \ldots + \left(\frac{4}{9}\right)^n\right)$ is a geometric series with n terms where the common ratio of $\frac{4}{9}$ is between -1 and 1, so its sum to infinity exists and is $\dfrac{\frac{4}{9}}{1 - \frac{4}{9}} = \frac{4}{5}$.

Hence, as n tends to infinity, then A_n tends to $1 + \frac{3}{4} \times \frac{4}{5} = 1\frac{3}{5}$.

(b) The length of one side of F_0 is x. At each stage the length of each side is divided by 3 so the length of each side in F_n is $x \times \left(\frac{1}{3}\right)^n$.

So the total perimeter of F_n is

$E_n \times x \times \left(\frac{1}{3}\right)^n = 3 \times 4^n \times x \times \left(\frac{1}{3}\right)^n = 3x\left(\frac{4}{3}\right)^n$.

Now as $\left|\frac{4}{3}\right| > 1$ then, as n tends to infinity, $\left(\frac{4}{3}\right)^n$ tends to infinity. Hence the perimeter of F_n does not converge to a limit.

Test yourself (p 41)

1 (a) 0.8 or $\frac{4}{5}$ **(b)** 10

(c) 50   **(d)** 0.189 (to 3 s.f.)

2 $\frac{2}{3}$

3 (a) Each term in the sequence is double the one before. Hence there is a common ratio of 2. So the sequence is geometric.

(b) 5×2^n is the prime factorisation of each term and, as the index of 5 is an odd number (1), then none can be a square number.

(c) 10230

4 118096

5 (a) A possible proof is:

$S_n = a + ar + ar^2 + \ldots + ar^{n-1}$

So $rS_n = ar + ar^2 + \ldots + ar^{n-1} + ar^n$

$\Rightarrow \quad S_n - rS_n = a - ar^n$

$\Rightarrow \quad S_n(1 - r) = a(1 - r^n)$

$\Rightarrow \quad S_n = \dfrac{a(1 - r^n)}{1 - r}$ as required.

(b) $r = 0.6$ or $\frac{3}{5}$, $a = 5$

(c) $12\frac{1}{2}$

6 (a) $\dfrac{1200}{1-r} = 960$

$\Rightarrow \quad 1 - r = \dfrac{1200}{960} = \dfrac{5}{4}$

$\Rightarrow \quad r = -\frac{1}{4}$ as required

(b) 0.023

(c) $960\left(1 - \left(-\frac{1}{4}\right)^n\right)$

(d) When n is odd $\left(-\frac{1}{4}\right)^n = -\left(\frac{1}{4}\right)^n = -0.25^n$

So the sum is $960\left(1 - \left(-\frac{1}{4}\right)^n\right)$

$= 960\left(1 - (-0.25^n)\right)$

$= 960\left(1 + 0.25^n\right)$ as required

7 49.70 (to 2 d.p.)

(a) The sum of the first three terms is $a + ar + ar^2$
$= 200 + 200r + 200r^2$ and the sum is 950

so $200r^2 + 200r + 200 = 950$

$\Rightarrow 200r^2 + 200r - 750 = 0$

$\Rightarrow \quad 4r^2 + 4r - 15 = 0$ as required

(b) 450

4 Binomial expansion

A Pascal's triangle (p 42)

A1 (a) $(a + b)^4 = a^4 + 4a^3b + 6a^2b^2 + 4ab^3 + b^4$

(b) Multiply the expansion in (a) by $(a + b)$.

A2 (a) Each number is the sum of the two numbers above it in the previous row.

(b) 1, 6, 15, 20, 15, 6, 1
$a^6 + 6a^5b + 15a^4b^2 + 20a^3b^3 + 15a^2b^4 + 6ab^5 + b^6$

(c) In the table for expanding $(a + b)^5$, the coefficients in the 'a' row are the row 1, 4, 6, 4, 1 from Pascal's triangle. So are the coefficients in the 'b' row. When like terms are combined, the coefficients are added, like this: 1 4 6 4 1
1 4 6 4 1

Exercise A (p 43)

1 $1 + 3x + 3x^2 + x^3$

2 (a) $1 + 6x + 12x^2 + 8x^3$

(b) $1 + 10x + 40x^2 + 80x^3 + 80x^4 + 32x^5$

(c) $1 - 6x + 15x^2 - 20x^3 + 15x^4 - 6x^5 + x^6$

(d) $1 - 18x + 135x^2 - 540x^3 + 1215x^4 - 1458x^5 + 729x^6$

(e) $1 + \frac{7}{2}x + \frac{21}{4}x^2 + \frac{35}{8}x^3 + \frac{35}{16}x^4 + \frac{21}{32}x^5 + \frac{7}{64}x^6 + \frac{1}{128}x^7$

3 (a) $1 - \frac{5}{2}x + \frac{5}{2}x^2 - \frac{5}{4}x^3 + \frac{5}{16}x^4 - \frac{1}{32}x^5$

(b) $8 + 12x + 6x^2 + x^3$

(c) $81 - 216x + 216x^2 - 96x^3 + 16x^4$

4 (a) $1 + 8x + 28x^2 + 56x^3$ (b) 2.136   (c) 0.424

B Arrangements (p 44)

B1 (a) 120   (b) $5 \times 4 \times 3 \times 2 \times 1$

B2 (a) 720   (b) 3 628 800

B3 (a) 12

(b) Because the two As can be put in two different orders

B4 (a) 120   (b) 6   (c) 20

B5 84

B6 (a) 15   (b) 126   (c) 184 756

B7 (a) 1 (b) 1

C The binomial theorem (p 47)

C1 $aaa + aab + aba + baa + abb + bab + bba + bbb$

C2 (a) $1 + 10x + 45x^2 + 120x^3$

    (b) $1 - 10x + 45x^2 - 120x^3$

Exercise C (p 49)

1 $1 + 12x + 66x^2 + 220x^3$

2 (a) 252 (b) 1140

3 1.23

4 (a) $1 + 18x + 144x^2 + 672x^3$

    (b) $1 - 24x + 252x^2 - 1512x^3$

    (c) $1 + \frac{15}{2}x + \frac{105}{4}x^2 + \frac{455}{8}x^3$

    (d) $1 - \frac{7}{5}x + \frac{21}{25}x^2 - \frac{7}{25}x^3$

5 (a) $1 - 10x + 40x^2$ (b) 159

6 (a) 5376 (b) -5376 (c) $145\,152$

7 (a) $1 + 8x + 28x^2 + 56x^3 + \ldots$

    (b) $(0.98)^8 = (1 + (-0.02))^8$

       $= 1 + 8 \times (-0.02) + 28 \times (-0.02)^2 + 56\,(-0.02)^3 + \ldots$

       $= 1 - 8 \times 0.02 + 28 \times 0.0004 - 56 \times 0.000\,008 + \ldots$

       $= 1 - 0.16 + 0.0112 - 0.000\,448 + \ldots$

       $\approx 0.8512 - 0.000\,448$

       $= 0.85$ (to 2 d.p.)

8 (a) $2916x + 1080x^3 + 36x^5$

    (b) $2916x + 1080x^3 + 36x^5 = 36(81x + 30x^3 + x^5)$

       So where x is an integer

       $(3 + x)^6 - (3 - x)^6$ is divisible by 36

9 $a = 64$, $q = \frac{3}{4}$, $b = 135$

10 (a) $1 + 5nx + \frac{25}{2}n(n-1)x^2 + \frac{125}{6}n(n-1)(n-2)x^3$

     (b) (i) $n = 11$ (ii) 55

11 (a) Coefficient of $x^3 = \dfrac{n(n-1)(n-2)}{6}k^3$

        Coefficient of $x^2 = \dfrac{n(n-1)}{2}k^2$

        So $\dfrac{n(n-1)(n-2)}{6}k^3 = \dfrac{2n(n-1)}{2}k^2$

        $\Rightarrow \qquad (n-2)k = 6$

        $\Rightarrow \qquad n - 2 = \dfrac{6}{k}$

        $\Rightarrow \qquad n = 2 + \dfrac{6}{k}$

     (b) $k = 1$, $n = 8$; $k = 2$, $n = 5$; $k = 3$, $n = 4$;

        $k = 6$, $n = 3$

12 4032

Test yourself (p 51)

1 $1 + 20x + 190x^2 + 1140x^3$

2 (a) 2240 (b) -960

3 $1 + 6x + 7x^2$

4 (a) $(1.04)^6 = (1 + 0.04)^6$

       $= 1 + 6 \times 0.04 + 15 \times (0.04)^2 + 20 \times (0.04)^3 + \ldots$

       $= 1 + 0.24 + 15 \times 0.0016 + 20 \times 0.000\,064 + \ldots$

       $= 1 + 0.24 + 0.024 + 0.00128 + \ldots$

       ≈ 1.26528

       $= 1.27$ (to 2 d.p.)

     (b) $(0.99)^8 = (1 - 0.01)^8$

       $= 1 + 8 \times (-0.01) + 28 \times (-0.01)^2$

       $\quad + 56 \times (-0.01)^3 + \ldots$

       $= 1 - 0.08 + 0.0028 - 0.000\,056 + \ldots$

       $= 0.9228 - 0.000\,056 + \ldots$

       $= 0.92$ (to 2 d.p.)

5 $p = \frac{3}{4}$, $A = -144$

6 (a) $1 + 3nx + \frac{9}{2}n(n-1)x^2 + \frac{9}{2}n(n-1)(n-2)x^3$

     (b) $n = 12$ (c) 40095

7 $n = 9$, $p = -2$

8 (a) $A = 64$, $B = 160$, $C = 20$ (b) $x = \pm\sqrt{\frac{3}{2}}$

9 (a) $512 + 576x + 288x^2 + 84x^3$

     (b) $(2.025)^9 = \left(2 + \frac{0.1}{4}\right)^9$

       $\approx 512 + 576 \times 0.1 + 288 \times 0.01 + 84 \times 0.001$

       $= 512 + 57.6 + 2.88 + 0.084$

       $= 572.564$

       So an estimate is 572.6.

10 (a) $\left(1+\dfrac{x}{k}\right)^{n} = 1 + n\left(\dfrac{x}{k}\right) + \dfrac{1}{2}n(n-1)\left(\dfrac{x}{k}\right)^{2}$

$\qquad + \dfrac{1}{6}n(n-1)(n-2)\left(\dfrac{x}{k}\right)^{3} + \dots$

$\qquad = 1 + \left(\dfrac{n}{k}\right)x + \left(\dfrac{n(n-1)}{2k^{2}}\right)x^{2}$

$\qquad + \left(\dfrac{n(n-1)(n-2)}{6k^{3}}\right)x^{3} + \dots$

The coefficient of x^3 is twice the coefficient of x^2 so

$\dfrac{n(n-1)(n-2)}{6k^{3}} = 2 \times \dfrac{n(n-1)}{2k^{2}}$

$n > 2$ so $\dfrac{n-2}{6k^{3}} = \dfrac{1}{k^{2}}$

$\Rightarrow \qquad n - 2 = 6k$

$\Rightarrow \qquad n = 6k + 2$ as required

(b) The coefficient of x^4 is $\dfrac{n(n-1)(n-2)(n-3)}{24k^{4}}$

and the coefficient of x^5 is

$\dfrac{n(n-1)(n-2)(n-3)(n-4)}{120k^{5}}$

Since these coefficients are equal we have

$\dfrac{1}{24k^{4}} = \dfrac{n-4}{120k^{5}}$

$\Rightarrow \quad 5k = n - 4$

$\Rightarrow \quad n = 5k + 4$

Since $n = 6k + 2$ and $n = 5k + 4$ then

$6k + 2 = 5k + 4 \Rightarrow k = 2$

So $n = 5k + 4 \Rightarrow n = 5 \times 2 + 4 = 14$

(c) $f(x) = 1 + 7x + \dfrac{91}{4}x^{2} + \dfrac{91}{2}x^{3} + \dfrac{1001}{16}x^{4} + \dfrac{1001}{16}x^{5}$

5 Trigonometry 1

All answers for this chapter are given to 1 d.p. unless otherwise required.

A Sine and cosine: revision (p 52)

A1 $OQ = 1 \times \cos\theta° = \cos\theta°$
$OR = PQ = 1 \times \sin\theta° = \sin\theta°$
Hence coordinates of P are $(\cos\theta°, \sin\theta°)$.

A2 (a) 1   (b) 0   (c) 1   (d) 0
     (e) 0   (f) 0   (g) −1   (h) 0

A3 (a) Positive   (b) Positive   (c) Negative
     (d) Negative   (e) Negative   (f) Positive
     (g) Negative   (h) Negative

A4 (a) Negative; $\cos\theta°$ is negative.
     (b) $\sin\theta°$ is positive.

A5

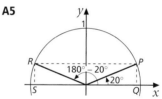

A proof such as:
$\sin 160° = SR = QP$ by symmetry
$\qquad\qquad = \sin 20°$

A6 A similar proof to A5

A7

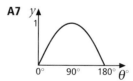

A8

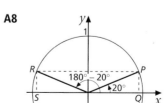

A proof such as:
$\cos 160° = OS = -OQ$ by symmetry
$\qquad\qquad = -\cos 20°$

A9 A similar proof to A8

A10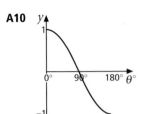

A11 $\theta° = 39°$; another angle is $141°$.

A12 $\theta° = 51°$; the obtuse angle is $129°$.

Exercise A (p 53)

1 (a) Positive   (b) Negative

(c) Positive   (d) Negative

2 (a) $20°$ (b) $20°$ and $160°$

3 (a) $64°$ and $116°$ (b) $26°$

(c) $27°$ and $153°$ (d) $117°$

(e) $32°$ and $148°$ (f) $58°$

(g) $4°$ and $176°$ (h) $94°$

4 An explanation such as: the line $y = k$ meets $y = \sin\theta°$ at either two or no points; it meets $y = \cos\theta°$ at one point.

B Cosine rule (p 54)

B1 (a) $PB = c - x$ (b) $h^2 = a^2 - (c - x)^2$

(c) $h^2 = b^2 - x^2$ (d) $a^2 = b^2 - x^2 + (c - x)^2$

(e) $a^2 = b^2 + c^2 - 2cx$ (f) $x = b\cos A$

(g) $a^2 = b^2 + c^2 - 2bc\cos A$

B2 $PB = c + x$
In $\triangle CPB$, $h^2 = a^2 - (c + x)^2$
In $\triangle CPA$, $h^2 = b^2 - x^2$
Hence $a^2 = b^2 - x^2 + (c + x)^2$
  i.e. $a^2 = b^2 + c^2 + 2cx$
In $\triangle CPA$, $x = b\cos\angle CAP$
           $= b\cos(180° - A)$
           $= -b\cos A$
Hence $a^2 = b^2 + c^2 - 2bc\cos A$

Exercise B (p 55)

1 (a) 4.1 cm   (b) 8.9 cm   (c) 6.0 cm

2 (a) $34.8°$ (b) $106.1°$ (c) $38.7°$

3 8.9 cm

4 $34.0°$, $101.5°$, $44.4°$ or $44.5°$

---

5 5.4 km

6 (a) $AC^2 = 4^2 + AM^2 - 2 \times 4 \times AM \times \cos\theta°$

(b) $AB^2 = 4^2 + AM^2 - 2 \times 4 \times AM \times \cos(180° -$
      $= 4^2 + AM^2 + 2 \times 4 \times AM \times \cos\theta°$

(c) $AC^2 + AB^2 = 2(4^2 + AM^2)$
     $6^2 + 7^2 = 2(4^2 + AM^2)$
         $AM = 5.1$

C Sine rule (p 56)

C1 (a) $h = b\sin A$ (b) $h = a\sin B$

(c) $b\sin A = a\sin B$ (d) $\dfrac{a}{\sin A} = \dfrac{b}{\sin B}$

C2 (a) $h = b\sin\angle PAC$

(b) $\angle PAC = 180° - A$
    $h = b\sin(180° - A)$

(c) $h = b\sin A$

(d) $h = a\sin B$

(e) $\dfrac{a}{\sin A} = \dfrac{b}{\sin B}$

Exercise C (p 58)

1 (a) 3.8 cm   (b) 10.5 cm   (c) 17.7 cm

2 (a)

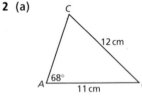

(b) $\sin C = 0.849\ldots$

(c) $58°$ and $122°$

(d) If $C = 58°$, $B = 54°$
    If $C = 122°$, $B = -10°$

(e) $C = 58°$ is the only possible answer.

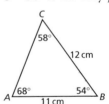

3 (a) $35.9°$ ($144.1°$ is impossible)

(b) $48.7°$ ($131.3°$ is impossible)

(c) $59.2°$ or $24.8°$

D Both rules

Exercise D (p 60)

1 (a) $E = 38.0°$, $F = 62.0°$, $DE = 7.2\,$cm
(b) $Q = 27.4°$, $R = 22.6°$, $PQ = 10.0\,$mm
(c) $M = 66.8°$, $N = 63.2°$, $LM = 11.7\,$m or
$M = 113.2°$, $N = 16.8°$, $LM = 3.8\,$m

2 (a) $RS = 11.4\,$cm, $R = 30.3°$, $S = 114.7°$
(b) $EF = 100.3\,$m, $E = 58.6°$, $F = 49.4°$

3 (a) $BC = 43.2\,$m, $C = 46.8°$, $B = 33.2°$
(b) $DE = 24\,$mm, $E = 16.3°$, $F = 73.7°$
(c) $J = 41.9°$, $K = 73.1°$, $40.1\,$cm
(d) $X = 58.4°$, $Y = 48.2°$, $Z = 73.4°$

E Area of a triangle

Exercise E (p 62)

1 (a) $5.6\,$cm^2 (b) $38.6\,$mm^2 (c) $11.8\,$m^2

2 (a) $R = 61.1°$ (or $S = 74.4°$ or $T = 44.5°$)
(b) Area $= 38.5\,$cm^2

3 (a) $11.2\,$cm^2 (b) $59.6\,$mm^2
(c) $1270\,$m^2 (3 s.f.)

F Radians and arcs (p 63)

F1 (a) π (b) $\dfrac{\pi}{2}$ (c) $\dfrac{\pi}{3}$
(d) $\dfrac{\pi}{6}$ (e) $\dfrac{3\pi}{2}$ (f) $\dfrac{\pi}{180}$

F2 $57.3°$

F3 (a) $2r$ (b) $\frac{1}{2}r$ (c) θr

F4 $2\,$cm

F5 (a)

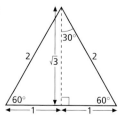

(b) $\sin 30° = \frac{1}{2}$ $\cos 30° = \dfrac{\sqrt{3}}{2}$ $\tan 30° = \dfrac{1}{\sqrt{3}}$

$\sin 60° = \dfrac{\sqrt{3}}{2}$ $\cos 60° = \frac{1}{2}$ $\tan 60° = \sqrt{3}$

Exercise F (p 65)

1 (a) $\dfrac{7\pi}{6}$ (b) $\dfrac{3\pi}{4}$ (c) $\dfrac{2\pi}{3}$
(d) $\dfrac{11\pi}{6}$ (e) $\dfrac{5\pi}{3}$

2 (a) $22\frac{1}{2}°$ (b) $18°$ (c) $1°$ (d) $45°$
(e) $150°$ (f) $225°$ (g) $75°$ (h) $315°$
(i) $40°$ (j) $240°$

3

Radians	Degrees	$\sin\theta$	$\cos\theta$	$\tan\theta$
$\dfrac{\pi}{6}$	$30°$	$\dfrac{1}{2}$	$\dfrac{\sqrt{3}}{2}$	$\dfrac{1}{\sqrt{3}}$
$\dfrac{2\pi}{3}$	$120°$	$\dfrac{\sqrt{3}}{2}$	$-\dfrac{1}{2}$	$-\sqrt{3}$
$\dfrac{3\pi}{4}$	$135°$	$\dfrac{1}{\sqrt{2}}$	$-\dfrac{1}{\sqrt{2}}$	-1
$\dfrac{5\pi}{6}$	$150°$	$\dfrac{1}{2}$	$-\dfrac{\sqrt{3}}{2}$	$-\dfrac{1}{\sqrt{3}}$

4 (a) $\dfrac{2\pi}{3}\,$m   (b) $4 + \dfrac{2\pi}{3}\,$m

5 (a) $11.5\,$cm   (b) $9.8\,$cm   (c) $21.3\,$cm

6 $81.9°$

7 $4.3\,$cm

G Area of a sector

Exercise G (p 67)

1 (a) $81.3\,$cm^2 (b) $69.8\,$m^2
(c) $52.8\,$cm^2 (d) $335.8\,$mm^2

2 (a) 8π (b) $\dfrac{100\pi}{3}$

3 $35.8°$

4 (a) $\theta = \dfrac{18}{r} - 2$ (b) Area $= 9r - r^2$

5 (a) $1600\,$m   (b) $80\,000$ people

6 (a) $r \sin\theta$ (b) $\frac{1}{2}r^2 \sin\theta$
(c) $\frac{1}{2}r^2 \theta$ (d) $\frac{1}{2}r^2(\theta - \sin\theta)$

7 (a) A proof such as:
By symmetry $BP = 10\,$cm and $OP = 10\,$cm
(radius), so $\angle BOP = 60°$.
Hence $\angle AOB = 120°$.
(b) $104.7\,$cm^2 (c) $43.3\,$cm^2 (d) $61.4\,$cm^2

8 (a) $12\theta\,$m^2
(b) $12\theta\,$m$^2 = 15\,$m^2, hence $\theta = \frac{15}{12} = 1.25$
(c) $19\,$m   (d) $40\,$cm

Test yourself (p 69)

1 (a) 3.2 cm   (b) 55.4° or 124.6°

    (c) 117.3°

2 (a) 4.7 cm²   (b) 17.5 cm² or 5.8 cm²

    (c) 21.3 cm²

3 (a) 6.8 cm   (b) 16.8 cm   (c) 17.0 cm²

4 39 cm

5 (a) $2\sqrt{3}$ cm   (b) 2π cm²

    (c) Perimeter $= AB + AC + $ arc BC

$$= 2\sqrt{3} + 2\sqrt{3} + 2\sqrt{3} \times \frac{\pi}{3} = 2\sqrt{3}\left(2 + \frac{\pi}{3}\right)$$

$$= \frac{2\sqrt{3}}{3}(\pi + 6)\ \text{cm}$$

6 (a) Area of X $=$ Area $ABCD + $ area of semi-circle

$$= 2d \times d + \tfrac{1}{2}\pi d^2 = d^2\left(2 + \tfrac{1}{2}\pi\right)$$

     Area of Y $= \tfrac{1}{2} \times (2d)^2 \times \theta = 2d^2\theta$.

     Hence $d^2\left(2 + \tfrac{1}{2}\pi\right) = 2d^2\theta;\ \theta = 1 + \tfrac{1}{4}\neq$

    (b) $3(4 + \pi)$ cm

    (c) $\tfrac{3}{2}(12 + \pi)$ cm

    (d) 12.9 mm

6 Trigonometry 2

A Sines and cosines (p 70)

A1 (a) Same   (b) Not   (c) Not   (d) Not

     (e) Same   (f) Same   (g) Same   (h) Same

A2 Let R be the reflection of P in the x-axis. By symmetry, the coordinates of R are $(\cos\theta°,\ -\sin\theta°)$, and $\angle QOR = -\theta°$. Hence $QR = \sin(-\theta)°$ $= -\sin\theta°$.

A3 (a) $\sin 20°$ (b) $-\sin 20°$ (c) $-\sin 20°$

    (d) $-\sin 20°$ (e) $-\sin 20°$ (f) $\sin 20°$

    (g) $\sin 20°$ (h) $-\sin 20°$ (i) $-\sin 20°$

    (j) $\sin 20°$

A4 (a) Not   (b) Not   (c) Same   (d) Same

     (e) Same   (f) Not   (g) Same   (h) Not

A5 In the diagram for A2, in $\triangle OQP$, $OQ = \cos\theta°$, and in $\triangle OQR$, $OQ = \cos(-\theta)°$. So $\cos\theta° = \cos(-\theta)°$.

A6 (a) $-20°$ (b) $160°$ (c) $340°$ (d) -200

A7 (a) $317°$ (b) $260°$

    (c) If one solution is $\theta° = \alpha°$, then the other solution is $\theta° = 360° - \alpha°$.

Exercise A (p 72)

1 (a) $110°$ (b) $430°$ and $470°$

2 (a) 5.28^c (b) 7.28^c and 11.57^c

3 (a) (i) $40°,\ 140°$ (ii) $50°,\ 310°$

       (iii) $197°,\ 343°$ (iv) $152°,\ 208°$

    (b) (i) $400°,\ 500°$ (ii) $410°,\ 670°$

       (iii) $557°,\ 703°$ (iv) $512°,\ 568°$

4 (a) $\dfrac{\pi}{6}, \dfrac{5\pi}{6}$ (b) $\dfrac{\pi}{2}$ (c) $\dfrac{\pi}{2}, \dfrac{3\pi}{2}$

5 (a) $-\dfrac{7\pi}{4}, -\dfrac{5\pi}{4}, \dfrac{\pi}{4}, \dfrac{3\pi}{4}$ (b) $-\dfrac{3\pi}{4}, -\dfrac{\pi}{4}, \dfrac{5\pi}{4}, \dfrac{7\pi}{4}$

(c) $-\dfrac{11\pi}{6}, -\dfrac{\pi}{6}, \dfrac{\pi}{6}, \dfrac{11\pi}{6}$ **(d)** $-\dfrac{4\pi}{3}, -\dfrac{2\pi}{3}, \dfrac{2\pi}{3}, \dfrac{4\pi}{3}$

6 (a) $-354°, -186°, 6°, 174°$

(b) $127°, 233°, 487°, 593°$

(c) $49°, 131°, 409°, 491°$

(d) $-248°, -112°, 112°, 248°$

B Transforming sine and cosine graphs (p 73)

B1 (a)

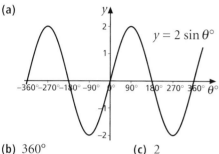

(b) $360°$ **(c)** 2

(d) A stretch in the y-direction, scale factor 2

B2 (a) A suitable graph   **(b)** $360°$ **(c)** a

(d) A stretch in the y-direction, scale factor a

B3 (a) 0 **(b)** $\dfrac{1}{\sqrt{2}}$ **(c)** 1 **(d)** 0 **(e)** -1

B4 (a)

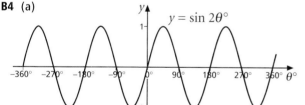

(b) Period $= 180°$, amplitude $= 1$

(c) A stretch in the θ-direction, scale factor $\dfrac{1}{2}$

B5 (a) A stretch in the θ-direction, scale factor $\dfrac{1}{b}$

(b) Period $= \dfrac{360°}{b}$, amplitude $= 1$

(c) A check of the answers

B6 (a) (i) $-30°$

(ii)

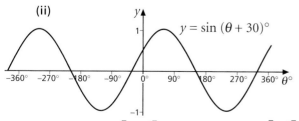

(b) A translation of $\begin{bmatrix} -30° \\ 0 \end{bmatrix}$ **(c)** A translation of $\begin{bmatrix} -c° \\ 0 \end{bmatrix}$

B7 (a) A translation of $\begin{bmatrix} 0 \\ d \end{bmatrix}$ **(b)** 1

B8 (a)

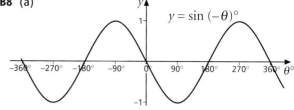

(b) $y = \sin(-\theta)°$ is the reflection of $y = \sin \theta°$ in the θ-axis.

(c)

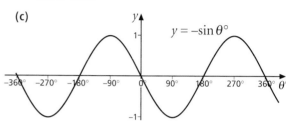

(d) $y = -\sin \theta°$ is the reflection of $y = \sin \theta°$ in the θ-axis.

Exercise B (p 75)

1 (a) A stretch in the y-direction, scale factor $\dfrac{1}{2}$; $y = \dfrac{1}{2}\sin \theta°$

(b) A stretch in the θ-direction, scale factor $\dfrac{1}{3}$; $y = \sin 3\theta°$

(c) A translation of $\begin{bmatrix} 45° \\ 0 \end{bmatrix}$; $y = \sin(\theta - 45)°$

(d) A translation of $\begin{bmatrix} 90° \\ 0 \end{bmatrix}$; $y = \sin(\theta - 90)°$

(e) A translation of $\begin{bmatrix} 0 \\ -1 \end{bmatrix}$; $y = \sin \theta° - 1$

(f) A translation of $\begin{bmatrix} -90° \\ 0 \end{bmatrix}$; $y = \sin(\theta + 90)°$

(g) A stretch in the θ-direction, scale factor 2; $y = \sin \dfrac{1}{2}\theta°$

2 (a) $\sin(\theta + 90)° = \cos \theta°$

(b) $\sin(\theta - 90)° = -\cos \theta°$

3 (a)

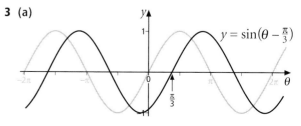

(b)

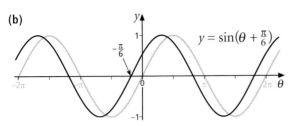

$y = \sin\left(\theta + \frac{\pi}{6}\right)$

(c)

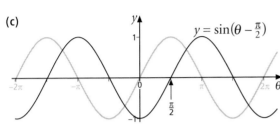

$y = \sin\left(\theta - \frac{\pi}{2}\right)$

4 (a)

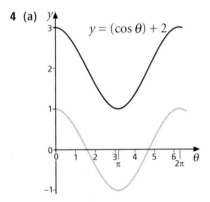

$y = (\cos \theta) + 2$

(b)

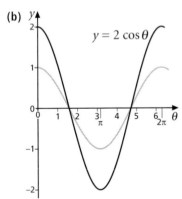

$y = 2\cos\theta$

(c)

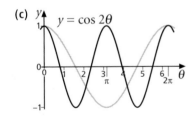

$y = \cos 2\theta$

(d)

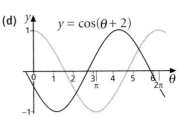

$y = \cos(\theta + 2)$

5 (a) A translation of $\begin{bmatrix} \frac{\pi}{4} \\ 0 \end{bmatrix}$; $y = \cos\left(\theta - \frac{\pi}{4}\right)$

(b) A translation of $\begin{bmatrix} 0 \\ 1 \end{bmatrix}$; $y = (\cos\theta) + 1$

(c) Stretch in the y-direction, factor 2; $y = 2\cos\theta$

(d) Stretch in the θ-direction, factor $\frac{1}{3}$; $y = \cos 3\theta$

(e) A translation of $\begin{bmatrix} -\frac{\pi}{2} \\ 0 \end{bmatrix}$; $y = \cos\left(\theta + \frac{\pi}{2}\right)$

or a translation of $\begin{bmatrix} \frac{3\pi}{2} \\ 0 \end{bmatrix}$; $y = \cos\left(\theta - \frac{3\pi}{2}\right)$

(f) Stretch in the θ-direction, factor $\frac{3}{2}$; $y = \cos\frac{2}{3}\theta$

6 (a)

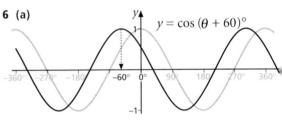

$y = \cos(\theta + 60)^\circ$

(b)

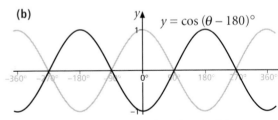

$y = \cos(\theta - 180)^\circ$

(c) The graph is identical to that in (b).

7 (a)

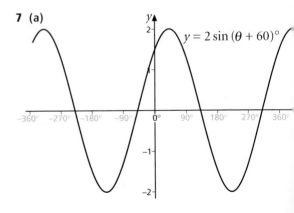

$y = 2\sin(\theta + 60)^\circ$

(b)

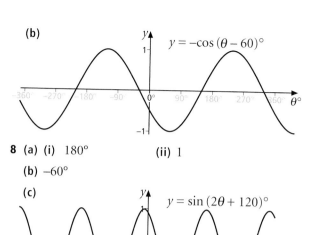

$y = -\cos(\theta - 60)°$

8 (a) (i) $180°$ **(ii)** 1

(b) $-60°$

(c)

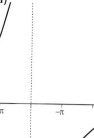

$y = \sin(2\theta + 120)°$

C Tangents (p 77)

C1 (a), (b)

$\sin\theta°$ +ve	$\sin\theta°$ +ve
$\cos\theta°$ −ve	$\cos\theta°$ +ve
$\tan\theta°$ −ve	$\tan\theta°$ +ve
$\sin\theta°$ −ve	$\sin\theta°$ −ve
$\cos\theta°$ −ve	$\cos\theta°$ +ve
$\tan\theta°$ +ve	$\tan\theta°$ −ve

C2 $\tan(-\theta)° = \dfrac{\sin(-\theta)°}{\cos(-\theta)°} = \dfrac{-\sin\theta°}{\cos\theta°}$

$= -\dfrac{\sin\theta°}{\cos\theta°} = -\tan\theta°$

Exercise C (p 78)

1 (a) $72°, 252°$ **(b)** $108°, 288°$

(c) $153°, 333°$ **(d)** $58°, 238°$

2 (a) $\dfrac{\pi}{3}, -\dfrac{2\pi}{3}$ **(b)** $-\dfrac{\pi}{6}, \dfrac{5\pi}{6}$

(c) $-\dfrac{5\pi}{4}, -\dfrac{\pi}{4}$ **(d)** $\pi, 2\pi, 3\pi, 4\pi, 5\pi$

3 (a) $y = \tan(\theta + 45)°$ **(b)** $\tan 2\theta°$

(c) $y = \tan(\theta - 45)°$ **(d)** $\tan\frac{1}{2}\theta°$

4 (a)

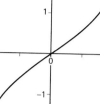

$y = \tan\frac{x}{3}$

(b)

$y = \tan x + 0.5$

(c)

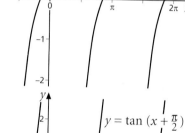

$y = \tan\left(x + \frac{\pi}{2}\right)$

(d)

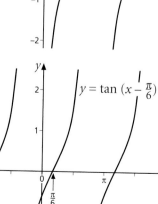

$y = \tan\left(x - \frac{\pi}{6}\right)$

D Solving further equations (p 79)

D1 $\theta° = 106°$ or $334°$

Exercise D (p 81)

1 (a) $231°$ or $329°$ **(b)** $294°$ or $346°$

(c) $116°$ or $296°$ **(d)** $22°, 68°, 202°$ or $248°$

(e) $22°, 98°, 142°, 218°, 262°$ or $338°$

(f) $6°, 96°, 186°$ or $276°$

2 (a) $\dfrac{\pi}{12}, \dfrac{5\pi}{12}, \dfrac{13\pi}{12}$ or $\dfrac{17\pi}{12}$

(b) $0, \dfrac{\pi}{2}, \pi, \dfrac{3\pi}{2}$ or 2π

(c) $\dfrac{\pi}{12}, \dfrac{5\pi}{12}, \dfrac{9\pi}{12}, \dfrac{13\pi}{12}, \dfrac{17\pi}{12}$ or $\dfrac{21\pi}{12}$

3 (a) $3.9°, 14.1°, 39.9°$ or $50.1°$

(b) $51.7°$ **(c)** $2.3°$ or $38.3°$

4 (a) $-107.7°, -72.3°, 12.3°, 47.7°, 132.3°$ or $167.7°$

(b) $-303.8°, -236.2°, -123.8°$ or $-56.2°$

(c) $-156.7°, -120.7°, -84.7°, -48.7°, -12.7°,$
$23.3°, 59.3°, 95.3°, 131.3°$ or $167.3°$

(d) $98.9°$ or $261.1°$

5 (a) $\dfrac{\pi}{3}$ or $\dfrac{4\pi}{3}$ **(b)** $\dfrac{5\pi}{6}$ or $\dfrac{11\pi}{6}$ **(c)** $\dfrac{2\pi}{3}$ or $\dfrac{5\pi}{3}$

6 (a) $10.1°, 134.9°, 190.1°$ or $314.9°$

(b) $62.4°, 83.1°, 152.4°, 173.1°,$
$242.4°, 263.1°, 332.4°$ or $353.1°$

(c) $56.4°$

(d) $25.8°, 115.8°, 205.8°$ or $295.8°$

E Further equations and identities (p 81)

E1 (a) $-\dfrac{2\sqrt{2}}{3}$ **(b)** $-\dfrac{1}{2\sqrt{2}}$

E2 (a) $2c^2 - 3c + 1 = 0$ **(b)** $(2c - 1)(c - 1) = 0$

(c) A check that one factor is $(c - 1)$

(d) $\theta° = 0°$ **(e)** $\theta° = 60°$

(f) A check of the solutions

E3 (a) $\cos^2 \theta° + \cos \theta° = 0$

(b) $\theta° = 90°, 180°$ or $270°$

Exercise E (p 84)

1 (a) $\cos \theta = \dfrac{\sqrt{15}}{4}$, $\tan \theta = \dfrac{1}{\sqrt{15}}$

(b) $\cos \theta = -\dfrac{\sqrt{15}}{4}$, $\tan \theta = -\dfrac{1}{\sqrt{15}}$

2 (a) $1 + \cos x° = 3 \sin^2 x°$
$\Rightarrow 1 + \cos x° = 3(1 - \cos^2 x°)$
$\Rightarrow 1 + \cos x° = 3 - 3 \cos^2 x°$
$\Rightarrow 3 \cos^2 x° + \cos x° - 2 = 0$

(b) $(3 \cos x° - 2)(\cos x° + 1) = 0$

(c) $x° = 48.2°, 180°$ or $311.8°$

3 (a) $\dfrac{2\pi}{3}, \dfrac{4\pi}{3}, 0$ or 2π **(b)** $\dfrac{\pi}{6}$ or $\dfrac{7\pi}{6}$

(c) $\dfrac{\pi}{3}$ or $\dfrac{5\pi}{3}$

4 (a) $\dfrac{\pi}{6}, \dfrac{5\pi}{6}, \dfrac{7\pi}{6}$ or $\dfrac{11\pi}{6}$ **(b)** $0, \pi$ or 2π

(c) $\dfrac{\pi}{3}, \dfrac{2\pi}{3}, \dfrac{4\pi}{3}$ or $\dfrac{5\pi}{3}$ **(d)** $0.46, 2.68, 3.61$ or 5.8

(e) $0, \pi$ or 2π **(f)** $\dfrac{3\pi}{2}$

5 (a) When $x = 1$, $x^3 - x^2 - 3x + 3$
$= 1 - 1 - 3 + 3 = 0$. Hence $(x - 1)$ is a factor
by the factor theorem.
$x^3 - x^2 - 3x + 3 = (x - 1)(x^2 - 3)$

(b) $\dfrac{\pi}{4}, \dfrac{\pi}{3}, \dfrac{2\pi}{3}, \dfrac{5\pi}{4}, \dfrac{4\pi}{3}$ or $\dfrac{5\pi}{3}$

6 (a) $(\sin x + \cos x)^2$
$= \sin^2 x + 2 \sin x \cos x + \cos^2 x$
$= \sin^2 x + \cos^2 x + 2 \sin x \cos x$
$= 1 + 2 \sin x \cos x$

(b) $\dfrac{6 - \cos^2 \theta}{\sin^2 \theta + 5} = \dfrac{6 - (1 - \sin^2 \theta)}{\sin^2 \theta + 5} = \dfrac{6 - 1 + \sin^2 \theta}{\sin^2 \theta + 5}$
$= \dfrac{5 + \sin^2 \theta}{\sin^2 \theta + 5} = 1$

7 $(1 + \sin \theta + \cos \theta)^2$
$= 1(1 + \sin \theta + \cos \theta) + \sin \theta(1 + \sin \theta + \cos \theta)$
$\quad + \cos \theta(1 + \sin \theta + \cos \theta)$
$= 1 + \sin \theta + \cos \theta + \sin \theta + \sin^2 \theta + \sin \theta \cos \theta$
$\quad + \cos \theta + \cos \theta \sin \theta + \cos^2 \theta$
$= 1 + 2 \sin \theta + 2 \cos \theta + 2 \sin \theta \cos \theta + \sin^2 \theta + \cos$
$= 1 + 2 \sin \theta + 2 \cos \theta + 2 \sin \theta \cos \theta + 1$
$= 2 + 2 \sin \theta + 2 \cos \theta + 2 \sin \theta \cos \theta$
$= 2(1 + \sin \theta + \cos \theta + \sin \theta \cos \theta)$
$= 2(1 + \sin \theta)(1 + \cos \theta)$

8 $\dfrac{x^2}{9} + \dfrac{y^2}{4} = 1$

Test yourself (p 85)

1 (a)

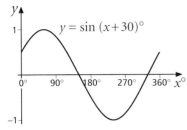

$y = \sin(x+30)^\circ$

(b) $(0, 0.5)$, $(150^\circ, 0)$, $(330^\circ, 0)$

(c) $x^\circ = 180^\circ$ or 300°

2 (a) 225° or 345°

(b) $22.2^\circ, 67.8^\circ, 202.2^\circ$ or 247.8°

3 (a) (i) $\dfrac{\sqrt{3}}{2}$ **(ii)** $\dfrac{\sqrt{2}}{2}$ or $\dfrac{1}{\sqrt{2}}$ **(iii)** $\dfrac{\sqrt{3}}{3}$ or $\dfrac{1}{\sqrt{3}}$

(b)

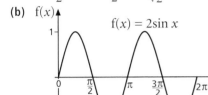

$f(x) = 2\sin x$

(c) $\left(\dfrac{\pi}{4}, 1\right)$, $\left(\dfrac{3\pi}{4}, -1\right)$, $\left(\dfrac{5\pi}{4}, 1\right)$, and $\left(\dfrac{7\pi}{4}, -1\right)$

(d) $\dfrac{\pi}{12}, \dfrac{5\pi}{12}, \dfrac{13\pi}{12}$ and $\dfrac{17\pi}{12}$

4 (a) 108.5° or 311.5° **(b)** 1.3° or 78.7°

(c) 59.8° or 239.8°

5 (a) $0.10, 1.47, 3.24$ or 4.61

(b) $0.82, 1.27, 2.92, 3.37, 5.01$ or 5.46

(c) 1.75

6 (a)
$$2\sin 2\theta = \cos 2\theta$$
$$\Rightarrow \quad 2\dfrac{\sin 2\theta}{\cos 2\theta} = 1$$
$$\Rightarrow \quad 2\tan 2\theta = 1$$
$$\Rightarrow \quad \tan 2\theta = \tfrac{1}{2} \text{ or } 0.5$$

(b) $13.3^\circ, 103.3^\circ, 193.3^\circ$ or 283.3°

7 (a)

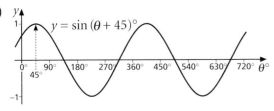

$y = \sin(\theta + 45)^\circ$

(b)

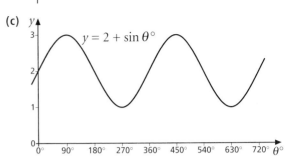

$y = \tfrac{1}{3}\cos\theta^\circ$

(c) $y = 2 + \sin\theta^\circ$

(d)

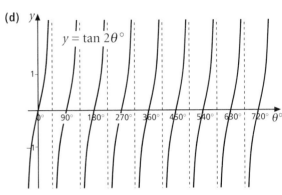

$y = \tan 2\theta^\circ$

8 (a)
$$\frac{3 - 2\cos^2\theta}{2\sin^2\theta + 1} = \frac{3 - 2(1 - \sin^2\theta)}{2\sin^2\theta + 1} = \frac{3 - 2 + 2\sin^2\theta}{2\sin^2\theta + 1}$$
$$= \frac{1 + 2\sin^2\theta}{2\sin^2\theta + 1} = 1$$

(b) $\tan\theta\sin\theta = \dfrac{\sin\theta}{\cos\theta}\sin\theta = \dfrac{\sin^2\theta}{\cos\theta} = \dfrac{1 - \cos^2\theta}{\cos\theta}$
$$= \frac{1}{\cos\theta} - \cos\theta$$

9 (a)
$$2\sin^2\theta = 2 + \cos\theta$$
$$\Rightarrow \quad 2(1 - \cos^2\theta) = 2 + \cos\theta$$
$$\Rightarrow \quad 2 - 2\cos^2\theta = 2 + \cos\theta$$
$$\Rightarrow \quad -2\cos^2\theta = \cos\theta$$
$$\Rightarrow \quad 2\cos^2\theta + \cos\theta = 0$$

(b) $\dfrac{\pi}{2}, \dfrac{2\pi}{3}, \dfrac{4\pi}{3}$ or $\dfrac{3\pi}{2}$

10 $0^\circ, 131.8^\circ$ or 228.2°

11 $-160.5^\circ, -19.5^\circ$ or 90°

7 Exponentials and logarithms

A Graphs of exponential functions (p 86)

A1 (a)

t (weeks)	0	1	2	3	4
A (m²)	1	2	4	8	16

(b), (f)

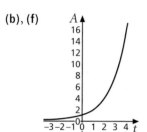

(c) The formula is $A = 2^t$.

(d) $A = 1.414$ to 3 d.p.

(e) $A = 3.249$ to 3 d.p.

A2 (a) $y = 1$

(b) y is large and positive.

(c) y approaches zero and is positive.

A3 (a) The family of graphs is shown.

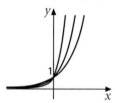

(b) All graphs of $y = a^x$ pass through $(0, 1)$.

A4 (a) y approaches zero and is positive.

(b) y is large and positive.

(c) $y = (\frac{1}{2})^x = \dfrac{1}{2^x} = 2^{-x}$ as required

(d) The graph of $y = (\frac{1}{2})^x$ is a reflection in the y-axis of $y = 2^x$.

A5 (a) If $x = 3$, then $y = 2^3 = 8$, so $(3, 8)$ is on the graph.

(b) $(3, 9)$

(c) The y-intercept is 2.

(d) $y = 2^x + 1$

A6 $y = 2^{x-3}$

A7 $y = 2^{x+1}$

A8 (a)

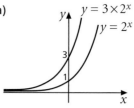

(b) $y = 3 \times 2^x$

A9 $y = 2^{\frac{x}{3}}$

A10 (a) $y = 16 \times 2^x$

$\qquad = 2^4 \times 2^x$

$\qquad = 2^{x+4}$ as required

(b) $y = 2^{x+4}$ is a stretch of $y = 2^x$ by scale factor 16 in the direction of the y-axis.

$y = 2^{x+4}$ is a translation by $\begin{bmatrix} -4 \\ 0 \end{bmatrix}$ of $y = 2^x$.

A11 $y = 2^{x+5}$ is a stretch of $y = 2^x$ by scale factor 32 in the direction of the y-axis.

$y = 2^{x+5}$ is a translation by $\begin{bmatrix} -5 \\ 0 \end{bmatrix}$ of $y = 2^x$.

Exercise A (p 88)

1

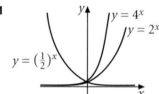

2 (a) The graph of $y = 5^{x+1}$ is a translation by $\begin{bmatrix} -1 \\ 0 \end{bmatrix}$ of $y = 5^x$ or a stretch of $y = 5^x$ by scale factor 5 in the direction of the y-axis.

(b)

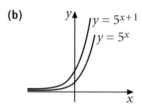

3 (a) $y = 6^{x-3}$ (b) $y = 6^x + 3$

4 (a) $f(x - 2) = 4^{x-2}$

(b) The graph of $y = f(x - 2)$ is a translation by $\begin{bmatrix} 2 \\ 0 \end{bmatrix}$ of $y = f(x)$.

5 (a) $g(3x) = 7^{3x}$

(b) The graph of $y = g(3x)$ is a stretch of $y = g(x)$ by scale factor $\frac{1}{3}$ in the direction of the x-axis.

6 (a) The graph of $y = 3^{-x}$ is a reflection in the y-axis of $y = 3^x$.

(b) The graph of $y = 3^x - 5$ is a translation by $\begin{bmatrix} 0 \\ -5 \end{bmatrix}$ of $y = 3x$.

(c) The graph of $y = 2 \times 3^x$ is a stretch of $y = 3^x$ by scale factor 2 in the direction of the y-axis.

(d) The graph of $y = 3^{x+4}$ is a translation by $\begin{bmatrix} -4 \\ 0 \end{bmatrix}$ of $y = 3^x$ or a stretch of $y = 3^x$ by scale factor 81 in the direction of the y-axis.

7 (a) $y = 16 \times 4^x$
$= 4^2 \times 4^x$
$= 4^{x+2}$ as required

(b) $y = 4^{x+2}$ is a stretch of $y = 4^x$ by scale factor 16 in the direction of the y-axis.
$y = 4^{x+2}$ is a translation by $\begin{bmatrix} -2 \\ 0 \end{bmatrix}$ of $y = 4^x$.

8 $y = 5^{x-1}$ is a stretch of $y = 5^x$ by scale factor $\frac{1}{5}$ in the direction of the y-axis.
$y = 5^{x-1}$ is a translation by $\begin{bmatrix} 1 \\ 0 \end{bmatrix}$ of $y = 5^x$.

B Logarithms (p 89)

B1 After 3.3 weeks the area covered is $10\,\text{m}^2$.

B2 (a) (i) $y = 4$ **(ii)** $y = 32$ **(iii)** $y = \frac{1}{2}$
(b) (i) $x = 0$ **(ii)** $x = 3$ **(iii)** $x = -2$

B3 (a) $\log_2 64 = 6$ **(b)** $2^7 = 128$

B4 (a) (i) $x = 1$ **(ii)** $x = 3$ **(iii)** $x = -1$
(b) (i) $x = 3$ **(ii)** $x = -2$ **(iii)** $x = -3$

B5 (a) $\log_5 625 = 4$ **(b)** $10^2 = 100$

B6 (a) $\log_3 81 = 4$ **(b)** $\log_7 343 = 3$
(c) $\log_8 0.125 = -1$

B7 (a) $3^2 = 9$ **(b)** $4^3 = 64$ **(c)** $9^{-1} = \frac{1}{9}$

B8 (a) $2^x = 2$ **(b)** $x = 1$

B9 (a) $2^x = 1$ **(b)** $x = 0$

B10 (a) $2^x = \frac{1}{2}$ **(b)** $x = -1$

B11 (a) $\log_a a = 1$ **(b)** $\log_a 1 = 0$
(c) $\log_a \left(\frac{1}{a} \right) = -1$

B12 (a) (i) $5^x = 5^2$ **(ii)** $x = 2$
(b) $\log_3 3^4 = 4$
(c) $\log_a a^x = x$

B13 (a) (i) $\log_2 x = \log_2 8$ **(ii)** $x = 8$
(b) $3^{\log_3 9} = 9$
(c) $a^{\log_a x} = x$

Exercise B (p 91)

1 (a) (i) $64 = 2^6$ **(ii)** $\sqrt{2} = 2^{\frac{1}{2}}$
(iii) $\frac{1}{8} = 2^{-3}$ **(iv)** $0.25 = 2^{-2}$
(v) $1 = 2^0$

(b) (i) $\log_2 64 = 6$ **(ii)** $\log_2 \sqrt{2} = \frac{1}{2}$
(iii) $\log_2 \frac{1}{8} = -3$ **(iv)** $\log_2 0.25 = -2$
(v) $\log_2 1 = 0$

2 (a) $3^{-2} = \frac{1}{9}$ **(b)** $8^0 = 1$
(c) $4^{2.5} = 32$ **(d)** $8^{\frac{2}{3}} = 4$

3 (a) $\log_6 216 = 3$ **(b)** $\log_3 243 = 5$
(c) $\log_4 \left(\frac{1}{64} \right) = -3$ **(d)** $\log_{27} 9 = \frac{2}{3}$

4 (a) 2   **(b)** 3   **(c)** −2   **(d)** 0
(e) $\frac{1}{4}$ **(f)** $\frac{1}{2}$ **(g)** 1   **(h)** −1

5 (a) 2   **(b)** −2   **(c)** $\frac{1}{2}$ **(d)** 7

6 $3^4 = p$ so $p = 81$

7 $t^{\frac{1}{2}} = 3$ so $t = 9$

8 (a) $x = 3$ **(b)** $x = 2$ **(c)** $x = 27$ **(d)** $x = 6$
(e) $x = 5$ **(f)** $x = \frac{1}{2}$ **(g)** $x = -1$ **(h)** $x = \sqrt{3}$

9 (a)

x	0.25	0.5	1	2	4	8
$y = \log_2 x$	−2	−1	0	1	2	3

(b)

(c) The graph of $y = \log_2 x$ is a reflection in the line $y = x$ of the graph of $y = 2^x$.

C Laws of logarithms (p 92)

C1 (a) (i) $\log_2 8 = 3$ (ii) $\log_2 16 = 4$
    (iii) $\log_2 128 = 7$

  (b) $8 \times 16 = 128$ becomes $2^3 \times 2^4 = 2^7$, so $a = 3$,
    $b = 4$, $c = 7$ and $a + b = c$.

  (c) Since $a = \log_2 8$, $b = \log_2 16$, and $c = \log_2 128$,
    it follows that $\log_2 8 + \log_2 16 = \log_2 128$.

C2 As with C1, $2 + 3 = 5$, but $2 = \log_3 9$, $3 = \log_3 27$
and $5 = \log_3 243 = \log_3 (9 \times 27)$
so $\log_3 9 + \log_3 27 = \log_3 (9 \times 27)$.

C3 $\log_5 12 = \log_5 (3 \times 4) = \log_5 3 + \log_5 4$
so $\log_5 12 = 0.6826 + 0.8614 = 1.544$

C4 Let $x = \log_a m$ so $m = a^x$ and
let $y = \log_a n$ so $n = a^y$.
$$\frac{m}{n} = \frac{a^x}{a^y} = a^{x-y}$$
so $x - y = \log_a \left(\dfrac{m}{n} \right)$

and $\log_a m - \log_a n = \log_a \left(\dfrac{m}{n} \right)$

C5 $\log_8 7 = \log_8 \left(\frac{21}{3} \right)$
       $= \log_8 21 - \log_8 3$
so $\log_8 7 = 1.4641 - 0.5283 = 0.9358$

C6 Let $x = \log_a m$ so $m = a^x$
$$\frac{1}{m} = \frac{1}{a^x} = a^{-x}$$
so $-x = \log_a \left(\dfrac{1}{m} \right)$

and $-\log_a m = \log_a \left(\dfrac{1}{m} \right)$

C7 Let $x = \log_a m$ so $m = a^x$
$m^2 = (a^x)^2 = a^{2x}$
so $2x = \log_a m^2$
and $2\log_a m = \log_a m^2$

C8 Let $x = \log_a m$ so $m = a^x$
$m^k = (a^x)^k = a^{kx}$
so $kx = \log_a m^k$
and $k\log_a m = \log_a m^k$

C9 (a) $\log_3 \frac{1}{2} = -\log_3 2 = -0.6309$

  (b) $\log_3 16 = \log_3 2^4 = 4\log_3 2 = 2.5236$

  (c) $\log_3 4 = \log_3 2^2 = 2\log_3 2 = 1.2618$

  (d) $\log_3 \sqrt{2} = \log_3 2^{\frac{1}{2}} = \frac{1}{2}\log_3 2 = 0.3155$

C10 (a) $\log_{10} \frac{1}{2} = -\log_{10} 2 = -0.3010$

  (b) $\log_{10} 1.5 = \log_{10} 3 - \log_{10} 2 = 0.1761$

  (c) $\log_{10} 4 = 2\log_{10} 2 = 0.6020$

  (d) $\log_{10} 5 = \log_{10} 10 - \log_{10} 2 = 0.6990$

  (e) $\log_{10} 6 = \log_{10} 3 + \log_{10} 2 = 0.7781$

  (f) $\log_{10} 9 = 2\log_{10} 3 = 0.9542$

  (g) $\log_{10} 16 = 4\log_{10} 2 = 1.2040$

  (h) $\log_{10} 20 = \log_{10} 2 + \log_{10} 10 = 1.3010$

Exercise C (p 94)

1 (a) $\log_a 10$ (b) $\log_a 4$ (c) $\log_a 9$
  (d) $\log_a 8a$ (e) $\log_a 32$ (f) $\log_a 8$

2 (a) $\log_5 5 = 1$ (b) $\log_5 9 = 1.3652$
  (c) $\log_5 \frac{1}{3} = -0.6826$ (d) $\log_5 \sqrt{3} = 0.3413$
  (e) $\log_5 15 = 1.6826$ (f) $\log_5 25 = 2$
  (g) $\log_5 0.6 = -0.3174$ (h) $\log_5 \frac{9}{25} = -0.6348$

3 (a) $\log_a \frac{x}{y} = \log_a x - \log_a y$

  (b) $\log_a xy = \log_a x + \log_a y$

  (c) $\log_a \frac{x^2}{y} = 2\log_a x - \log_a y$

  (d) $\log_a \frac{\sqrt[a]{y}}{x} = \frac{1}{a}\log_a y - \log_a x$

4 $\log_5 5! = \log_5 (5 \times 4!) = 2.9746$

5 (a) $\log_a p^2 q$ (b) $\log_a ap^3$ (c) $\log_a \left(\dfrac{\sqrt{p}}{q^4} \right)$

6 (a) After t hours the size of the colony is
    multiplied by 2^t. If the population is 1000
    times bigger then $2^t = 1000$.

  (b) $\log_2 1000 = t$
    $2^9 = 512$ and $2^{10} = 1024$, so $9 < t < 10$

  (c) $t = 9.97$

7 (a) $x = 4$ (b) $x = 4$ (c) $x = 9$
  (d) $x = 11$ (e) $x = 2$ (f) $x = -2, 6$

D Equations of the form $a^x = b$ (p 95)

D1 Answers for C10 checked using calculator; slight
differences are due to rounded values being given
for the logs in C10.

D2 (a) $\log 2^t = t \log 2$

(b) $\log 2^t = \log 1000$
$t \log 2 = \log 1000$
$t = 9.97$ to 2 d.p.

D3 (a) 1% represents a monthly growth factor of 1.01. After m months the amount in the account will be 1000×1.01^m.
There will be £2000 in the account when $1000 \times 1.01^m = 2000$.
Dividing by 1000, $1.01^m = 2$

(b) $\log 1.01^m = \log 2$
$m \log 1.01 = \log 2$
$m = 69.66$
The amount will be a little over £2000 after 70 months.

D4 (a) A decrease of 5% represents a growth factor of 0.95.

(b) After t years the population has reduced to 0.95^t of its original value, so $0.95^t = \frac{3}{5}$, or $0.95^t = 0.6$.

(c) $\log 0.95^t = \log 0.6$
giving $t = 9.96$
After 10 years the population is just under $\frac{3}{5}$ of its original value.

Exercise D (p 97)

Answers are given to 3 d.p. unless otherwise required.

1 (a) $x = 5$ (b) $x = 2.5$ (c) $x = 2.667$
(d) $x = 2.100$ (e) $x = 1.379$ (f) $x = 2.711$

2 $n = 2.899$ years

3 $t = 5.0$ days

4 (a) $n = 250 \times 3.7^t$

(b) $t = 2.82$ hours $= 2$ hours 49 minutes

5 The time when there is $\frac{1}{5}$ of the original charge left is given by $0.9^t = 0.2$.
$t = 15.28$ seconds

6 $n \log 2 > 132 \log 50$
$n > 744.99$
The smallest possible integer to satisfy $2^n > 50^{132}$ is $n = 745$.

7 (a) 1.06   (b) $P = 250\,000 \times 1.06^t$
(c) 8 years

8 (a) After t years the amount of isotope has reduced to 0.925^t of its original value. So if it is half of its original value then $0.5 = 0.925^t$.

(b) $t = 8.891$ years

9 The investment has increased by 25% after 7.0 years.

10 (a) $x = 2.465$ (b) $x = -0.087$
(c) $x = -0.834$ (d) $x = 12.425$
(e) $x = 0.115$ (f) $x = 8.417$

11 (a) $y = 2, 3$
(b) $2^x = 2$ giving $x = 1$ or $2^x = 3$ giving $x = 1.585$

12 (a) $3^x = 3$ giving $x = 1$ or $3^x = 1$ giving $x = 0$
(b) $5^x = 4$ giving $x = 0.861$ or
$5^x = 2$ giving $x = 0.431$
(c) $2^x = -5$ which is not possible or
$2^x = 2$ giving $x = 1$

13 (a) $a = 1.1776$
(b) After 16 more years the population will have increased to 1800.
(c) If the population exceeds 2000, then
$$\frac{2000a^t}{4 + a^t} > 2000$$
$$\Rightarrow \quad \frac{a^t}{4 + a^t} > 1$$
but $a^t > 0$, so $4 + a^t > a^t \Rightarrow \dfrac{a^t}{4 + a^t} < 1$

Thus the population cannot exceed 2000.

14 (a) $p = \log_a x \Rightarrow a^p = x$
$$\log_b a^p = \log_b x$$
$$\Rightarrow \quad p \log_b a = \log_b x$$
$$\Rightarrow \quad p = \frac{\log_b x}{\log_b a}$$
$$\Rightarrow \quad \log_a x = \frac{\log_b x}{\log_b a}$$

(b) (i) $x = \log_5 8$

(ii) $\log_5 8 = \dfrac{\log_{10} 8}{\log_{10} 5} = 1.29$ to 3 s.f.

Test yourself (p 99)

Answers are given to 3 d.p. where rounding is required.

1 (a) The graph of $y = 3^{x+2}$ is a translation by $\begin{bmatrix} -2 \\ 0 \end{bmatrix}$ of $y = 3^x$.

(b) The graph of $y = 3^{-x}$ is a reflection in the y-axis of $y = 3^x$.

(c) The graph of $y = 4 \times 3^x$ is a stretch of $y = 3^x$ by scale factor 4 in the direction of the y-axis.

(d) The graph of $y = 3^x - 1$ is a translation by $\begin{bmatrix} 0 \\ 1 \end{bmatrix}$ of $y = 3^x$.

2 (a) $5^3 = 125$ so $\log_5 125 = 3$

(b) (i) $\log_5 (125)^4 = 4\log_5 125 = 12$

(ii) $\log_5 \left(\dfrac{1}{\sqrt{125}} \right) = \log_5 (125)^{-\frac{1}{2}} = -\dfrac{3}{2}$

3 (a) $y = 2^{x+3}$ is a translation by $\begin{bmatrix} -3 \\ 0 \end{bmatrix}$ of $y = 2^x$ or a stretch of $y = 2^x$ by scale factor 8 in the direction of the y-axis.

(b) $p = 8$

4 (a) -1 **(b)** $\log_2 \dfrac{p^3}{\sqrt{q}} = -3 - \dfrac{t}{2}$

5 (a) $\log_q 2 = \dfrac{p}{4}$ **(b)** $\log_q(8q) = \dfrac{3p}{4} + 1$

6 $\log_a x = \log_a 7 + 3\log_a 2$
$\qquad = \log_a 7 + \log_a 2^3$
$\qquad = \log_a 7 + \log_a 8$
$\qquad = \log_a (7 \times 8)$
$\qquad = \log_a 56$
$\Rightarrow x = 56$

7 (a) $3 + 2\log_2 x = \log_2 y$
$\qquad 3 + \log_2 x^2 = \log_2 y$
$\qquad\qquad 3 = \log_2 y - \log_2 x^2$
$\qquad\qquad 3 = \log_2 \dfrac{y}{x^2}$
$\Rightarrow \dfrac{y}{x^2} = 2^3 \Rightarrow y = 8x^2$

(b) $\alpha = \frac{1}{4}, \beta = 1\frac{1}{2}$

8 (a) $\dfrac{x^2 + 4x + 3}{x^2 + x} = \dfrac{x + 3}{x} = 1 + \dfrac{3}{x}$ **(b)** $x = \frac{1}{5}$

9 (a) $x = 2.292$ **(b)** $x = 6.170$ **(c)** $x = 0.631$

10 The half-life is given by $0.88^t = 0.5$.
$t = 5.422$
The half-life is 5.422 years.

11 $(3^x - 4)(3^x - 1) = 0$
$3^x = 1$ giving $x = 0$ or $3^x = 4$ giving $x = 1.262$

8 Differentiation

A Increasing and decreasing functions

Exercise A (p 101)

1 Decreasing

2 (a) Decreasing **(b)** Increasing

3 $p = 0, q = 4$ (i.e. $0 < x < 4$)

4 $x < -3, x > 3$

5 $-5 < x < 5$

6 $0 \le t < 10$

B Stationary points (p 102)

B1 (a) $f'(x)$ is decreasing at $x = 1$.

(b) $f''(x)$ is negative at $x = 1$.

(c) $f''(x)$ is positive at $x = 3$.

Exercise B (p 103)

1 (a) $15x^2 - 6x + 7$ **(b)** $30x - 6$

2 (a) $12x^3 + 6x^2$ **(b)** $36x^2 + 12x$

3 Maximum at $(1, 8)$; minimum at $(3, 4)$

4 (a) (i) Maximum at $(-5, 183)$;
minimum at $(3, -73)$

(ii)
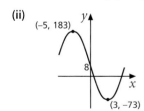

(b) (i) Maximum at $(\frac{1}{2}, 3\frac{3}{4})$;
minimum at $(2, -3)$

(ii)
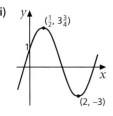

(c) (i) Maximum at $(-6, -5)$;
minimum at $(-2, -37)$

(ii)
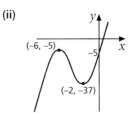

(d) (i) Minimum at $(-\frac{1}{2}, -2\frac{1}{2})$;
maximum at $(1\frac{1}{2}, 13\frac{1}{2})$

(ii)
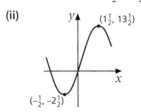

(e) (i) Maximum at $(-1, 18)$;
minimum at $(2\frac{1}{2}, -67\frac{3}{4})$

(ii)
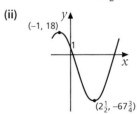

(f) (i) Maximum at $(-6, 0)$;
minimum at $(2, -256)$

(ii)
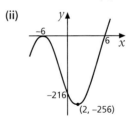

5 (a) $x = 9$, minimum

(b) $x = 2$, minimum; $x = -2$, maximum

6 (a) $(2, 8)$

(b) (i) y gets larger and larger

(ii) y gets larger and larger

(c)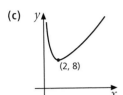

C Stationary points of inflexion (p 104)

C1 (a)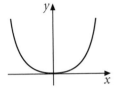

(b) $f'(0) = 0, f''(0) = 0$

(c) Minimum

(d) $f'(0) = 0, f''(0) = 0$ and $(0, 0)$ is a maximum

D Optimisation

Exercise D (p 105)

1 $\dfrac{dF}{dv} = 1 - 0.02v$

For maximum fuel economy, $\dfrac{dF}{dv} = 0$,

so $v = \dfrac{1}{0.02} = 50$.

The most economical speed is 50 m.p.h.

2 (a) (i) $P = 500 + 100t$

(ii) $\dfrac{dP}{dt} = 100$

This represents the rate at which the population increases.

(b) (i) $\dfrac{dP}{dt} = 100 - 50t$

When $t = 1, \dfrac{dP}{dt} = 50$; when $t = 2, \dfrac{dP}{dt} = 0$;

when $t = 3, \dfrac{dP}{dt} = -50$.

(ii) P is a maximum when $\dfrac{dP}{dt} = 0$,

i.e. when $t = 2$.

When $t = 2, P = 600$.

(iii) The population would decrease to zero.

3 (a) Length of side parallel to hedge $= 60 - 2x$

$A = x(60 - 2x) = 60x - 2x^2$

(b) $\dfrac{dA}{dx} = 60 - 4x$

For maximum A, $60 - 4x = 0$ so $x = 15$

(c) Maximum area $= 15 \times (60 - 30) = 450 \, \text{m}^2$

4 (a) Length of card $= w + l + w + l = 2w + 2l$

So $2w + 2l = 160$

$\Rightarrow \qquad w + l = 80$

$\Rightarrow \qquad l = 80 - w$

(b) Width of card $= \frac{1}{2}w + h + \frac{1}{2}w = w + h$

So $w + h = 50$

$\Rightarrow \qquad h = 50 - w$

(c) $V = whl = w(50 - w)(80 - w)$

(d) $V = w^3 - 130w^2 + 4000w$

$\dfrac{dV}{dw} = 3w^2 - 260w + 4000$

For maximum V, $3w^2 - 260w + 4000 = 0$

$\Rightarrow \qquad (3w - 200)(w - 20) = 0$

$\Rightarrow \qquad w = 20$ or $66\frac{2}{3}$

$w = 66\frac{2}{3}$ is impossible, so $w = 20$ gives the maximum volume.

The dimensions of the box are 20 cm, 30 cm, 60 cm.

5 (a) Length of tray $= 8 - 2x$

Width of tray $= 5 - 2x$

So volume $V = x(8 - 2x)(5 - 2x)$

(b) V is a maximum when $x = 1$.

The dimensions are 6 cm, 3 cm, 1 cm.

6 (a) Total surface area $=$ top $+$ bottom $+$ 4 sides

$= x^2 + x^2 + 4hx$

$= 2x^2 + 4hx$

(b) (i) $2x^2 + 4hx = 384$

$\Rightarrow \quad h = \dfrac{384 - 2x^2}{4x}$

(ii) $V = x^2h = x^2\left(\dfrac{384 - 2x^2}{4x}\right) = \dfrac{384x}{4} - \frac{1}{2}x^3$

$= 96x - \frac{1}{2}x^3$

(iii) V is a maximum when $x = 8$.

The corresponding value of h is 8.

(iv) $512 \, \text{cm}^3$

7 (a) Area of each end $= 6x^2$

Area of rectangular faces $= 3xl + 4xl + 5xl$

$= 12xl$

Total surface area $= 12x^2 + 12xl$

$12x^2 + 12xl = 64$

$\Rightarrow l = \dfrac{64 - 12x^2}{12x} = \dfrac{64}{12x} - \dfrac{12x^2}{12x} = \dfrac{16}{3x} - x$

(b) Volume = area of end × length

$$= 6x^2 l = 6x^2\left(\frac{16}{3x} - x\right) = 32x - 6x^3$$

(c) $\dfrac{dV}{dx} = 0$ when $32 - 18x^2 = 0$

$$\Rightarrow \quad x^2 = \tfrac{16}{9}$$

$$\Rightarrow \quad x = \tfrac{4}{3} \ (-\tfrac{4}{3} \text{ impossible})$$

When $x = \tfrac{4}{3}$, $V = 32 \times \tfrac{4}{3} - 6 \times (\tfrac{4}{3})^3$

$$= \tfrac{128}{3} - \tfrac{128}{9} = \tfrac{384 - 128}{9} = \tfrac{256}{9} \text{ cm}^3 = 28\tfrac{4}{9} \text{ cm}^3$$

8 Let the price per bike be £P. The number sold drops by 40 for each increase of £1 in the price, and so the number sold is

$5000 - 40(P - 100) = 9000 - 40P$

Total revenue = £$(9000 - 40P)P$

Total costs = £$(50\,000 + 85(9000 - 40P))$

Profit = revenue − costs

$$= £(-815\,000 + 12\,400P - 40P^2)$$

$\dfrac{d(\text{Profit})}{dP} = 0$ when $12\,400 - 80P = 0$,

i.e. $P = 155$

Number sold = $9000 - 40P = 2800$

Approximately 2800 should be manufactured and they should be sold at a price of £155 each.

Mixed questions (p 108)

1 Maximum at $(-1, 2)$; minimum at $(1, -2)$

2 (a) $6x^2 - 20x + 1$ **(b)** $12x - 20$

3 (a) $(0, 3), (3, 0), (-\tfrac{1}{2}, 0)$

(b) 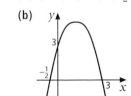   **(c)** $\left(\tfrac{5}{4}, \tfrac{49}{8}\right)$

4 (a) $4x^3 - 4x$

(b), (c) $(-1, 3)$ minimum; $(0, 4)$ maximum; $(1, 3)$ minimum

(d)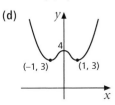

5 (a) $24x^2 - 6x$

(b) $48x - 6$

(c) $f'(1) = 24 - 6 = 18$
$f'(1) > 0$, so f is increasing

(d) $f'(x) = 0$ when $24x^2 - 6x = 0$

$$\Rightarrow \quad 6x(4x - 1) = 0$$

$$\Rightarrow \quad x = 0 \text{ or } \tfrac{1}{4}$$

(e) $f''(0) < 0$, so y is a maximum when $x = 0$
$f''(\tfrac{1}{4}) > 0$; so y is a minimum when $x = \tfrac{1}{4}$

6 (a) $\dfrac{dC}{dv} = -\dfrac{160}{v^2} + \dfrac{v}{50}$

$\dfrac{dC}{dv} = 0 \Rightarrow \dfrac{160}{v^2} = \dfrac{v}{50} \Rightarrow v^3 = 8000$

$$\Rightarrow v = 20$$

So C is stationary when $v = 20$.

(b) $\dfrac{d^2C}{dv^2} = \dfrac{320}{v^3} + \dfrac{1}{50} > 0$ when $v = 20$.

So C is a minimum when $v = 20$.

(c) 12, £30

7 $f'(x) = 15 - 12x - 3x^2$

$$= 3(5 - 4x - x^2)$$

$$= 3(5 + x)(1 - x)$$

	-5		1	
$5 + x$	$- \ -$	$0 \ +$	$+ \ + \ + \ +$	$+$
$1 - x$	$+ \ +$	$+ \ +$	$+ \ + \ 0$	$- \ -$
$(5 + x)(1 - x)$	$- \ -$	$0 \ +$	$+ \ + \ 0$	$- \ -$

$f'(x) > 0$ in the interval $-5 < x < 1$
so $a = -5$ and $b = 1$

8 (a) Length of shelter = $4 - 2x$
Height of shelter = $2 - x$
So $V = x(4 - 2x)(2 - x)$

$$= x(8 - 8x + 2x^2)$$

$$= 2x^3 - 8x^2 + 8x$$

(b) $\dfrac{dV}{dx} = 6x^2 - 16x + 8$

$\dfrac{dV}{dx} = 0$ when $6x^2 - 16x + 8 = 0$

$$\Rightarrow \quad 2(3x^2 - 8x + 4) = 0$$

$$\Rightarrow \quad 2(3x - 2)(x - 2) = 0$$

$$\Rightarrow \quad x = \tfrac{2}{3} \text{ or } 2$$

$x = 2$ is impossible, so $x = \tfrac{2}{3}$

(c) $\tfrac{64}{27}$ m^3 or 2.37 m^3 (to 3 s.f.)

9 (a) $\dfrac{256}{x^2}$

(b) $A = \text{base} + \text{sides} = x^2 + 4x\left(\dfrac{256}{x^2}\right)$

$\qquad\qquad\qquad\quad = x^2 + \dfrac{1024}{x}$

(c) 8

10 (a) $4x^3 - 16x$

(b) $(0, 3), (2, -13), (-2, -13)$

(c) $(0, 3)$ maximum; $(2, -13), (-2, -13)$ minima

(d) $x - 12y - 49 = 0$

11 (a) $h = \dfrac{515}{x^2}$

(b) $A = \text{base} + \text{top} + \text{sides}$

$\qquad = 2x^2 + 2x^2 + 6xh$

$\qquad = 4x^2 + 6x\left(\dfrac{515}{x^2}\right)$

$\qquad = 4x^2 + \dfrac{3090}{x}$

(c) $\dfrac{dA}{dx} = 8x - \dfrac{3090}{x^2}$

$\dfrac{dA}{dx} = 0 \Rightarrow 8x^3 = 3090 \Rightarrow x = 7.28$ to 3 s.f.

(d) 636

(e) $\dfrac{d^2A}{dx^2} = 8 + \dfrac{6180}{x^3} > 0$ when $x = 7.28$

So A is a minimum.

12 (a) (i) Area of cross-section $= \frac{1}{2} \times 3x \times 4x = 6x^2$
Volume, $V = 6x^2h$

(ii) Total area of base and top $= 12x^2$
Area of sides $= 3xh + 4xh + 5xh = 12xh$
$\Rightarrow S = 12x^2 + 12xh$

(b) $S = 12x^2 + 12xh = 12x^2 + 12x\left(\dfrac{100}{6x^2}\right) = 12x^2 + \dfrac{200}{x}$

(c) $\dfrac{dS}{dx} = 24x - \dfrac{200}{x^2}; \dfrac{d^2S}{dx^2} = 24 + \dfrac{400}{x^3}$

$\dfrac{dS}{dx} = 0$ when $24x^3 = 200 \Rightarrow x = 2.03$

When $x = 2.03$, $\dfrac{d^2S}{dx^2} > 0$; hence minimum S

13 (a) $y = x^2(x - a) = x^3 - ax^2$

$\dfrac{dy}{dx} = 3x^2 - 2ax$

$\dfrac{dy}{dx} = 0$ when $x = 6$, so $108 - 12a = 0$
$\qquad\qquad\qquad\qquad \Rightarrow \quad a = 9$

(b) $y = (x - 3)^2(x - b)$
$\quad = (x^2 - 6x + 9)(x - b)$
$\quad = x^3 - (b + 6)x^2 + (6b + 9)x - 9b$

$\dfrac{dy}{dx} = 3x^2 - 2(b + 6)x + 6b + 9$

$\dfrac{dy}{dx} = 0$ when $x = 6$,

so $108 - 12(b + 6) + 6b + 9 = 0$,
$\qquad\qquad\qquad \Rightarrow \quad b = 7\frac{1}{2}$

(c) $y = x(x - c)^2$
$\quad = x(x^2 - 2cx + c^2)$
$\quad = x^3 - 2cx^2 + c^2x$

$\dfrac{dy}{dx} = 3x^2 - 4cx + c^2$

$\dfrac{dy}{dx} = 0$ when $x = 6$, so $108 - 24c + c^2 = 0$
$\qquad\qquad \Rightarrow \quad (c - 6)(c - 18) = 0$
$\qquad\qquad \Rightarrow \quad c = 6$ or 18

Test yourself (p 111)

1 (a) $(-5, 0), (1\frac{1}{2}, 0), (0, 15)$

(b) **(c)** $(-1\frac{3}{4}, 21\frac{1}{8})$

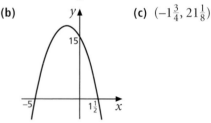

2 (a) Length of tray $= 50 - 2x$, width $= 40 - 2x$,
height $= x$

Volume $= x(50 - 2x)(40 - 2x)$
$\qquad\quad = x(2000 - 180x + 4x^2)$
$\qquad\quad = 4x(x^2 - 45x + 500)$

(b) $0 \le x \le 20$

(c) 7.36 (to 3 s.f.)

(d) $\dfrac{d^2V}{dx^2} = 24x - 360 = -183$ when $x = 7.36$
This is < 0 so value of V is a maximum.

3 (a) $\dfrac{dy}{dx} = 3x^2 - 6x - 9$

(b) When $x = 0$, $\dfrac{dy}{dx} = -9$.

$\dfrac{dy}{dx} < 0$, so the function is decreasing.

(c) $(3, -27), (-1, 5)$

(d) $\dfrac{d^2y}{dx^2} = 12$ when $x = 3$

$\dfrac{d^2y}{dx^2} = -12$ when $x = -1$

So $(3, -27)$ is a minimum and $(-1, 5)$ is a maximum.

4 (a) (i) $V = 2x^2h$ **(ii)** $A = 2x^2 + 6xh$

(b) $A = 2x^2 + 6x\left(\dfrac{288}{2x^2}\right) = 2x^2 + \dfrac{864}{x}$

(c) $\dfrac{dA}{dx} = 4x - \dfrac{864}{x^2}, \dfrac{d^2A}{dx^2} = 4 + \dfrac{1728}{x^3}$

$\dfrac{dA}{dx} = 0$ when $x = 6$. For this value of x, $\dfrac{d^2A}{dx^2} > 0$.
Hence A is a minimum when $x = 6$.

9 Integration

A Linear graphs: area function (p 112)

A1 (a)

x	0	1	2	3	4
A(x)	0	$\frac{1}{2}$	2	$4\frac{1}{2}$	8

(b)

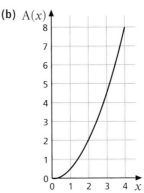

A(x)

(c) A$(x) = \frac{1}{2}x^2$

A2 (a)

x	0	1	2	3	4
A(x)	0	1	4	9	16

(b) The graph of A$(x) = x^2$

(c) A$(x) = x^2$

A3 A$(x) = \frac{1}{2}x^2 + x$

A4 A$(x) = 3x$

A5 A$(x) = x^2 + 3x$

A6 (a)

Graph	Area function A(x)
$y = 3$	$3x$
$y = x$	$\frac{1}{2}x^2$
$y = 2x$	x^2
$y = x + 1$	$\frac{1}{2}x^2 + x$
$y = 2x + 3$	$x^2 + 3x$

(b) The area function is the indefinite integral (but without the constant of integration).

(c) $\frac{1}{3}x^3$

B Area function for $y = x^2$ (p 114)

B1 (a) The areas are 0.5, 2.5, 6.5, 12.5, 20.5, 30.5

(b) Overestimate

(c)

x	0	1	2	3	4	5	6
$A(x)$	0	0.5	3	9.5	22	42.5	73

(d) The values of $\frac{1}{3}x^3$ (to 2 d.p.) are:

0, 0.33, 2.67, 9, 21.33, 41.67, 72

There is close agreement, especially for larger values of x.

C Definite integrals

Exercise C (p 116)

1 (a) $\int_2^4 \left(3x^2 - 5\right) dx$ **(b)** $\left[x^3 - 5x\right]_2^4 = 46$

2 $\left[\frac{1}{4}t^4 + \frac{1}{3}t^3 + \frac{1}{2}t^2 + t\right]_1^3 = 34\frac{2}{3}$

3 (a) $\frac{1}{6}$ **(b)** 8   **(c)** $2\frac{1}{3}$ **(d)** $3\frac{5}{6}$ **(e)** 3   **(f)** $17\frac{2}{3}$

4 The information given leads to the equation
$a^2 + 3a - 4 = 24$ from which $a = 4$ (or -7, which is rejected since $a > 1$).

5 (a) (i) $18\frac{2}{3}$ **(ii)** $18\frac{2}{3}$

(b)

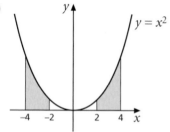

The areas are equal because of the symmetry of the graph.

6 $69\frac{3}{4}$

7 (a) $20\frac{4}{5}$ **(b)** $115\frac{1}{5}$ **(c)** $9\frac{1}{3}$

8 (a)

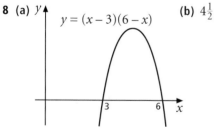

(b) $4\frac{1}{2}$

9 $4\frac{1}{2}$

10 $\frac{1}{30}$

11 (a) $\frac{4}{9} = 0.444$ (to 3 s.f.)   **(b)** $\frac{1}{10}$ **(c)** 53.3

12 $k = 33$

D Areas below the *x*-axis (p 117)

D1 (a) Area $= \left[x^3 - 6x^2\right]_1^3 = (27 - 54) - (1 - 6)$

$$= -27 + 5 = -22$$

(b) Because the area is below the *x*-axis, where values of *y* are negative

Exercise D (p 117)

1 (a) -18 **(b)**

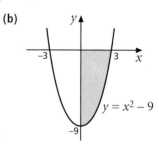

2 (a) $x = -1$ and $x = 5$ **(b)** -36

3 (a) $x = 0$ and $x = 3$ **(b)** $-13\frac{1}{2}$

4 (a)

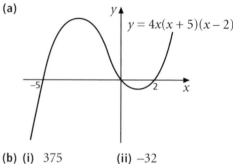

(b) (i) 375   **(ii)** -32

5 The value of the integral is 0. The negative and positive areas cancel each other out.

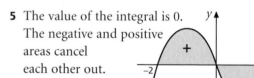

E Area between a curve and a line

Exercise E (p 119)

1 (a) $A\,(2, 12)$ $B\,(6, 12)$ **(b)** $10\frac{2}{3}$

2 (a) $(3, 8)$ **(b)** 4.5

3 (a)

(b) $1\frac{1}{3}$

4 (a) $A\,(-1, 2)$ $B\,(3, 2)$ (b) $10\frac{2}{3}$

5 (a) $A\,(-2, 11)$ $B\,(3, 6)$ (b) $20\frac{5}{6} = 20.8$ (to 3 s.f.)

F Numerical integration: the trapezium rule
(p 120)

F1 Too small, because the curve is above the line segments

F2 (a) 1 (b) 1.67, 1.92, 2.05; area = 6.64

F3 (a) 6.64

(b) Make h smaller and increase the number of ordinates.

Exercise F (p 121)

1 (a) 5.79

(b) Underestimate, because the curve is above the line segments

2 (a) 2.98 (b) 2.96

3 (a) 4.65 (b) $\frac{14}{3} = 4.666...$

4 (a)

x	2	2.2	2.4	2.6	2.8	3
y	1.58	1.63	1.68	1.73	1.78	1.83

(b) 1.705

Mixed questions (p 123)

1 (a) 4 (b) $2\frac{2}{3}$

2 $-\frac{1}{3}$

3 (a) $y = x(x^2 - 6x + 9)$
    $= x(x - 3)^2$
    A is $(3, 0)$.

(b) $(1, 4)$ (c) 6.75

4 (a) 2.23

(b) Overestimate

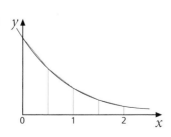

5 (a) $-\frac{1}{2}$

(b) $\left(\frac{1}{4}, \frac{1}{4}\right)$

(c) $\dfrac{dy}{dx} = \dfrac{1}{2\sqrt{x}} - 1$

When $x > \frac{1}{4}$, $\sqrt{x} > \frac{1}{2} \Rightarrow \dfrac{1}{\sqrt{x}} < 2 \Rightarrow \dfrac{1}{2\sqrt{x}} - 1 < 0$

As $\dfrac{dy}{dx} < 0$, y is decreasing.

(d) $\frac{1}{6}$

6 $\frac{2}{9}$

7 (a) $\frac{1}{4}x^4 - \frac{5}{3}x^3 + x^2 + 8x\ (+\ c)$

(b) $-5\frac{1}{3}$ (area below axis)

8 (a) $a = 2$ (b) 32

9 134 (to 3 s.f.)

10 (a) $\frac{1}{3}$ (b) $\frac{1}{9}$

Test yourself (p 125)

1 (a) $\frac{2}{5}$ (b) $51\frac{3}{4}$

2 (a) 5 (b) 20.8 (to 3 s.f.)

3 (a) $A\,(1, 2)$ $B\,(4, 5)$ (b) 4.5

4 (a) $p = 1.357$, $q = 1.382$ (b) 2.59

Index